Louis Searchwell

# Development of a Medium for Teaching Online Courses

Louis Searchwell

# Development of a Medium for Teaching Online Courses

## Test of an Effective E-Learning Model

VDM Verlag Dr. Müller

## Impressum/Imprint (nur für Deutschland/ only for Germany)

Bibliografische Information der Deutschen Nationalbibliothek: Die Deutsche Nationalbibliothek verzeichnet diese Publikation in der Deutschen Nationalbibliografie; detaillierte bibliografische Daten sind im Internet über http://dnb.d-nb.de abrufbar.

Alle in diesem Buch genannten Marken und Produktnamen unterliegen warenzeichen-, marken- oder patentrechtlichem Schutz bzw. sind Warenzeichen oder eingetragene Warenzeichen der jeweiligen Inhaber. Die Wiedergabe von Marken, Produktnamen, Gebrauchsnamen, Handelsnamen, Warenbezeichnungen u.s.w. in diesem Werk berechtigt auch ohne besondere Kennzeichnung nicht zu der Annahme, dass solche Namen im Sinne der Warenzeichen- und Markenschutzgesetzgebung als frei zu betrachten wären und daher von jedermann benutzt werden dürften.

Coverbild: www.purestockx.com

Verlag: VDM Verlag Dr. Müller Aktiengesellschaft & Co. KG
Dudweiler Landstr. 99, 66123 Saarbrücken, Deutschland
Telefon +49 681 9100-698, Telefax +49 681 9100-988, Email: info@vdm-verlag.de
Zugl.: Bangor, University of Wales, Bangor, ‚Diss., 2007

Herstellung in Deutschland:
Schaltungsdienst Lange o.H.G., Berlin
Books on Demand GmbH, Norderstedt
Reha GmbH, Saarbrücken
Amazon Distribution GmbH, Leipzig
**ISBN: 978-3-639-15547-1**

## Imprint (only for USA, GB)

Bibliographic information published by the Deutsche Nationalbibliothek: The Deutsche Nationalbibliothek lists this publication in the Deutsche Nationalbibliografie; detailed bibliographic data are available in the Internet at http://dnb.d-nb.de.

Any brand names and product names mentioned in this book are subject to trademark, brand or patent protection and are trademarks or registered trademarks of their respective holders. The use of brand names, product names, common names, trade names, product descriptions etc. even without a particular marking in this works is in no way to be construed to mean that such names may be regarded as unrestricted in respect of trademark and brand protection legislation and could thus be used by anyone.

Cover image: www.purestockx.com

Publisher:
VDM Verlag Dr. Müller Aktiengesellschaft & Co. KG
Dudweiler Landstr. 99, 66123 Saarbrücken, Germany
Phone +49 681 9100-698, Fax +49 681 9100-988, Email: info@vdm-publishing.com
Bangor, University of Wales, Bangor, ‚Diss., 2007

Printed in the U.S.A.
Printed in the U.K. by (see last page)
**ISBN: 978-3-639-15547-1**

# Acknowledgements

I would like to thank the staff at Research Institute for Enhancement Learning, especially Romy Lawson my supervisor, John Fazey (Department Director), and Judy Lloyd (Department Secretary) for the invaluable information and seminars given during the course of producing this book.

A 'thank you' also goes to the BTC Group employees who have helped and provided the opportunity to produce this book.

I would also like to thank all the authors whose work have enabled me to complete this book

Thank you to Russ Bromley who has been my supervisor throughout the TCS and all those involved at University of Wales, Bangor.

I would also like to thank all my friends for their encouragement in particular Zlatka, Tom Kirkham and relationships built through the TCS scheme.

A special thank you also goes to my family who has provided encouragement over the years. And last but not least to my father who has inspired and provide me with invaluable skills during his lifetime. 'May God bless'.

# Table of Contents

# List of Figures

# List of Tables

# Chapter - 1

# Introduction

The late 90s and the beginning of the century saw a surge in the e-learning market when the role electronic medium could provide for distant learning opportunities was realised. On this premise, the concept of theLearningBusiness (tLB) e-learning platform was conceived to provide learning with greater interaction between tutor and student over distance. tLB was developed over the 4 years proceeding the turn of the century along with many other systems. A flood of e-learning systems and Web based e-conferencing systems erupted on the market during 2004 – 2005 as high market growth rates encouraged entrance. tLB was not able to compete on a similar basis as many of the new platforms coming onto the market mainly because of budgetary restrictions; It therefore had to compete on differentiation by pedagogical focus and quality in delivering higher education (HE) courses. Pedagogical focus bought advantages as very few of the vendors within the e-learning environment were concerned with this at this stage. Many of them later realised the importance of how people learn in e-learning environments. This brings us to the purpose of this book which is to review the literature and examine methods of learning theory application into e-learning platforms, followed by a study of these theories in practice.

The review begins with Chapter 2 which provides an insight to the conception of tLB and the purpose for which it was developed whilst the following chapters give some inclination of the markets, competition and pedagogy and management information systems that provides for the rest of this document, followed by a number of studies to endorse the findings within the review of the literature.

The use of the electronic medium to convey information is a practice developed initially by the scientific community for the very same purpose e-learning has been used today. Chapter 3 delves into the history of e-learning and the management of knowledge which plays an important role in the way information is conveyed on a platform. The Learning Management System(LMS) and Learning Management Content System(LMCS) mentioned in Chapter 3 and 4 are important tools in planning and control of information based on small chunks of information

1

of which the learning byte, influenced by cognitive psychologist Miller (1956), is the basic unit. Chapter 4 also takes a brief look at standards and the use of learning theories in development of the LMS.

E-learning technology has emerged at a very competitive time where during the period of evolvement, has experienced market shakeout and has seen investment drop as a consequence of failure of technology companies known as Dot Coms, as explained in Chapter 5. In the last few years there has been an astonishing increase in the number of e-learning systems entering the market. Chapter 5, demonstrates comparisons of some of the major competitors to see where tLB fits amongst them, and also takes stock of training trends within the industry.

Pedagogy is generally overlooked by developers, in the early stages of e-learning design as evidence tends to show particularly when designing course work. One of the major drawbacks in e-learning is motivation and many of the theories in Chapter 6, provide insight into pedagogical design. Some of the leading psychologists and educational theorists have involved themselves in the conjecture of e-learning e.g. Laurillard (1999), & Pask (1985) and 'theory of special variation' Fazey & Marton (2002) these thories can be adapted to an e-learning context to improve the teaching and learning process. Chapter 6 examines some of these theories in great detail where Chapter 7 examines its application and the relationship between industrial design and pedagogy. Chapter 7 also considers the principles of communities of practice a concept tLB platform was designed on.

The use of learning theory in pedagogical design is further developed in Chapter 8 where active learning is discussed as a tool for learning on an e-learning platform along with the risk it entails. The role of reflective practices is highlighted in Kolb's framework but it also plays a major role in active learning on an e-learning platform. Also the inclusion of such practices as online journals, learning logs and journals serve to highlight their use in working practices for e-learning.

Active learning practices are generally associated with motivation and engagement of learners as well as deep learning. One of the key areas of importance in online-learning is motivation which Chapter 8 attempts to address the links with active learning. Motivation appears to be one of the factors that have helped to rescind e-learning from its original state and brought about the phrase 'blended learning'. Theorists such as Karesenti (1999) articulate a perceived gap between the 'virtual classroom and the university classroom'; motivation is the key to its reduction. Chapter 9 attempts to appreciate some of the key issues and examine techniques for elimination of attrition. Correspondence, papers and vocal converse have also highlighted motivation as one of the main concerns preventing e-learning from achieving its potential growth. Chapter 9 provides a much deeper examination of some of the key motivational issues and attempts to address them. One of the drawbacks in this area and others where e-learning is concerned is the lack of comprehensive research. It is beyond this study to cover research into these areas but it perfectly reasonable to address the issues.

Armed with pedagogical theories and motivational principles and knowledge of repositories and LMS from previous chapters, Chapter 10 looks at development of instruction through a number of frameworks which takes into account important attributes within the design process. The aim is to use the tools provided to design motivational activities to reduce attrition rates in e-learning in which the importance of the role of the coach/tutor/facilitator is apparent. The role of the coach/trainer in e-learning is fundamentally different to traditional face to face; Chapter 11 examines online coaching and looks at the role and demands of today's e-trainer/e-coach by examination of requirements and expectations. It takes into consideration moderating and facilitation through clarification of demands and expectations. The coach has a facilitative role in which he/she is required to acquire skills to provide for a collaborative environment where a learner is able to develop deep learning. The arguments for deep learning in an e-learning environment revolve around the student having the ability to learn understand and convey the knowledge within a community of learners. Chapter 11 tries to emphasise this in some depth as it links into the motivational factors mentioned in Chapter 9. Without the reductions in student drop-out rates, e-learning will fail, it therefore makes sense to understand the relationships between platform, facilitator, learner and materials and motivation advocated by leading

3

educationalist 'Biggs' with is theory of 'constructive alignment'. The facilitator/coach/tutor/moderator can be classed as a practitioner as Biggs (1999) would advocate which makes adequate sense as the theories of learning begin to diffuse among these groups. Practitioners need to keep pace with these and reflect on current practices in order to bring in new ideas as research into e-learning is still has a way to go.

The difference between learning outcomes and learning objectives is very subtle but can be differentiated as in Chapter 12 where clear distinction is drawn between that of objectivism and active learning. It also highlights how a particular approach to learning can make the difference between the surface and deep learners. This again is covered to some extent in Chapter 10 which explains the role of instructional design and how using a pedagogical approach improves on learning. It mustn't be forgotten as illustrated in Chapter 7 it is holistic principles within the model that constitute the system on whole and not the architecture or the technology. The convergence of technology and pedagogy creates a meaningful system but emphasis must be on the learner not the architecture.

Chapter 12 also looks at how asynchronous and synchronous tools and tracking devices can be used as a means of assessment. Many universities are now using assessment which falls in line with many of the theories advocated by the experts advocating students acting as *collectors, evaluators and conduits of information*, (Thomas J., 2004).

The development of a model for e-learning requires a comprehensive examination of the available technology. Again the convergence of technology and pedagogy can provide a system of learning but is it consistent with application of trainer/coach, utilisation of materials plus exploiting the collaborative aspects of the system to engage and enhance learning? Chapter 13 in summarisation of the preceding chapter's attempts to provide a typical model based on convergence through researching the literature and observation from online practice on the tLB taking into account modern coaching practices.

## Study Section

There are three studies within this section. One major study covers the evaluation the tLB platform and courses. Two smaller studies include: one to determine the sense of community on the platform through connectedness and learning; and the final study looks at facilitative approach to varied methods of learning.

One of the main areas of study in this section is the evaluation system of which its application is covered in the Methodology section Chapter 14. Chapter 15 attempts to justify the evaluation system and provides a guide into its adaptation and implementation. The expected outcomes and feedback into the design is an important factor within the system because it provides purpose and ultimately, it is expected that improvements to the system will be provided through this process. An additional reason for its existence is to evaluate five main areas of the e-learning courses delivered on tLB platform: the learning, operating system, usability, technology and motivation. This chapter analyses the data from the study and correlates the results from which it authenticates the conclusion and discussion for recommendations from tLB platform.

Community's concept plays an important role in the active learning processes provided on the learning business and it measurement can tell us if not only if it is working but whether many of the theories advocated e.g. Pask (1985), Laurillard (1999, See Chapter - 6) are functioning within the environment of the platform. The theories interpreted by way of a sense of community provide two measurements: learning and connectedness. Chapter 16 provides the study for a sense of community and covers the design, methodology, procedure and analysis of data.

The final study uses the concept of variation raised in chapter 6 to determine the *effect on levels of understanding and provision* amongst a group of students from the British Council on a distant learning platform. The varied learning was based on learning styles, learning experiences and reflection amongst the group. Again the theories of Pask (1985), Laurillard (1999), and Fazey & Morton (2002) come into play underpinned by theories of Marton & Säljö (1976), Entwistle (2000) and Atherton (2002) on 'deep and surface learning'.

The three studies as a part of this book try to incorporate the theories and reviews on e-learning to measure the quality of the system holistically and from a sub system approach. The outcome reflects on much of what has been reviewed as the relationships between the sections. In general the theorists have suggested an e-learning environment is not only suitable for most types of learning but can also enhance and improve on it through reflective practices and quality facilitation. The conclusion of the studies in chapter 18 argues this case, although further investigations are recommended.

# Chapter – 2
# theLearningBusiness Platform

## 2.1 The Evolution of theLearningBusiness Platform

Development of theLearningBusiness (tLB) platform began in 1999 - 2000 with the intention to deliver training in the workplace on a system simple to use. It originated from theories of active learning (Active Learning see chapters 7, 9 & 10) and coaching principles. In general it was a system developed for coaching at distance but in keeping with constructivism, the philosophy surrounding the principles of Active Learning.

The tLB was originally developed to support learning on a teaching/learning and development degree programs very much at the embryonic stage of the e-learning phenomena around the beginning of this century. It was originally built from Learning Space 4.0 an IBM Lotus product which also housed Domino and Sametime 2.0 Server. Sametime Server is the Virtual Learning Environment (VLE) and Domino lotus the backend database. Because of its inability to meet the needs of learners; difficult navigation, poor usability, and lack of collaborative aspects, the decision was taken to develop an e-learning model around the communities' concept (see chapter 7). This new platform was developed in Java and Java Script programming language built around HTML language using Tomcat as the Script server. The main content was housed at the Internet Service Provider (ISP) which allowed easy access for content developers. The approach was to build the communities around Learning Space (LS) for course support but the platform eventually become more and more independent where it was eventually discarded. HTML file format are used to build content providing independency from programmer support. The system is server-side therefore all files are kept on the main server. Having all the content and materials based on server side technology, or within the ISP allows users to access an account from any Browser with Internet access.

## 2.2 The Current System

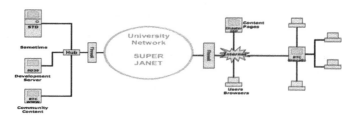

**Figure 1 - tLB Schematic**

As can shown in Figure 1 there are 3 completely isolated servers to prevent applications conflict. Sametime 3.0 delivers the support tools i.e. the Live Session functionality and provides synchronized collaborative interaction within the VLE supported by Audio and Video plus control tools to keep order during a live session. The community content server provides the functionality facilities and work space access whilst the development server replicates the main server. The main development work is tested on the development server prior to going live.

The platform is developed as a hierarchical community based system where different groups within an organisation are able to collaborate together on various subject areas. This consists of:

- Discussions, File Share and Web Share facilities,
- Who's Here to show members of a community with a personal profile,
- Email to allow all members to communicate on the platform. Originally the email was confined to the system for security reason but the importance of linking it with individuals external mailing systems became apparent for motivational issues (see chapter 9).

As the system evolved, a Library system was further added providing File Share and Web Share facilities confined to subject area and community. This allowed publication and privatisation of materials. The coach and administrators use this facility to share materials between the communities on a one to one basis. The development of coaching facilities has also emerged from requirements, including Page Editing facilities. This allows the coach to edit their own materials and personalise the course material to each community which reduces administrative responsibilities.

Furthermore the format for delivery of online courses using an action learning approach became apparent, reducing the need for a hyperlink based system and opting for use of Java Script dropdown menus. This allows more material to be placed on a single page without the user being lost in a labyrinth of pages. The user has the ability to arrive at any section of the course through the dropdown menu. This theme is part and parcel of the learning business and follows the general concept of making the system simple to use.

The latter covers the asynchronous facilities of tLB platform. Alongside this are the synchronous including live classroom, chat facilities, live document share, White Board, Audio and Video facilities, Polling and a Web follow me facility

A shopping cart system to allow users to automatically purchase a course through credit card transactions using a banking merchant was later added to the system. This brought about a changed of the development method of a course and syllabus based courses were now being delivered through the platform whilst keeping in touch with the action learning principles.

There were many additions to the learning business to allow coach's to moderate communities remotely. Facilities for editing pages using a HTML editor and adding own material on the page where necessary. Other facilities included; allow the coach to read students learning logs, similarly a one to one library relationship between coach and student allows upload of materials. The use of JAVA drop-down menus provides the capacity for structuring materials with almost an unlimited number of links. It in essence provides a means of structuring course material into modules and structures which help to arrange course work in a simple format for user access.

To summarise: main additions to the Platform is the facility for administrators and coaches who can now access Libraries edit the welcome page, track users and read Learning Log's. The coaches also had the facility to create Libraries, File Share and Web Share areas, Download and Upload Pages to the be exhibited on the platform and provide users with the ability to create their own page . There was also access to any page within a community on tLB platform including the Java Script drop-down menus used to deliver course material and tasks.

The main requirement for the platform was to enhance collaboration between tutor and student by delivery of Active Learning instruction within the work place. It is important that moderator/coach has access to distant students and the tLB platform aids this process.

# Chapter – 3

## The History of E-Learning

The Internet originated from the RAND Corporation an American think-tank whom recognised the need for a failsafe means of communication in likelihood of a nuclear war. They produced a solution based on a packet switched network. The objective was for a packet to travel through any route or node in order to reach its destination as opposed to end to end synchronous connection in a closed loop system the 'circuit switched network'. They believed that if ever the circuit switched network was destroyed there would be no way of communicating and set about producing a fail-proof system to achieve this.

The first Laboratory was set up in United Kingdom by The National Physical Laboratory but demands from the Pentagon's Advanced Research Projects Agency (DARPA) provided funding for a much larger project within the USA (Berling). Whatever the intention of the military after the first nodes were installed in 1969 at UCLA; the scientists found uses for high speed data transmission and sharing of resources over distance. By the 1970's there were fifteen nodes and up to 32 by 1972. The use of the network however had changed by this time and the collaboration on projects, a method of sharing information had already begun. This was one of the first signs of communities collaborating through a digital medium known as the electronic mail system (email). Mailing lists and news groups were soon to emerge from the practices taking place at this time. The increased density of transistors on a chip, promoted an increase in the number of nodes within the network, leading to a further growth of Internet connectivity. As the technology improved anyone with the knowledge to work this equipment was able to add further nodes by using a simple personal computer sitting in a household or office. Figure 2 shows the exponential growth of the number of internet hosts between 1994 and 1997 where there were approximately 75 million users worldwide. A further fall in the price of hardware has also helped the number of Internet hosts to reach these proportions. The effect of the Internet on way of life has been phenomenal in the Western world. It has influenced many areas of society including; politics, the stock market, economics and education. There is very little the Internet has not influenced or will affect in the future.

> *The Internet has revolutionized the computer and communications world like nothing before. The invention of the telegraph, telephone, radio, and computer set the stage for this unprecedented integration of capabilities. The Internet is at once a world-wide broadcasting capability, a mechanism for information dissemination, and a medium for collaboration and interaction between individuals and their computers without regard for geographic location.* Barry (2000), page 1

The fact that the price of a computer has fallen to an affordable level, has added to growth in the number of hosts on the Internet which has now expanded into the hypothetical world of Cyberspace.

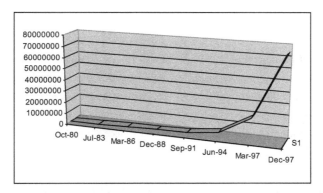

**Figure 2 - Growth in the Number of Internet Hosts**

The term Cyberspace was invented to determine the expectations of the activities on the Internet, Dodge (1998), whilst changes in activities over the Internet have meant a re-defining of the term. A general definition sums up the meaning of Cyberspace as:

12

*'a conceptual world of information and electronic networks accessible via the Internet, which occasionally is compared to an unexplored frontier whose boundaries seem limitless* (Whittle 1996)' Narushige, page 2

The packet switched network has added to its capabilities whilst wireless, satellite and radio, as a means of communicating on asynchronous and synchronous networks have had a large influence in the expansion of cyberspace. It is expected that within the near future, almost every person in the western world will have a stake in cyberspace and there will be at least one or more computers in each household. This increased bandwidth in the shape of broadband networks has laid the way for open access learning over the network. The UK government have put forward a model for future learning where students attend lessons by attending a computer centre as opposed to the present class room. The infrastructure is in the process of being set for e-learning the real challenge is to get people motivated to use it.

### 3.1 Definition of E-learning

The definition of the process of online-learning can be very subjective because of the lack of discipline behind research and technological invention. However standards are beginning to appear and collective discipline and strategic approach are presently converging technologies to allow producers to standardise. The way online-learning is used in this book can define the method in which learning takes place and serves to include the majority of definitions simply meaning, learning with use of an electronic digitized system indirectly over the Internet or directly through an Intranet using a asynchronous and synchronous means of communication. E-learning is similar in term and definition in which the 'e' represents the word electronic which defines the way digitisation is used to transfer information across a physical medium with a set of protocols or rules and standards to ensure its safe delivery. In this book both these words are used in the same context. E-learning is very subjective and can be realised in a variety of definitions and entitlements, but it can be assumed that this book will base it in on the context of developing an e-learning platform. It is differentiated from other e-learning systems by the pedagogical approach with an affinity for learning and coaching theories in the form of constructivism and action learning, although other theories will be briefly touched upon.

E-Learning is not a recent concept, it has been around for approximately 35 years but most would agree that its establishment began in the early 80's but not in way we would consider it within in today's markets e.g. VLE's with Audio and Video portray a sign of complexity yet is still unlikely to reach its potential. Modern e-learning could be considered to be in its early stages of advancement and as a consequence, new terms are appearing constantly and sometimes appear to share meaning, reason being, research itself overlaps and is duplicated creating definitions of similarity. This cannot be avoided but consolidation and standardisation in the industry should help to reduce this problem. For the moment all that can be done is to try and consolidate the terms to bring some understanding.

E-learning appears to be a natural progression from distant learning: it has brought distant learning closer in both time and interaction. Consider the Open University which could be said to be one of the bastions of distant learning with 250,000 students worldwide and is acknowledged globally as exceptional quality. On-line learning is quite a demanding task according to Scigliano & Miller (2000); it requires many resources and a different skill-set to normal face to face. The gathering and management of knowledge has an important role to play alongside the resources and skill sets required for e-learning.

## 3.2 Knowledge Management and Learning Management Systems

Knowledge Management which is neither an e-learning, nor a recent term has an important role within an organisation and was particularly important in the early stages of e-learning. Origins of knowledge management are quite controversial and probably designed in consideration of both tacit and explicit knowledge although the first conference attributed to knowledge management originated in 1993 at Boston. It may also have derived from the digitisation of knowledge or to explain the knowledge in the building block of capabilities of the combined efforts of an organisation Prusak (1999). It could also have been inherited from areas such as Enterprise Resource Planning (ERP) or Product Data Planning (PDP) and derives from collation and

14

categorisation of data. The fact that tacit knowledge is a key resource which should be captured in its entirety, if at all possible, is something to be considered within an e-learning platform. Knowledge on learner access and contribution to e-learning system discussions and chats or participation in online activity on the system has already been seen acknowledged as means of formative & summative assessment in academic courses. It allows the tutor to determine depth of learning relative to taxonomy (see Chapter 12 - Figure 18.). The role of the tutor is to assess the level of learning so it is quite acceptable to use this method of assessment to determine a student's level or ability.

In many industries it had always been realised that individuals were able to hold an organisation to ransom simply because most knowledge remained tacit. Experience is essential to organisational function and consequently; important to be made explicit where possible. This is also the case in areas where the use of a knowledge base is important to an outcome for example in law or a call centre. The knowledge base, although used for thousands of years, was derived from this concept and was used in the automation of many manufacturing processes.

Generally speaking a knowledge base is simply 'an organised collection of information' such as the way a library organises books into categories of authors, book titles or subject areas, Warner (2000). Using this process requires a person to be at a point where knowledge is extracted. The emergence of Artificial Intelligence (AI) has changed the way we capture knowledge because it captures it in the process and makes judgments on what is required. This method is more efficient than the original because the knowledge becomes relevant and timely i.e. it is provided on demand so the expert is only required to provide what is necessary. A knowledge base can very quickly be built on relevant information using artificial intelligence. Knowledge management can be defined as a concept and processes used to control information such as in Artificial Intelligence (AI) or Product Data Planning.

The use of Learning Content Management Systems as an e-learning platform is a digitised version of a library containing text books for learners to learn. In addition the class room is based on community members exchanging information between each other facilitated by a

15

moderator or coach. The librarian allowing a customer to take out a book is analogous to the administrator giving user access to a community of learners, containing categorised and indexed learning materials.

The use of communities brings together groups of people who require access to a similar knowledge base and can easily diverge into other communities where other knowledge requirements are necessary (see chapter 7). The association is based on ownership and peer connection. Members feel a sense of connection with community members where they can provide and gain information which provides a sense of ownership. It is sometimes left to experts to provide the knowledge but ideally the members should provide demand for knowledge and as an outcome of collaborative activity, provide a significant amount of that knowledge entitled 'experiential learning' for which a system is built to manage. In future, the Learning Content Management System (LCMS - see chapter 4), as they become more sophisticated, will perform the AI role of knowledge capture and supply has e-learning systems evolve but for now it is the role of the author and instructor to police and manage it within the e-learning system.

### 3.3 The Learning Bite as a Unit of Knowledge

The knowledge base is a fundamental concept which covers a subjective topic thus e-learning requires some kind of definition for the unit. This has emerged as a 'learning bite', that is, a basic unit of knowledge.

In 1956, Miller a cognitive psychologist discovered that our learning pattern is more suitable to absorbing knowledge in small chunks hence the learning bite. In his experiments he acknowledged concepts that realised impositions on the limitation of memory. His belief was the 'span of absolute judgement' limit the amount of information that one was able to 'receive, process, and remember' leading to the theory of organising information in chunks to increase the amount taken in.

> *First, the span of absolute judgment and the span of immediate memory*
> *impose severe limitations on the amount of information that we are able*

*to receive, process, and remember. By organizing the stimulus input simultaneously into several dimensions and successively into a sequence or chunks, we manage to break (or at least stretch) this informational bottleneck. (Miller 1956, page 14)*

Miller's research was based on uni-dimensional stimuli and multidimensional stimuli which he entitled absolute judgments. The experiments involved users recognising musical pitch tones which were based on uni-dimensional attributes or intensity of different concentration of salt solutions based on multidimensional attributes, Miller (1956), page 8. This research has provided the basis for much application in Web Design and according to Harkus (1990). Miller's 7±2 theory is disputed in Harkus's paper where they looked at *pushing the memory beyond the 7±2 limitation* through reference to Miller's work where they suggested altering the conditions of the test would push the memory beyond the suggested limits. She argues that the Miller's theories were based on subjects such as pitch and taste none of which related to text. According to Harkus (1990) designers fail to relate to the environment in which the user works where the memory is supported by *visuals, words and sounds*. The 7±2 principles were tested using navigational structures: Larson & Czerwinski set up 3 different navigational structures of 8x8x8, 16x32 and 32x16 primary navigation properties based on 512 pages from Encarta encyclopaedia. They expected the users to browse more successfully on the 8 primary navigation structures. They found that the 16x32 and 32x16 provided optimal performance because of the distinctive category labels with which they labelled the scent. Larson and Czerwinski believed that these navigation category labels provided better memory attainment allowing better decision making. The results from Harkus (1990) gives food for thought when designing materials for courses but there needs to be more evidence to this effect.

Course builders are creating materials in bite size chunks on the basis of Millers 7±2 theory which are suitable to pattern searches. It is also suitable to online learning vending because knowledge can be purchased at its basic level as opposed to purchasing a novel or a newspaper. You pay for exactly what you need similar to purchase of a paper from a journal. This is today being nurtured, as the future method of material vending evolves on the Web.

The learning bite is basically a digestible chunk of knowledge capable of being learned based on theoretical arguments such as Miller (1956) argument about what people can remember.

The learning bite and a learning outcome share a relationship. The learning outcome is more in tune with modern methods of learning, as used within an e-learning platform, and will replace the learning bite to some extent. The learning bite is likely to be associated with objectives of learning which doesn't integrate into active learning processes readily therefore, will be considered in this light because of the possibilities of use of materials designed outside of the e-learning platform.

The 'learning bite' is a basic unit of information and collectively forms a repository as can be said for an active learning process. The learning bite, a unit, can be built up to form a learning bite as learning objectives pertains to an active learning process. They differ by the fact that the 'learning bite' is more likely to be an item of knowledge where as the active learning process would be classed as a means or approach to gaining knowledge therefore more difficult to categorise in terms of knowledge bites. The e-learning systems created to manage these concepts are known as Learning Management Systems (LMS).

# Chapter - 4

## Learning Management Systems

There are two dominant types of LMS:

- Learning Management System (LMS)
- Learning Content Management System (LCMS)

These LMS & LCMS are similar in concept but differ in functionality yet are sometimes defined as similar systems:

The concept of learning management systems is often confused as training record systems, authoring tools competency management systems, virtual classrooms and various other systems. As defined by IDC:

> *The term 'learning management system' (LMS) embraces just about any use of web technology to plan, organise, implement and control aspects of the learning process.* Shepherd (2002), page 1

The concept of learning object is in close correlation to LMS and is defined as:

> *IDC defines a learning object as a standing piece (a.k.a. "chunk") of education that contains content and assessment based on specific learning objectives and that has descriptive meta-data wrapped around it (see Figure 3).*

The learning object is a specific piece of information similar to a learning bite that can be tracked or measured as a unit of a personal goal for the learner. In Figure 3, it shows the metadata which engulfs the learning object and provides an index and catalogue data. The content is basically the medium for conveying materials such as text, audio, video or materials developed by a variety of applications i.e. Authorware, Dreamweaver or Microsoft Office Applications such as PowerPoint.

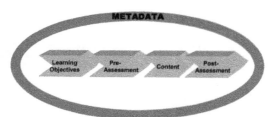

**Figure 3 - Metadata (Source - IDC 2001)**

Figure 3 shows the pre-assessments are determined by learning objectives followed by the content which conveys the learning objectives. The pre-assessment and post-assessment determines the competency of the user in relation to the learning objective. Ideally a form of reflective process should precede or follow the post assessment and likewise, linked to the learning objectives would be some form of goal setting process, or personal management. A system that is more akin to incorporating these processes and concepts is the Learning Content Management System (LCMS) which differs greatly from the LMS but is spoken of in a similar context. IDC defines the LCMS as:

> *'a learning content management system as a system that is used to create, store, assemble, and deliver personalised e-learning content in the form of learning objects.'* (Brennan, Funke & Anderson (2002), page 4)

LCMS can differ accordingly, it depends solely on the provider but according to the IDC, most share the similarities depicted in Figure 4.

The Learning Object Repository (LOR), as shown, in Figure 4 acts as a storage and management point for the learning content. Materials stored in the database are in bite size chunks which can be *'dispensed to users individually'* or grouped together to form a course or module. The dynamic delivery can be in the form of a web application or a bespoke interface such as CD ROM or printed text. An authoring tool can be used to put together content from the depository or form objects from existing organisational material or other objects to create templates for

20

materials to be used in a course or module. Generally authors from various backgrounds will design a course from the learning objects present in the repository from which they are able to create a variety of courses. The administrative application deals with the admin functions such as; setting up students, adding additional materials to course catalogue, tracking and analysis, and other general admin functions. Admin is considered a function of the wider LMS which provides the architecture for LCMS. The Dynamic Delivery Interface allows the LMS to tailor the provision of information to the individual as well as deliver contents on web pages which reflect the organisations look and feel. It is this interface that links to the information that personalises the user interface. It is therefore central to provision of learner profiles, tracking the user, pre-testing and logging user queries, '*the focus of an LCMS is to manage and deliver content that the learner needs when he needs it*'. This implies a learner focused system with the fundamentals for personalised tracking process.

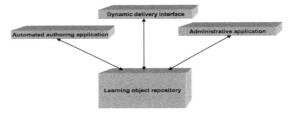

**Figure 4 - Components of a Learning Content Management System (Source - IDC 2001)**

## 4.1 The LCMS, LMS and Evaluation Systems

**Figure 5** demonstrates how the LMS interacts with the LMCS. The role of an LMS is administration of courses and student registration and tracking, launches courses and course tracking of learners; it also allows administration of courses and possibly competence mapping using skill assessments. The evaluation is also a part of the LMS which doesn't seem to play a huge part but its outcome indirectly influences LCMS i.e. it provides feedback to fine tune all the outputs. One of the roles of the evaluation system is to fine tune these processes and check if it is satisfactory to learners. The personal profile of the user is also a function that is required to give instructor an idea of learner particulars. This additional function can be linked into the virtual classroom tools from which the instructor gains access.

21

The LMS monitors the processes and quality of the system and indicates any deviation from quality. The focus of an LMS is to manage and deliver content and compile the learning objects in a format that allows more extensive tracking. The LMS linear sequential tracking approach interacts with LCMS providing a platform for greater personalised interaction with the user. It should also not be forgotten that learning theories and behaviours can be integrated into the learning system via the LCMS. Simple reflective and active learning processes can easily be incorporated at the automated authoring or dynamic delivery systems as well as considered in the way the learning objects are utilised and stored in the content repository. The IDC quotes the LMS as a manager of communities of users which can be said of 'tLB'. Each user within the 'tLB' has its own community and personalised pages. What is lacking on tLB are authoring tools and more extensive managing of the learning content, linear sequence tracking capabilities and catalogue of courses.. A further stage of tLB could be to provide this functionality but requires XML programmers following standards that use metadata. Adherence to standards will allow incorporation of learning objects from other sources.

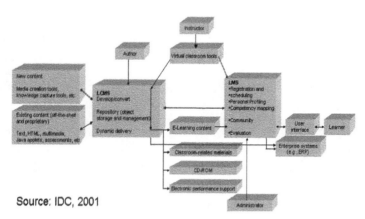

Source: IDC, 2001

**Figure 5 - LMS-LCMS Integration in a Learning Ecosystem**

## 4.2 Standards in E-learning

Standards were originally an initiative of governments and have become an important issue in e-learning design and many application builders are encouraging its usage. A reason for this is to allow learning objects to be used on multiple platforms, environments thus transformation or purchase of materials becomes a performable task.

*The goal of standards is to provide fixed data structures and communication protocols for e-learning objects and cross-system workflows1.*

The call for consistency in Metadata for example allows indexing across platforms. XML, SAML are standards used in both security and attribute processing and enables, for example, cross platform access and sharing of information about learners. Shared content across platform require standards and protocols that allow this to take place. Many of the LCMS & LMS are built on standards such Instructional Management System Global Learning Consortium (IMS) which is body of an interrelated consortium entitled Sharable Content Object Reference Model (SCORM). Other bodies include: Advanced Distributed Learning Network (ADLNet), the Aviation Industry CBT Committee (AICC), the Institute of Electrical and Electronics Engineers (IEEE). Many businesses including the US federal government are demanding that providers are SCORM compliant which is pushing it towards an e-learning de facto Standard throughout the globe.

## 4.3 Theories of Learning in LCMS

In Summary, knowledge management should form part of the LMS system. LCMS is more in tune with knowledge management although it is considered in a different context. LCMS makes use of the knowledge base to create learning objects which are stored in the repository and made available for the LMS courses or personalised tracking. It also provides content for learning resources such as CD ROM and traditional classroom materials. Content is made available to users via the LMS which also tracks courses and makes content available through communities

---

1  (Ellis R, 2005, http://www.e-learningcentre.co.uk/eclipse/Resources/contentmgt.htm)

or as a result of competency mapping. The LCMS can also provide input into Product Data Planning or Enterprise Resource Planning systems which integrates e-learning with resource planning. An integration of this nature provides links in the value chain similar to ERP or PDP. This implies, as the same data becomes available and is passed throughout the value chain, firms are able to be trained on products quite quickly, regardless of where they are produced. The emphasis is on the importance of standards like IMS which is a member of SCORM to make this work. It is also important that the pedagogy is considered in the learning process and design. This tends to get overlooked particularly in the authoring process.

The shift from traditional to online learning has now rapidly advanced although the subject has been addressed for at least 35 years or more (Scigliano, 2000). It seems more of a push than pull as demand is not as predicted in the growth market. Schools, Universities and Colleges have adopted distant learning with utilisation of electronic systems as a contact means for students alongside the mailing methods and traditional classroom learning. Online learning has expectations of astronomical growth during this next decade as can be seen by the number of developers that have switched resources to designing systems but, it seems users are slow to adapt and many vendors have returned to the distant learning approach of a combination of traditional classroom learning with online learning. The Open University for example combines e-mail with classroom and mailed materials traditionally. In theory there are great opportunities for the LMS: in practice the take up has been very slow but appears to be getting there.

The LMS or LCMS is the basis for development of e-learning systems and like many economic markets is susceptible to laws of demand and supply. The influx of resources into these markets is an indication of expected demand as there are many suppliers creating similar systems. The requirement for companies shifting production and services to cheaper markets in other areas of the world raises the demand for browser based systems. Most commercial LMS systems are developed to work on distributed networks and are able to be accessed from an Internet linked computer anywhere in the world. The next chapter therefore investigates the market expectations and trends for such systems.

# Chapter - 5

## E-Learning Technology

### 5.1 The E-Learning Market

The emergence of online learning had created great confusion amongst organisations but according to the financial times it had a very aggressive growth market and it was believed that the use of technology could make training more efficient and more relative to organisational goals (Fisher, 2002).

> *"'There's still going to be very aggressive growth.' Technology, he says, can make learning more effective and related to business goals. As with other business processes, he believes that IT must be used to wring out inefficiencies in training activities"* (Fisher, 2002).

The world of e-learning is an advancing economy that is expected to fully establish itself during the next decade. Considering the market growth rate which is expected to reach $112 billion within the next 5 years, expectations are high.

> *"the market research company, forecast last year that the global corporate e-learning market will be worth some Dollars 23bn in 2004"* (Brennan, Funke & Anderson, 2003).

The above statements were made in 2002 and the figures from the history of Dot.COMS's influenced the future of e-learning hence the reason for early shake-out during this period. Organisations such as Smart Force and Skillsoft had invested heavily into e-learning and suffered the consequences because of the lack of take-up. The market place had been slightly weary because of the collapse of the Dot COM's and the fall of the NASDAQ during the end of the 90's so investment at this time was at a minimum yet e-learning development still advanced at an alarming rate. The market place had witnessed a slight decline in the take up and a number of the big players have felt the pinch.

25

*This month sees further consolidation in the e-learning market, as SkillSoft and SmartForce confirm their merger. With the number of recent high-profile collapses within the e-learning market, we watch with interest to see how the remaining players fare.* BlueU[2]

Figures from BlueU Website showed a portfolio of $50,000 investment into e-learning companies would have had a ROI of - 4.8%. Not all fell over in the period in fact some had made gains from 2% to 42% which is an indication that all was not bad in the e-learning market. However there are fundamental differences to e-learning as it was considered in a different light to the Dot COM's although they are both classed as e-business. E-learning is e-business because cash transactions are being conducted over the net but it is still yet to fully integrate itself into e-business markets but it took time for society to adapt to the idea of life-long learning and for organisations to start to realise the benefits and reward for those that participated. However, e-learning is generally about delivery of training, training materials and simulation over the Web which is a difficult market economy where there is consumer caution in online purchases. Two main vendors that can be considered to have established themselves in e-businesses in the e-learning world were Learndirect and Click-to-learn who took a syllabus based approach to providing courses over the Web. In the market, it is mainly the content providers that are losing ground which may be related to entry barriers being very low thus competition was a little stiffer. According to BlueU the main take up was with catalogue courses but there had been a rise in bespoke systems over the years. If surveys are to be believed it was expected that a rise in organisations using e-learning from 45% that presently use it to 85% within 2 years. In contrast to Training ZONE, BlueU claim that e-learning is best used for IT training and soft skills followed by company products and procedures. Many of the large vendors were producing systems where companies and individuals are able to purchase time on their systems, where others were creating systems to enable e-coaches to provide services over a medium.

One of the dangers in e-learning failure is organisational focus on cost savings which could

---

[2] http://www.blueu.com

explain the reason for rollback into blended learning as a combined consequence of rejection and bad material. Blended Learning had suddenly become an important synonym in the world of e-learning.

> *"Saving money is also an attraction of e-learning, if executed properly, but it should not be the main factor, says Claire Schooley, an analyst with Giga Information Group. "It cannot be the only reason or web-based training will fail"* BlueU[2.]

The change in fortunes of the NASDAQ greatly affected the advance of e-learning. Only those organisations such as Smart Force benefited from investment because of its early entry. It was difficult to get funding because investors had been bitten by the collapse of many Dot COMS. The reluctance to invest was instrumental in the market shakeout this was further damaged by precaution in world markets due to the 9/11 attack. These factors had a profound effect on the global economy causing further setbacks in investment and hence, the advancement of e-learning.

## 5.2 Training Trends

The e-learning environment was sending mixed messages to prospective clients and its users, it became important to examine trends and find out what exactly was happening. A study commissioned by Training ZONE to find out the state of play in the work place with e-learning predicted the following for 2002:

- *As with last year, 2002 is expected to see a huge increase in the use of online training, but attitudes to using e-learning are less enthusiastic than they were, with fewer respondents regarding the method as 'convenient' or 'engaging'.*

- *Personalising learning looks set to be a key theme, with a significant increase in coaching and mentoring expected and in the amount of individual self-study taking place.*

- Classroom training is still thriving and does not seem to have been affected by the rise of e-learning as a method of training delivery.

- *Blended learning, although much vaunted as a replacement for e-learning, has yet to establish itself properly as an alternative method.*

- Individuals are having a greater say in their own development, and are sharing responsibility for making sure their training needs are met with their line managers.

*Evaluation continues to grow in importance, with around a quarter of respondents progressing past the 'happy sheet' stage* (Phillips S., Training Trend, 2002).

The main outcome of this survey indicates there was a future for e-learning but not necessarily in the soft skills market. The important factor in the survey concerning evaluation was its significance. As the last point shows it continued to grow in importance' mainly due to justification of expenditure but 57% of those surveyed said the need for evaluation was essential and 89% of respondents stated they used feedback and validation and only 2% were not using any evaluation method.

The method of training delivery showed significant trends towards delivery of information and IT skills but slightly effective in working towards qualifications. This is the market tLB was hoping to make inroads along with delivery of information and e-coaching. The virtual learning environment was designed for both delivery and working towards training goals. There are functions such as goal setting designed into applications for this purpose. It appears that the culture of classroom based training was not easy to break. Again e-learning was in its infancy, if it was compared to fashion it would take a significant amount of time before users begin to accept it into normal everyday practice. A comparison between Figure 6 and Figure 7 shows respondents still favoured towards classroom based training as a more effective method hence the shift towards blended learning by e-learning providers. The distant learning respondents had lesser knowledge on the subject therefore the response becomes diffused therefore the judgment will be indifferent.

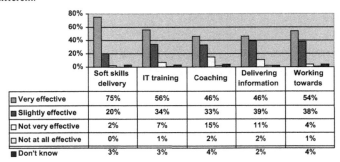

| | Soft skills delivery | IT training | Coaching | Delivering information | Working towards |
|---|---|---|---|---|---|
| ☐ Very effective | 75% | 56% | 46% | 46% | 54% |
| ■ Slightly effective | 20% | 34% | 33% | 39% | 38% |
| ☐ Not very effective | 2% | 7% | 15% | 11% | 4% |
| ☐ Not at all effective | 0% | 1% | 2% | 2% | 1% |
| ■ Don't know | 3% | 3% | 4% | 2% | 4% |

**Figure 6 - Classroom-based training - Training Trend (2002)**

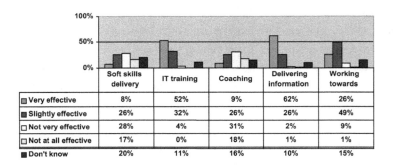

| | Soft skills delivery | IT training | Coaching | Delivering information | Working towards |
|---|---|---|---|---|---|
| ☐ Very effective | 8% | 52% | 9% | 62% | 26% |
| ■ Slightly effective | 26% | 32% | 26% | 26% | 49% |
| ☐ Not very effective | 28% | 4% | 31% | 2% | 9% |
| ☐ Not at all effective | 17% | 0% | 18% | 1% | 1% |
| ■ Don't know | 20% | 11% | 16% | 10% | 15% |

**Figure 7 - E-learning - Training Trend (2002)**

In general one to one tutoring was favoured best by respondents as the most effective method followed by classroom based training. E-learning shows a significant mark in IT training and delivery of information but would be more suitable in a soft skills market where users are able to train in their own time.

29

E-learning had not reached the growth predicted for 2004 it was presumed that businesses and users were apprehensive but nevertheless producers of learning materials were growing. A survey by Epic shows a slow uptake to e-learning in UK organisations where it was at less than 20% at one point but within 2 years 57% were using it and 76% were expecting to use it in 5years.

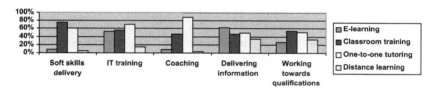

**Figure 8 - Percentage of respondents rating training method as 'very effective' Training Trend (2002)**

There are a growing number of developers in the e-learning arena where the major players include Blackboard and Smart Force who had established themselves in the educational market. Learndirect had also established itself as major soft skills and IT player and SmartForce had made inroads to corporate markets in competition with bespoke systems. IBM developed learning space and Sametime which provided the VLE for tLB platform and was involved with establishing e-learning in the corporate environment. Oracle had also developed Oracle iLearning which was displayed at the e-learning exhibition Wembley in May 2002 and made inroads in the Asian markets. Oracle made a $5.5 Billion bid for Peoplesoft as a strategic decision which was an indication of intent with the organisations e-learning policy and also an indication of where the e-learning market was going.

It is no surprise to know that most of the major e-learning players operated out of the USA where there is greater entrepreneurial spirit and investment. The list in Appendix B shows some of the main suppliers and their main competences.

## 5.3 Comparison of Players in Today's E-learning Market

There are a number of main providers in the e-learning market most of the larger organisations such as Blackboard, Smart Force, First Class are global players (Oracle doesn't feature in this comparison because at the time of writing, the specifications are not available). tLB deploys Sametime as a virtual learning environment therefore used in this comparison. Brandon Hall was the source of the table of comparisons between a number of players that mainly operate out of the USA and Canada.

The University of Bangor e-learning investigative team when considering its e-learning applications decided on market players of which Black Board and First Class were selected as the main contenders. In light of this, Black Board, First Class was included in this comparison. Click2Learn Toolbook, Saba Learning Enterprise, and WebCT was also used in comparison because these are major player in the UK market. Saba was not as UK established as the others but was an up and coming application and used widely in Europe

The climate today in the e-learning market place sees a push towards consolidation through strategic alliances. Some of the organisations for example, Ascot systems and many of the content providers, had opted to differentiate realising there is a market for providing VLE to accompany LCMS and LMS systems. It is those content providers that had opted to creating alliances early on that were likely to survive of which many other e-learning vendors were presently pursuing this policy. The e-learning market had realised the way forward is to consolidate resources between suppliers. There are very few vendors with complete systems because to go it alone ate up resources and those that did, tended to find their resources stretched to the limits. As mentioned previously the stock market was very wary of investment therefore capitalisation became scarce. Smart Force had invested $100 million in a complete system but were quickly laying people off, had they pursued a collaborative strategy, costs would have been reduced. It poses questions on being first into this type of market when academic research is limited and market research is difficult to establish.

The table of comparison of application is provided by Centre for Curriculum and Transfer of

Technology. The comparison is made within three main subject areas with categories above a listing of subheadings: (See Appendix A for glossary and B for comparative table)

1  Learner Tools: web browsing, asynchronous and synchronous sharing, student tools.
2  Support tools: course, lesson, data, resource, administration, helpdesk
3  Tech Info: server platform, client platform, pricing, extra, limitations of package, extra considerations.

It is easier to follow the order of the table to begin with learner tools with the focus on Learning Space: It appears that Learning Space falls over in its Web Browsing capacity with accessibility along with Click to Learn and Saba. Most of the applications have bookmarks function and Learning Space fears well on Asynchronous Sharing with e-mail, newsgroups and bulletin board file exchange it is only Saba that falters in this area. In the synchronous category Learning Space lacks in voice chat and virtual space similar to Click2Learn but has Video and Audio Conferencing facilities which only Click2Learn share. Although Black Board doesn't have video and audio conferencing it has a voice chat facility. Webct, First Class and Saba are lacking in the Synchronous areas. First Class does not have any synchronous facilities apart from chat and virtual space whereby Webct have only chat, white board and application sharing. Learning Space seems to be well blessed in the asynchronous and synchronous functions which makes it a cut above the rest. It also has a full complement of student tools i.e. Self assessment, progress tracking, searching, motivation building, study skill building. All the applications share these facilities apart from Click2Learn which has only progress tracking and study skill building and First Class is lacking only in study skill building.

In Support Tools, Most of the applications have a full complement of course tools apart from Saba who have no course customising facility. It also lacks in instructional design and information presentation where all the other applications have these facilities apart from first class that is lacking in instructional design. All applications are also very good on data with online      marking,      records      management      analyzing      and      tracking.

For resource planning only Black Board and Learning Space have a full complement of curriculum management, knowledge building, team building and motivation building. Click2Learn has none of these facilities and First Class and Webct are lacking in curriculum management and building motivation. On the administration front Learning Space has no on-line fee handling facility which is the same for all applications apart from Black Board and Saba. Apart from that Learning Space fears well on all other administration facilities, where Black Board has a full complement. Saba is lacking here in resource monitoring and crash recovery and Cli2Learn in the latter.

### 5.3.1 Technical Information

The technical information section shows all applications apart from First Class are unable to run on an Apple Server, although they are all capable on Windows NT and Unix Servers. The other important factor in the technical area is the limitations and standards. Only Webct, Learning Space and Saba comply with IMS standards. Learning Space, Click2Learn, and First Class are also limited by number of courses, number of students, number of connections and number of instructors.

This comparison gives a basic idea of what facilities are available and how some of the major players compare. In this comparison Black Board appears to rise above most but is lacking in provision of video and audio conferencing facilities and not being IMS compliant. Learning space seems to fare well and would come out second apart from the limitations on numbers which Black Board doesn't have it matches well against the others. (Note: These findings were based on the systems at the time of writing.)

### 5.3.2 tLB Platform

The reasons for including learning space in this comparison was it forms the live classroom in tLB. What was not included in the comparison was the community's side of tLB much of which replicated Learning Space. However, what most others lacked was a facility to create communities of learners or if present, the potential has not been considered as a major functionality within the system. Virtual space and break out chats or group facilities could be placed in the same category as communities but the intention was not within Communities of Practice (CoP) which was a function of the active learning process. Goal setting and learning logs were features unavailable in most if not all of the applications which play an important role in reflective learning.

### 5.3.2 How does tLB compare

As previously mentioned tLB carries Sametime, a feature of Learning Space but it also approaches e-learning with pedagogy in mind. The fundamental difference between tLB and other systems is in the design process. The design process is based on active learning principles (see Active Learning - Chapter 8) which differentiate it from most other e-learning systems. The communities within e-learning have easy access and navigation and supplies learning logs and journals with simple user access. It allowed a coach/tutor access to materials with the capability of uploading and downloading pages which promotes more of an e-coaching system. The file access was also simple to operate and confined to materials for a particular community. There were also web links that allowed users to access material similar to the file access service. tLB does not function as a LCMS as it lacked a course catalogue and a tracking process although these functions were in the pipeline. It boasted many other functions such as a library and editing facilities for coaches.

The future roadmap of tLB suggested it would have the ability to perform much of the tasks these other systems conveyed but with additional coaching functions which if perform correctly could place it at the top of the e-learning market. The pedagogical process within tLB determined the markets in which it operated which were predominantly within industry although; it was equally capable of operating within the educational sector. It was of significant importance that industrial markets and how e-learning systems are designed was well understood in relation to development.

# Chapter – 6

# Learning Theory

## 6.1 Theories of Learning

Modern methods of teaching is adopting new theories of learning some of which are deemed suitable to e-learning. E-learning is fundamentally different to traditional practices although the intention is similar: appropriate theories of learning have to be adapted for use on e-learning platforms. It is important to include pedagogy in the design process by selecting appropriate theories that lend themselves to the online coaching process. Three of the traditional theories regularly associated with teaching are:

- Constructivism - Bruner (1973)
- Behaviourism – Skinner (1953)
- Phenomenography - Marton & Entwistle (1983)

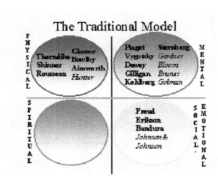

Figure 9 - The Integration Model – Boatman (1998)

Past literature tends to focus on the two main theories of learning as constructivism and behaviourism, whilst some refers to phenomenography and behaviourism. Behaviourism suggests there is no distinction between mental and physical events, it generally thinks behaviour

35

is predicted and can be changed by doing, Skinner (1953 & 1987). Behaviourism is disputed and generally criticised because it is believed the mind is more complex and cognitive responses and non predictable behaviour cannot be explained in a similar context, it requires more materialistic explanations relating mental states with neural activity. Of late a number of modern theories have arisen which have displaced the role of behaviourism in teaching & learning: Two of these theories include 'conversation' Laurillard (1999), & Pask (1985) and 'theory of understanding space of experiential variation' Fazey & Marton (2002)

Pask (1975) set out to make knowledge explicit through conversation and within the subject context. The theory suggested that three exclusive but relative 'languages' could be used:

- *Natural Language – Suitable for general discussion*
- *Object Language – Suitable for subject matter discussions*
- *Met Language – Described dialogue about learning and about language*

The learning strategies behind the theories were identified as:

- Serialists: *Who progress through an entailment structure in a sequential fashion* Bodomo (2001)
- Holists: *Who look for higher order relations* Kearsley (1994-2000)


Boyd (1993) determined further levels of conversation: *task, explanatory, manipulative, purposive and meta-cognitive* (Kaminski J.) summarised by a statement from Laurillard:

> *Through the lens of conversation theory, the learning environment is one of social and internal relation where content and process are interdependent,* Laurillard (1999).

Laurillard (1999) developed conversational theory based on the works of Vytgogsky (1962, 1978), who uses a social learning theory approach based on social interaction as a means to

36

cognitive development within limited time span entitled 'zone of proximal development' (ZPD). Laurillard (1999) emphasises the necessity of dialogue for higher level learning at theoretical and practical levels to enable the student to *link theory with practice*. The role of the student acting as collectors, evaluators and conduits of information as highlighted by Thomas J. readily relates to Laurillard's conversational theory as does the 'theory of understanding space of experiential variation' Fazey & Marton (2002), where practise is emphasised as key to learning. Laurillard has noted these points which are considered tacit therefore generally overlooked and are a basis for the conversational framework:

- *narrative - this involves the telling or imparting of knowledge to the learner;*
- *interactive - this is based on the outcome of the learning. The tutor provides feedback to students based on the outcomes of tasks students undertake in order to help consolidate learning and improve performance;*
- *In addition, the tutor uses this information to revise what learning has occurred and, if necessary, change the focus of dialogue (adaptive);*
- *Communicative/discursive - the tutor supports processes where students discuss and reflect upon their learning.*
- *The tutor and student agree learning goals and task goals, which can be achieved using 'productive' media, such as online presentations* (Laurillard, 1999).

It is the *experiences in thinking about variation,* considered 'the space of experiential variation', Fazey & Marton (2002), and due to become an important concept in learning. Considering Thomas, Laurillard, and Vytgogsky whom have all in some way associated social aspects of learning with dialogue and considered them in different aspects of approach where the results are fed back into the process. Variation theory examines concepts from each viewpoint, and concludes to a point of learning and understanding resulting in cognitive development with the understanding; many different viewpoints are the road to mastery. Therefore, as this written chapter provides the evidence, the concept of variation grasps a dimension in learning which is overlooked. For example, consider the theories of these authors which have helped to develop understanding by association which is evident. A varied perspective can help to improve the learning and it should be within the skill set of the facilitator to understand and develop learning procedures based on these concepts. Variation concept readily interacts with the *conversational approach* which is based on further *interaction between the teacher and learner with a slightly more humanistic angle*, Atherton (2003) i.e. The perceptions and interactions between tutor and student are as much a part of the learning which helps to determine further outcomes within a collaborative relationship. The concepts and theories to constructivist theory and lend themselves to learning with technologically and active learning processes within e-learning collaboration.

Constructivism is considered to be a more appropriate theory of learning and is based on the fact that humans cannot immediately respond to theory; they construct knowledge through experiences. This implies that one person will interpret knowledge in ways they find more comfortable to them. In other words we all think differently therefore will respond to stimuli in a variety of ways.

The past has seen behavioural theories incorporated into teaching which have been difficult to discard and evident within the approach of material designers for online-learning environments. Most organisations have yet to take on new theories of learning therefore are lagging behind and lack efficiency which can import itself into design of materials for any new learning particularly online. Papert (1993) attempts to signify the differences between behavioural and constructivist approach:

> *Papert characterizes behavioural approaches as "clean" teaching whereas constructivist approach are "dirty" teaching:*

> *Papert illustrates the differences between behavioural and constructivist teaching by contrasting the way Baby learned to dance in the movie Dirty Dancing with the traditional method:*

> *Clean learning reduces dance to formulas describing steps, and clean learning reduces maths to formulates describing procedures to manipulate symbols. The*

*formula for the fox-trot box step is strictly analogous to the formula for adding fractions or solving equations.*

*Dirty learning, by contrast, is emotional, complex, and intertwined with the learner's social, cultural, and cognitive context* (Papert, 1993, Page135).

Therefore to learn by engaging in exercises where theories are constructed from post & prior experiences and understanding is gained within the context of how one learns and the learning environment. These are further explained by cognitive processes from which constructs are drawn, and therefore to engage in *meaningful activities,* improves our learning. The online learning environment can be a useful tool for constructs as long has the activities are meaningful thus can be achieved within active learning processes. The online environment makes an ideal active learning environment, provided it is moderated and instructed correctly, because students are able to engage in asynchronous and synchronous activities and collaborate on subjects. Online-learning platforms can be a perfect active learning setting providing the design of the system and materials consider theories to keep students motivated.

## 6.2 Piagetian Theories and Information Systems

The online-learning environment can be considered as a knowledge information system but when used correctly as a learning tool, this could be disputed, but most Web sites are generally just this. The tLB is partially designed to impart information and it is how this is achieved that postulates the essentials in the learning environment. The challenge is to turn this information system into an environment for active learning. Piagetian theories suggest information is issued in different approaches, for example, problem solving or games.

The Piagetian theories are based on cognitive learning which is closely related to Constructivism. Here are two key Piagetian principles for teaching and learning that illustrates this:

*Learning is an active process: Direct experience, making errors, and looking for solutions are vital for the assimilation and accommodation of information. How*

39

*information is presented is important. When information is introduced as an aid to problem solving, it functions as a tool rather than an isolated arbitrary fact.*

***Learning should be whole, authentic, and "real":*** *Piaget helps us to understand that meaning is constructed as children interact in meaningful ways with the world around them. Thus, that means less emphasis on isolated "skill" exercises that try to teach something like long division or end of sentence punctuation. Students still learn these things in Piagetian classrooms, but they are more likely to learn them if they are engaged in meaningful activities (such as operating a class "store" or "bank" or writing and editing a class newspaper). Whole activities, as opposed to isolated skill exercises, authentic activities which are inherently interesting and meaningful to the student, and real activities that result in something other than a grade on a test or a "Great, you did well" from the computer lesson software, are emphasized in Piagetian classrooms. (ebook)*

[3]Phenomenology and constructivism are also closely related according to Biggs (1999). Phenomenology tends to be more aesthetically orientated. Theories of teaching and learning are likely to be a combination of these by way of meaning and interpretation of the world we live in and how it is viewed in relation to the concepts we create. These two theories focus on the activities the student does and the approach of the student and their world view therefore determines what is learnt. The different cognitive levels of engagement are determined by the interpretation of meaning which can either produce surface learning or deep learning. A low level of cognitive engagement produces a fragmented outcome where as a deeper approach should be encouraged because it give the student more understanding. There are arguments that suggest the traditional methods of learning are likely to produce surface learners although some students will show a natural preference to deep learning. The motivation of the student can be an indicator of a particular approach.

---

[3] http://pratt.edu/~arch543p/help/phenomenology.htm

## 6.3 Deep & Surface Learners

Approaches to learning are defined as deep and surface Marton & Säljö (1976); Entwistle (2000), Atherton (2002) where deep learning uses are intrinsically motivated (see Chapter 9 for explanation of intrinsic and extrinsic motivation) using high level cognitive skills relative to Figure 14 (Chapter 8.2) where activity involves theorising and reflecting. Surface learning is linked to extrinsic motivation or *passive processing* Jocelyn (2004) where the student is more concerned with memorizing and note taking. A simple definition provides a correlation between constructivist and objectivist tradition and deep and surface learning. Intrinsic motives of deep learners drive them to relate tasks more readily than extrinsic learners, whom prefer to achieve just enough to obtain the grade.

| Surface Learners (Objectivism) | Deep Learners (Constructivism) |
|---|---|
| *Focuses on the signs and unrelated part of the task* | *Focuses on what is signified and relates previous knowledge to new knowledge* |
| *Treats the task as external imposition and focuses on assessment.* | *Generates intrinsic motivation for the task and puts emphasis on understanding aspects of realty.* |
| *Memorises information for assessments and associates facts and concepts unreflectively and fails to distinguish principles from examples.* | *Relates knowledge from different courses, relates theoretical idea to everyday experiences and distinguishes evidence and argument.* |

**Table 1 - Deep and Surface Learners (Enoroth 2002)**

A clear distinction is made between the two types of learners but it is argued by Enoroth (2002), that deep learning is not always appropriate to the situation or indeed the learner which is commendable. The statement is justified by the distinction between learning and knowledge. Knowledge requires deeper learning in contrast to surface learning which is dependent on knowledge demand. Whether you are there to impart knowledge or gain information from learning for something specific required speedily, it mustn't be forgotten that in most online systems time is a resource thus there are limitations to how much can be done in a given period.

Constructivist theories in active learning processes appears to provide a more learner centred environment so we need to take a closer look at how they can be included in e-learning which is explained in the next chapter.

# Chapter – 7

## Pedagogy in Online Learning

### 7.1 Definition of Pedagogy

The consideration of Pedagogy is an important subject area when building any e-learning platform. The term pedagogy pertains to the arts and craft of teaching in a child context but in this paper it is used to mean both adult and child. The correct term to use in an adult context is androgogy (Knowles, 1978) which generally is defined in the context of a shift from the normal didactic approach to facilitation, reflection and learner centred principles. The National Board for Teaching Standards defines pedagogy in the context below:

> *Content pedagogy refers to the pedagogical (teaching) skills teachers use to impart the specialised knowledge/content of their subject area(s). Effective teachers display a wide range of skills and abilities that lead to creating a learning environment where all students feel comfortable and are sure that they can succeed both academically and personally. This complex combination of skills and abilities is integrated in the professional teaching standards that also include essential knowledge, dispositions, and commitments that allow educators to practice at a high level.* (Knowles, 1978, page 54-55)

The pedagogy in e-learning refers to teaching and learning which addresses such issues concerning goals/objectives, content, design approach, organization, methods and strategies, and medium of e-learning environments. Various e-learning methods and strategies include: presentation, demonstration, drill and practice, tutorials, games, storytelling, simulations, role-playing, discussion, interaction, modelling, facilitation, collaboration, debate, case studies, and motivation.

## 7.2 Relationship between Pedagogy and Instructional Design

It is understood that it is very much relative to environmental and pedagogical approach as to the quality of learning. In online learning the pedagogical approach is all the more important within the facilitation of the learning and lesser in the technology, Leiblein (2000). The use of technology can only improve the learning process because it allows students to become more engaged thus appeal to a greater conscientiousness. Mason (1998) suggests that '*analysis of these cultures will lead to a range of new practices*' with reference to communities and activities within them. Students tend to learn more in this type of environment because they are more active.

The emphasis on the quality of the pedagogy and not the technology is essential as many have found to cost. The technology is not always able to function and when the learning focuses on the consequences of this, it takes the onus away from the intention. Technology is simply the foundation for learning and according to MacLoughlin and Oliver (1999), the introduction to teaching creates a dynamic environment and the fact that students are able to collaborate helps to introduce new learning experiences therefore transform and shape learning. Technology thus has this dynamic affect allowing the emergence of new teaching and learning practices. The fact that it can encapsulate the wider community and different cultures and has the ability to gain access to electronic data on a global scale aids the advancement of learning. The sociocultural theory looks at technology resources as a tool for learning and communication such as computers and sees them as a means of expression and creation not only in objective wisdom but in subjective manner. Such a relationship between technology and culture is not new and has always been the case throughout time, Mason (1998) but the quality of the convergence, and speed has it continues to emerge requires first-rate practitioners. The resources help to create dialogue and communication and support the learning but has a practitioner the role is to ensure a good pedagogical relationship with the technology. The technology is the infrastructure for learning whilst the tutors and learners are participants within a holistic process. The role of the tutor is to facilitate knowledge within a community utilising sociocultural and constructivist theories in the process.

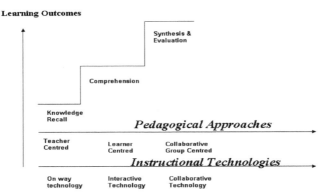

**Learning Outcomes**

Synthesis &
Evaluation

Comprehension

Knowledge
Recall

*Pedagogical Approaches*

Teacher
Centred

Learner
Centred

Collaborative
Group Centred

*Instructional Technologies*

On way
technology

Interactive
Technology

Collaborative
Technology

**Figure 10 - The Interaction between Leaning Outcomes, Pedagogies and Technologies - Mason (1998)**

Figure 10 is an example of the relationship between pedagogy and instructional technologies and indicates that higher level learning occurs more as the technology becomes more interactive. The learning outcome requires higher level participation thus the greater the collaborative activity. Convergence of the pedagogical approach and instructional technologies can provide a constructive learning environment in which students can participate in experiential learning. The collaborative or group centred activity tends to create communities of likewise learners who work towards a similar outcome. It therefore makes sense to create architecture to promote this type of learning. Discussion boards, VLE's, chat facilities, learner & grouping facilities are all functional within learning communities. The marriage between technology and pedagogy begins to become clear when understood in a learner centred context.

## 7.3 Communities of Practice

'Communities of Practice' (CoPs) have been around almost has long as learning has existed and are defined as '*a feeling that members have as belonging, a feeling that members matter to one another and to the group. And a shared faith that members needs will be met through their commitment to be together*' (Rovai, 2002, Page 2). Many of the great institutions such as Oxford and Cambridge were initially derived from gathering of scholars who shared a faith and commitment. The term 'communities of practice' appears to reflect the practice of gathering of scholars which is analogous to today's online communities. Online communities are, relative to learners coming together in order to embark upon a common cause or achieve a particular outcome just has scholars strived for success by pursuing this commonality towards a goal. It is inevitable that if e-learning systems existed in those days society would have advanced more rapidly, the advancement of society since the arrival of the processor has given provision to collaboration. Groups of people have always learned together and shared thoughts and ideas in order to develop higher level processes. Schools, Colleges and Universities are the product of the approach to thought sharing in order to create an educated society. Deep learning is a consequence of many factors but can be encouraged with practice particularly with like minded people or otherwise.

The tLB communities of practice are designed to achieve higher order learning through 'feelings *of connectedness, cohesion, spirit, trust and interdependence*' (Rovai, 2002). Communities can be quickly built and are hierarchical or a flatter in construct. To consider use of communities within an organisation, a typical community would be as in Figure 11. Sales, Marketing and Payroll are bought together in a single cross functional community of managers. The sales team have their own community of which the sales manager is also a member. This makes him a member of 2 communities. All three managers are members of communities concerning their own staff and a community of managers. This is a typical approach to build up of communities on the tLB platform with the introduction of collaborative tools such as a VLE, where synchronous meetings can take place.

**Figure 11 - Community Structure**

46

In each community are File and Web Share Facilities, Discussion Forums, Live Session and access to Chat. There are also opportunities to offer bespoke functionality such as Business Clinics, Specific Links to web sites, course material. It is limited only by the extent of the functionality of the web page.

## 7.4 Role of Communities in E-Learning

McLoughlin and Oliver (1999) and Mason, (1998) highlight the importance of the role of communities in e-learning. It has already been stated that the collaborative environments leads to higher level learning. To assist this, learning communities are created within the context of the learning. Like-minded students and learners whom share common tasks are able to communicate. Rovai (2002) suggests a community has shared learning goals based on more than just *'interpersonal skills'* and *'community membership'* but should also include *'strong feelings of community'* which is a sense of belonging and *'satisfaction of needs'* through *'active participation'*. This advocates that a community is more than just a place to pursue common goals and is not an arbitrary environment where users come and go. The community has a common boundary, common meeting place and a shared history which identifies a hierarchy of needs and relationships.

> *Proper attention must be given to community building in distant education programs because it is a 'sense of community' that attracts and retains learners.*
> (Rovai, 2002, page 199)

McLoughlin and Oliver (1999) emphasises this further in definition:

> *A community is formed as learners come to know each other, value what each other has to offer, focus on inquiry, share responsibility and control, learning through reflection and establishing a learning atmosphere that is predictable but has choices. In summary this community involves shared experience and a common commitment to method of enquiry.* (McLoughlin and Oliver, 1999, page 33)

47

Rovai (2002) and McLoughlin and Oliver (1999) refer to what is termed '*scaffolding* or *supporting others in a zone of proximal development*' Vitgotsky (1962 & 1978) which refers to cognitive development from an accommodating environment of tutors and students. The referral to teachers as practitioners highlights the ongoing skill requirement for scaffolding within active learning online environments. Cognitive learning occurs within socio-cultural activities but guidance is required to orchestrate and organise the learners. The facilitator has to not only understand the pedagogy within the learning processes but be aware of the technical issues that arise. In defining communities, Rovai (2002) and McLoughlin and Oliver (1999) have failed to emphasise the role of the practitioner within the community. An application of community in within a course context requires input from a facilitator to prevent it exceeding the boundaries of the learning objectives. It is agreed that the sense of belonging can inspire the need for motivation but a drift of users can slow the community down. Rovai (2002) suggests attention should be given in the building of communities, addressed with the application of learning theories to provide some of the motivational factors that help to keep users engaged.

## 7.5 Application of Learning Theories

The more we know about the way students learn allows the reflection on teaching methods for improvement. According to Biggs (1999) 'learning is the result of constructive activity of the student' thus in order to ensure the student learning approach is deep as opposed to surface effective teaching methods are required. Biggs (1999) thus uses a theory based on 'constructive alignment' where a more student centred system supports 'teaching methods', 'learning activities and assessments.

> *The system is called constructive alignment, based as it is on the twin principles of constructivism in learning and alignment in teaching, (Biggs, 1999, Page 11 )*

In the context of e-coaching applying suitable learning theories to ensure a learner centred environment is essential. Biggs (1999) uses the 3P Model to illustrate constructive alignment by bringing together some of the factors mentioned in this chapter:

The 3P model describes '*three points in time at which learning-related factors are placed*':

- *Presage: Before learning takes place*
- *Process: During learning*
- *Product: the Outcome of Learning*

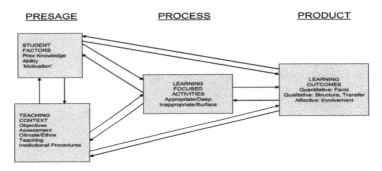

**Figure 12 - The 3P Model of Teaching & Learning - Biggs (1999)**

The *Presage* takes into account the student factors e.g. the ability, prior knowledge and motivation of the student. It also considers the teaching context including the institutional procedures which interact with both the learning activities and learning outcomes. This model suggests that all the factors should align and interact together to produce an appropriate learning environment. To consider these factors in an e-learning context it is similarly important they are conveyed in the environment. One important attribute missing from the *Process* is feedback it is important to convey student progress by formative and informative feedback to ensure the environment and all the tools involved are continuously assessed for improvement Hootstein (2002). The concepts of the process and learning outcomes are examined in Chapter 6 - Learning Theory and Chapter 11 - Online Coaching - 'the role of the coach in e-learning'. Motivation (Chapter 9) is also an important issue in e-learning that warrants greater scrutiny. Pedagogy and learning theory have provided evidence of the integration of active learning into the e-learning environment to produce activities that engage students into deep and meaningful learning. This will be examined in the next chapter.

49

# Chapter – 8

## Active Learning in an Online Environment

Passive learning generally tends towards greater *listening & concentration skills* Silbeman (1996), and allows very little reflection, whereas active participation strengthens learning Harasim et al (1997). It is therefore appropriate that only a minority of learners absorb knowledge through traditional means of course delivery. It can therefore be assumed that learning institutions originally evolved from learners capable of unsupervised engagement in higher level learning. However, society has changed and it is stated that one in three people leaving school or college now attend higher education institutions. There is a requirement for change in our teaching and learning methods to ensure greater depth in learning. Active learning, group dynamics and problem based learning as a legacy of constructivism theory, play an important role in e-learning systems to engage users in collaborative environments.

Active learning is about changing behaviour by development of higher order thinking skills which improves subconscious activity. It based on the cognitive principles *'when students hear, see, discuss, and do what they are taught'* is when the learning is taking place i.e. they are actively engaged in the learning process. The action learning approach is said to be more motivational because of active engagement and students tend towards this preference (Campbell and Piccinin, 2003).

The Online-Learning environment provides an ideal platform for the active learning strategies Silberman (1966) because of its ability to engage in participation. A typical VLE has Discussion Forums, Polling Facilities and White Board that allows the student to be online and take place in live discussions (New Teacher Toolkit).

The principles of active learning involve opening lines of communication that allow students to be more interactive and reflective, Austin, Nadine & Mescia (2003). Some of the characteristics of active learning are listed below:

50

- *Student responsibility and initiative to promote ownership of learning and transferable skills.*
- *Intentional learning strategies, explicit methods or learning, reflection on learning processes, metacognitive skills.*
- *Goal-driven, problem solving tasks and projects generating learning products of value.*
- *Teachers as facilitators, coaches, and guides, not sources of knowledge, requiring discussion between teachers and learners.*
- *Authentic contexts for learning, anchored in real-world problems.*
- *Authentic assessment strategies to evaluate real-world skills.*
- *Cooperative learning.*

(Characteristics of Active Learning Bostock, 1997, p. 226)

The teachers and moderators take on a facilitative role that encourages students to collaborate. The use of real world strategies and with real world assessments runs in parallel with the tLB philosophy, design and functionality. A guide to aid real world application in distance-learning shows there is very little distinction between provisions of good activity online or offline and these activities should be incorporated into the program (Mantayla, 1999):

1. Have a definite beginning and end
2. Have a clear purpose of objectives
3. Contain complete and understandable directions
4. Have feedback mechanism
5. Include a description of the technology or tool being used in the exercise

The table below delivers some of the possible active learning strategies that can be adopted.

| Activities | Study Type | Delivery |
|---|---|---|
| Assessment-tests and quizzes that provide immediate feedback | Reading case studies | Discussions(virtual chat, bulletin board) |
| Writings (reflective | Projects – group or | Experiential Learning: |

| journals, summaries, essays, critiques) | individual | Internships/ Preceptor ship/ Externships |
|---|---|---|
| Demonstrations with questioning (video clips) | Study/support groups | Visual-based instruction (streamed video or CD) |
| Games & Simulations | Problem Solving | Online presentations |
| Community building | Role – Play | Directed research |

**Table 2 - Active Learning Activities**

Assessments tests and quizzes will give student feedback and provide information very quickly on the student's ability. Case studies provide the subject matter for the assessments and quizzes which can be delivered in a VLE. Goal setting processes and journals allow students to reflect on their learning, whilst an interactive medium with games and simulation allow a more engaged approach. Community building provides an environment for experiential and aggregated learning. Active learning is considered a modern and effective approach but there are risks involved particularly if not applied in the correct way.

## 8.1 Risks in Active Learning

There is a tendency to assume that active learning is the 'be all and end all' of educational activity whilst this can be so far from the truth because active learning can be a high risk strategy:

> *'Active learning strategies, however, are often high risk. Students can fail to respond adequately to tasks, or fail to respond at all. Students can also produce responses that lack an appropriate amount of detail, are totally misguided, or that completely misunderstand the nature of the task. Active learning tasks can also be time consuming, and can appear to eat up valuable contact time'* (Mitchell 2002, page 4).

The risk is something that many coaches tend to overlook but encounter a situation where students have trouble grasping the concepts require contingency. This requires careful consideration in online environment because of the lack of body language it might proved difficult to establish such a situation is occurring. The skill of the facilitator is of significant importance, risks are therefore higher in an online learning situation where response and engagement is more difficult to evaluate. A lasting thought from Mitchell (2002) suggests that the '*risks involved are worth the rewards*' as one student from the tLB course would authenticate:

'*It was a shock to realise I was going to have to think for myself throughout! Most courses I have attended/worked through recently have been mere box-ticking exercises designed to keep the training providers' numbers up and get me through as quickly as possible. This one has actually made me think about marketing*' (Page 104).

A learning theory that is readily associated with active learning is experiential learning. Experiential learning is interpreted in many ways but the basic meaning is learning by doing i.e. hands on and practice. A theory closely associated to experiential learning is Kolb's Learning Cycle.

## 8.2 Kolb's Learning Methods as a E-Learning Framework

Kolb's learning cycle originated from 1956 and was designed on the basis that learning by doing and reflection on what has been done followed by conceptualisation which is the understanding of what has been done. Further experimentation on what has been done with a view of what to do next, completes the cycle. Completion of the cycle ensures that learning has occurred. It is understandable that the cycle can be entered at any point. Research shows that the more senses involved in learning the greater the learning that takes place so a multimedia situation online can maximise learning. This is something to be considered when designing materials and courses for e-learning environment.

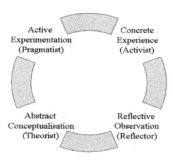

**Figure 13 - Kolb's Learning Cycle**

As can be seen in Figure 13, different components of the cycle tend to favour different types of learners therefore it is important that the cycle is completed in a learning environment thus all is catered for. A general explanation of the cycle is given below:

*Concrete experience:*
*An experienced-based, involved approach to learning. An individual needs to feel and experience the new information in a real way.*

*Abstract conceptualization:*
*A conceptually-based, analytic approach to learning. An individual needs to understand or have the new information explained logically.*

*Active experimentation:*
*An action-based, active approach to learning. An individual needs to try out or apply new learning*

54

*Reflective observation:*

*An observation-based approach to learning. An individual needs to reflect on and examine new learning.*

The adaptation of Kolb's learning cycle for online learning is depicted in the Table below.

| Active Experimentation (Planning) | Concrete Experience (Doing) |
|---|---|
| Simulation | Students carry out exercises online – Learn by Doing |
| Writing assignments | Discussions forums |
| Online learning logs and journals | Collaborative sessions |
| Setting goals | Reading |
| Preparation for online seminars (Questions) | Online lectures |
| Collaborative participation | Group work – Seminars |
| **Abstract Conceptualisation (Concluding)** | **Reflective Observation (Reviewing)** |
| Writing up material | Students carry out exercises online – Learn by Doing |
| Revision for online session | Writing up learning logs and journals |
| Linking various disciplines | Take part in online seminars |
| Experiencing web pages and making links | Follow me sessions |
| Take part in online seminars | Note taking |
| Follow me sessions | Discussion Boards, Chat and Email |

**Figure 14 - Kolb's Learning Cycle for Online Learning, Mitchell (2002)**

Action learning and the notion of experiential learning and Kolb's cycle is readily incorporated into an online environment as does learning outcomes because the journey taken is based on arrival at a conclusion and not concluded by the number of objectives that are met. The learning outcome doesn't necessarily discard objectives - it takes a more natural route dependent on the individual and is considered to be a more effective way of learning. To follow Kolb's cycle in an active learning process ensures effective learning but an important aspect of this is reflection.

In action learning Double Loop Learning is considered an important concept in organisational strategy. Double loop learning (Argyris,1976) involves examining the relationship between the 'espoused theory' and the 'theory in use'. This theory is based on implementing action within the organisation and associated with leadership and professional management. The principle is based on 4 steps:

1. Discovery of espoused and theory in use
2. Invention of new meanings
3. Production of new actions
4. Generalization of results

These four principles are applicable to the active learning process used in work place training. Consider it in the concept of Kolb cycle – Discovery of theory is relative to active experimentation, invention of new meaning can sit between active experimentation and abstract conceptualisation, production of new actions is relative to concrete experience and reflective observation is generalization of results. The fundamental difference with double loop learning is it reflects on generalizations with a view to review the situation. For example if you take a situation within an organisation with a negative view, expectation will be negative. In double loop learning you will see the situation in a positive light in order to affect the outcome in a more positive way Argyris, (1976).

As the design of the tLB is based on the learning within an organisation it is important that this concept is understood in an e-learning context.

## 8.3 Reflection

Reflection can be considered in many forms the typical experiential learning where the learner reflects on original conceptualization either during or following the process. Reflection can also be considered in the form of re-framing the problem and looking at it from different directions again it can be considered in light of the way practice takes place by alternating the approach. The problem is continuously reframed and reflected upon.

## 8.4 Online Journals and Learning Logs

Online journals, goal setting processes and learning logs can act has a reflective process in the assessment and the learning.

The Evaluation review (Chapter 15) has revealed the conclusion to the purpose of writing a learning journal was categorised as follows:

- *To record experience*
- *To facilitate learning from experience*
- *To support understanding and the representation of that understanding*
- *To develop critical thinking or the development of a questioning attitude*
- *To encourage metacognition*
- *To increase active involvement in, and ownership of, learning*
- *To increase ability in reflection and thinking*
- *To enhance problem solving skills*
- *As a means of assessment in formal education*
- *To enhance reflective practice*
- *For reasons of personal development and self empowerment*
- *For therapeutic purposes or as means of supporting behaviour change*
- *To enhance creativity*
- *To improve writing*
- *To improve or give 'voice'; as a means of self expression*
- *To foster communication; in particular reflective and creative interaction within a group*
- *To support planning and progress in research or a project*
- *As a means of communication between one learner and another*

(Moon, 2003)

To consider the above points it illustrates a greater degree of higher order thinking. The relationship between reflection and higher order thinking is evident therefore should be encouraged in online communities. It is for this reason the facilities for setting out journals, learning logs, and goal setting provides are provided on the tLB platform.

The thought of critical and purposeful reflection is not something a student readily takes on board. Provision of learning logs readily available to the learner enables the coach to encourage its usage. The coach/tutor should periodically allow group reflection using learning logs and goal setting features. This ensures commitment and replicates the norm in many colleges and universities today. Learning logs, journals, portfolios, reflective diaries are a much part of the reflective process as it is an element of life-long learning or personal development plan. The availability of such functionality provides an instant reflective process. It is advantageous to the tutor/coach over the duration of the course, to have readily available journals that can be incorporated into the assessment process.

The reflective process and the relationship to higher level process and deep learning requires incorporation into the assessment process. This is something that coaches/tutors should take on board as a method of summative assessment.

Portfolios have become significant in this type of assessment so there is no reason why learning logs and journals should not be also. Moon (2003) examines the assessment of the reflective process and provides some pointers to criteria:

- *Length*
- *Presentation and legibility*
- *Number of entries or regularity of entries*
- *Clarity and good observation in presentation of events or issues*
- *Evidence of speculation*
- *Evidence of a willingness to revise ideas*
- *Honesty and self-assessment*
- *Thoroughness of reflection and self-awareness*
- *Depth and detail of reflective accounts*
- *Evidence of creative thinking*

- *Evidence of critical thinking*
- *Evidence of a deep approach to the subject matter of the journal*
- *Representation of different cognitive skills (synthesis, analysis, evaluation etc)*
- *Relationship of the entries in the journal to any relevant coursework, theories, etc*
- *Match of the content and outcomes of the journal work to course objectives, learning outcomes for the journal or purposes that the journal is intended to fulfil.*
- *Questions that arise from the reflective processes and on which to reflect further*

The relationship between the criteria and assessment can easily be replaced by Bloom's or SOLO taxonomy (See chapter 12). The use of criteria for assessment is more extensively covered in Moon (2003) and is recommended reading for anyone unfamiliar with the use of journals and assessment criteria.

A last consideration in reflective writing, it could be considered as a course in itself and unless students are familiar with this type of work they are going to require coaching. They will also require motivating into performing many of the concepts involved in active learning. The levels of learning within an educational taxonomy, such as Bloom's, serves to determine the levels of motivation applicable to student work input. As Mitchell (2002) points out, there are risks to be addressed many of them lie within the subject of motivation in which the application of active learning processes and the approach the tutor/coach takes is essential to arriving at a suitable learning outcome.

# Chapter – 9

# Motivation

## 9.1 Theories of Motivation

Although these definitions have various backgrounds the basic theories that drive motivation is taken from many of the prominent learning theories which will be used to examine the implications on e-learning in an active learning context.

Active learning motivation can be thought of in an organisational context where e-learning leans towards theoretical learning in the work place and covers the learner's motivation to succeed in the job role and within an e-learning context where the motivation tends towards learning online. Considering these factors it is difficult to simply define motivation in the context of e-learning. All factors play their part as summarised by Huitt (1998): motivation is considered as a need or desire which conditions and drives behaviour where the following definitions help to summarise its meaning:

- *internal state or condition that activates behaviour and gives it direction;*
- *desire or want that energises and directs goal-oriented behaviour;*
- *influence of needs and desires on the intensity and direction of behaviour.*
- *the arousal, direction, and persistence of behaviour.*
- *influence of needs and desires on the intensity and direction of behaviour.*

A definition in an organisational context states: *"forces within an individual that account for the level, direction, and persistence of effort expended at work,"* (Schermerhorn, et al p.101 – 121).

In the case of an organisational context the internal state that activates behaviour is driven from the will to succeed. For organisations to take on e-learning from an active learning perspective, staff needs to be motivated to achieve in their job role, motivated towards organisational goals, and motivated to take on e-learning. The type of organisation and its management procedures and selection processes have significant influence on this. What is certain for online courses, a great deal more self-determination is required in consideration to normal courses; Deci and Ryan, (1991). Deci & Ryan theory on motivation looks at the environment from a dynamic perspective where *'individual's motivation is determined by a need for self determination and competence, complemented by the need for affiliation'*. Thus to influence these three factors would affect the motivation of the individual. Karesenti (1999) takes an argument from a study of the virtual classroom: The perceived gap between the university classroom and the virtual classroom is difficult to bridge. Students may not be ready for autonomy of self-determination when it comes to the 'virtual classroom' and there is a marked decline in student motivation after only four weeks of an online-course. This has huge implications on e-learning thus various signs show this could become evident in practice.

## 9.2 Intrinsic & Extrinsic Motivation

The relevance of the subject of motivation in online learning can be summarised by this statement:

> *"Behaviourism, with its emphasis on the external environment, missed the significant role of internal motivation in learning. This is in contrast to overwhelming evidence that can be summed up simply as –we really only learn when we want to'. Motivation is, in essence, an internal cognitive issue."*
> (http://www.utm.edu/research/iep/b/behavior.htm)

The general clarification of online motivation questions the fact as to whether it is intrinsic (internal to the person) *'Intrinsic sources and corresponding theories can be further subcategorized as either body/physical, mind/mental or transpersonal/spiritual'* Huitt (1998), or extrinsic (outside the person). Figure 15 further categorises these motivational factors.

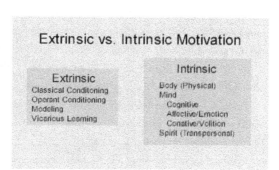

**Figure 15 - Extrinsic vs Intrinsic Motivation - Huitt (1998)**

Lepper (1998) suggests the general consensus is that intrinsically motivated students tend to think deeper and are likely to take a deeper approach and gather more information to complete a complex task. Whilst Condry and Chambers (1978) imply extrinsically motivated students tend to migrate to low cognitive tasks and tend to use just enough effort to accomplish the task. A conclusion can be drawn that intrinsically motivated students are likely to be deep thinkers, whereas the extrinsically motivated students are likely to take a surface approach, Atherton (2002). So what motivates learners? Biggs (1999) uses the expectancy value theory of motivation to explain why students do or do not learn. This states:

> *"...if anyone is to engage an activity, he or she needs to both value the outcome and to expect success in achieving it. Value and expectancy are said to multiply, not add, because both factors need to be present; if either one is zero, then no motivated activity occurs"* (Biggs, 1999, p56).

### 9.3 Emotion & Motivation

Psychologists have suggested that emotion differs from motivation because it occurs as a result of interaction between perception of environmental stimuli, and neural/hormonal responses to these perceptions. In other words people's feelings are based on their perceptions and stimulation from the real world. Thus facial expressions are linked to emotions but there is only a small core of them perhaps six or eight. Thus those feelings can be recognised and perhaps altered by the changes in facial expression hence motivation is a way of accessing those feelings and it is said that there is always a greater affinity towards happiness. Consider concentration and facial expression: if this is correct, long periods of concentration on a VDU requires endurance and can only be achieved by practice. After long lengths of concentration facial expressions begin to change. These expressions cannot be seen in a VLE, but possibly in synchronous communication using video streaming one can detect some emotion but not in enough detail to realise the relevance of emotional actions taking place. The delay affects the synchronisation between video and audio therefore renders the emotions more difficult to relate to. It is therefore important to know how to appeal to these emotions of altered facial expressions and to know when this has been achieved.

Maybe other reactions occur as a result of expressional alterations e.g. the way we write or communicate. This is an area for further research, 'What are the indicators of physiological changes to express the level of motivation in an online environment'?

From the latter it is possible to deduce the relative ease one can be de-motivated online. As some of theLearningBusiness studies have suggested some of the more important issues are based on technical aspects; hence imagine the problems that can occur in a technical environment and the effect it has on concentration and motivation. If the facial expression is an indicator of happiness and motivation is relative to emotion to any extent, it could be significant as to how moderators and facilitators relate to users and how they collaborate between themselves. The relationship with emotive responses and motivation highlights the importance of getting the right balance, as achieving this is relative to keeping users motivated.

Presently much research is being carried out on the problems associated with lack of face to face contact or more specifically eye contact. An extract from the article 'Closing the Gap' (see Web Site Reference) indicates the research level taking place in this category:

*On grander scale, researchers at Microsoft are developing a software solution to the eye-contact problem, which has traditionally plagued videoconferencing. The lack of gaze-awareness in standard video conferencing has contributed to its lack of popularity, says Jim Gemmel a researcher in Microsoft's Telepresence Research Group, part of the Bay Area Research Center (BARC) in San Francisco.*

*"Being able to make eye contact is a major component to making video compelling," Gemmel says. "Gaze is such a powerful social cue-it affects something deep in the psyche."* [4]

Gemmel and his colleagues were developing software, which wouldn't be on the market for a few years and was geared towards small groups of users. It uses computer-vision techniques to track participants' head and eye movements. This tracking information, which is transmitted along with the video stream, is then used to graphically place the head and eyes in a 3-D environment that provides gaze awareness and a sense of space.

Presently, facilitators and tutors can only deal with this by subjective judgment in mannerisms of online students as they interact for example, monitor behavioural pattern changes. More research is required in this area which is beyond the scope of this book.

### 9.4 What Can Be Done To Help Unmotivated Students?

In the first instance the greater the reduction in technological interference the more students will go on to complete the course. If tutors gain an understanding of the technical issues or has available to them instant support, the more likely students will be reassured. If for example, every week something goes wrong or the VLE or discussions are consistently off-line, the users will drift away. It is much the same with the information portrayed on a site. Students prefer activity; therefore it is up to the course providers to ensure that they get it.

---

[4](http://www.elearnmag.org/subpage/sub_page.cfm?article_pk=2761&page_number_nb=1&title=FEATURE%20STORY)

There is an issue between the use of technology and its purpose. It has been said that the technology is not the 'be all and end all', but it is the process of learning that has significance so should it be considered as a de-motivator when it doesn't function properly? Returning to the argument of the learning process and technology supporting the learning, the importance of the tutor and the theoretical application of the learning processes, it is possible to overcome technological problems. The students should be focused on the learning and not the infrastructure of that learning. If the technology fails then the learning can continue by some other means, email for example or use of an alternative chat or even telephone. More emphasis should be placed on learning outcomes rather than the architecture where expectations are far more students will remain motivated. The secret is not to dwell on the technology if it goes wrong, always have a contingency plan. The technological issues are relevant but what is far more important are the learners and the many different approaches i.e. motivation completing a course.

All the factors considered as apathy or cheating and procrastination are to protect the worth of individual and ties into extrinsic factors. Methods such as attribution training, encourage the students and help them concentrate on tasks rather than worry about the fear of failure. The use of reflective practice helps to remove the distraction of fear and failure as Biggs (1999) highlights in constructive alignment and the 3P Model (see Chapter 7 - Pedagogy in Online Learning - Figure 12). If the system is such that there are other means of solving a problem e.g. by removing the frustration, and reasons for giving up:

> *Portray effort as investment rather than risk, portray skill development as incremental and domain-specific, focus on mastery (*Brophy 1986, page 76*).*

The objective is to get learners into the frame of mind for valuing learning for its own sake; thus the role of the teacher is to develop within students the motivation to learn.

Motivation is an important factor in online–learning if we are to consider dropout rates are 20 to 50% of distant learners). Many of the students who enrol for e-learning courses are generally highly motivated to apply for the course in the first instant (Moore and Kearsley, 1996). Many people are de-motivated by bad experiences of learning from school or university and associate learning with boredom or stress or even memorising for an exam. The same can be said for bad technical experiences in online courses and lack of tutor commitment. There are many angles to motivation but one of the main issues involves how to re-motivate students.

Motivation as we have said depends on both intrinsic and extrinsic factors. Some of the factors required to instil in students are:

- Change their beliefs
- Create enthusiasm
- Use activities so student enjoys the learning
- Create a positive approach so student will take risks to learn
- Teach them patience and how to accept setbacks disappointments

Developing levels of motivation consists of five factors as Honey, P lists on his Website in Learning Motivation – Five Factors:

*1. Beliefs about Learning*
- *The extent to which you hold beliefs that underpin your willingness to invest effort in continuous learning. This includes:*
- *believing that everything that happens has learning*
- *potential*
- *believing it is helpful to have a personal development plan*
- *believing you are never too old to learn*
- *believing you are solely responsible for your own learning and development.*

*2. Enthusiasm - The extent to which in your feelings and behaviour you maintain an ongoing enthusiasm for learning. This includes:*
- *volunteering for extra tasks where you see a learning gain*
- *being keen to share your experiences with other people*

- *looking forward to participating in conferences, courses and*
- *workshops*
- *learning for the fun of it without a clear idea of why or how*
- *it will be of use to you.*

3. *Curiosity - The extent to which you habitually adopt behaviours that*
  - *demonstrate curiosity and inquisitiveness. This includes:*
  - *assuming you can learn something interesting from*
  - *everyone you meet*
  - *feeling exhilarated by the cut and thrust of a debate*
  - *being intrigued by the challenge of keeping learning fresh and continuous*
  - *keeping abreast of the latest developments in your field and*
  - *up-to-date with world events in general.*

4. *Courage - The extent to which you have the courage to take risks in order to learn. This includes:*
  - *relishing the prospect of tackling something new or different*
  - *experimenting with something where the outcome is*
  - *uncertain*
  - *being prepared to have a go and risk looking foolish/inept in*
  - *front of others*
  - *rising to the challenge of being stretched/taken outside*
  - *your comfort zone.*

5. *Resilience - The extent to which you stick with learning through setbacks, disappointments and frustrations. This includes:*
  - *persevering when you 'peak' or reach a learning plateau*
  - *maintaining a strong desire to make a difference*
  - *bouncing back after disappointments*

- *an unswerving conviction that the more you put in the*
- *more you stand to gain.*

## 9.5 Why do students drop out?

Drop-out rates in online-learning is a recent subject and very little study has been done. Arle (2002), faculty chair of life sciences at Rio Salado College, has made keeping students engaged his crusade and suggests keeping students motivated is generally an ordeal but doesn't need to be. Some of the problems he highlights are as follows:

- Instructors failing to engage and support students
- In online learning talking is done with the fingers within the VLE, those that can't keep up may have problems with active involvement. (Technical Skills)
- Lack of support and poor communication hence the need of good instructors.
- Lack of general ambience – i.e. sound activity and social stimulation that engage
- Students in a traditional classroom environment. Students find themselves out of sorts without this.
- Over booked courses
- Students expect an easy ride
- The instructor skills level and ability to facilitate
- Students forced into engagement in a e-learning environment when they are used to doing the minimum
- Lack of social stimulation as in traditional
- The moderator fails to keep student engaged – Lack of communication
- Lack of technical skills required to keep in contact with the course

## 9.6 What Makes Students Stay

Tutors and students have yet to realise they are required to work hard in an e-learning environment according to The retention rates bear witness to this and can vary from 50% to 60% in relation to the traditional 60% or more Arle (2002). Some of the factors for making students stay are highlighted in the text below:

68

- *Instructor skills - Train instructors in e-coaching and to utilise some of the Virtual Community tools such as chat, application sharing, and whiteboards. The suggestion from American university Spalding is to use the storytelling method.*
- *Build students technical skills and inform them of the skills required for browsing and discussions. Encouragement to increase their keyboard skills may be necessary.*
- *The enrolment procedure and access procedures should be easy to follow. Usability is an important to motivations as users become disparaged if find difficulty in access (See Jacob Nielson, 2002)[5].*
- *Provide technical support - this is essential to student retention. Again if the student feels as if logging on is more trouble than it's worth they are likely to avoid it.*
- *Group dynamics are essential as a motivational factor - It seems that students will migrate likewise forming own groups. Split into small groups because they are easier to manage*
- *Give students lots of up front information and advising. Students new to the online world need plenty of advice on accessing Web materials, participating in discussions, completing online assignments and the like, says Broughton, of Washington Online. Specially appointed advisers help, as do preparatory tutorials or courses, such as one called "Succeeding in Distance Learning," offered by Spalding University Online.*
- *Make registration easy. The easier it is to enrol in online courses, the more likely students are to sign up and stay in them, for example, the director of student services walks each student through course registration. And at the University of Phoenix, the computer system automatically enrols students in courses that follow sequentially in degree programs.*
- *Ensure that students feel connected right away. The class must "immediately become real to students or else they might start off disengaged," says Moore, at Washington State University. He advises that instructors use name-games, real-time chats and other icebreaker activities to get students talking. He also advises making an assignment and providing immediate feedback in the first week.*

---

[5] http://www.useit.com

- *Offer tech support. Since e-learning can pose technical difficulties, more institutions are beefing up tech help desks and sending students tutorials on using the Web and trouble-shooting. Washington State even offers students on-the-ground learning centres, complete with flexible hours and staffed computer labs.*

- *Provide academic support. Faculty "have to reach out to students-they can't wait until students contact them," says Edge. Regular calls, e-mails and chats are a must, he says, as are faculty receptivity and availability. At the tutoring service, Smarthinking.com, for example, students can call on "e-structors" any time-day or night. That level of access "really reduces students' anxiety levels and frustration," says Christopher Gergen, the firm's president.*

- *Assign students to teams. Linking students to each other helps link them to a course or entire degree program, says Digiovanni, CEO of the University of Phoenix Online. His institution is well-known for sending students through its programs in small teams or cohorts. "Some people think e-learning is almost solitary," Digiovanni T. "But it's quite the opposite here." Also beneficial to students, he says, is giving them plenty of group work and encouraging their participation in online discussions.*

- *Track students and check in with them regularly. Online students can easily lie low, so monitoring their progress is crucial, says Moore. At his school, staff checks whether students turn in assignments on time and call them if they haven't. And Rio Salado College, faculty use a course-management system to track how long students stay online*

(Arle, 2002)[6]


The importance of LCMS and tracking systems to keep in touch with student progress can help student motivation by recognising the activities the role of the coach and all those involved in the creation and upkeep. It is clear that concerns have encouraged some of the US University's & college's to look into some of the factors of motivation in e-learning which is essential its survival.

---

[6]http://www.elearnmag.org/subpage/sub_page.cfm?article_pk=2761&page_number_nb=1&title=
FEATURE%20STORY

### 9.6.1 Interactivity

Another means of keeping students engaged and increasing motivation is interactivity Wagner (1997) of which a number of types are suggested:

- *interaction to increase participation*
- *interaction to develop communication*
- *interaction to receive feedback*
- *interaction to enhance elaboration and retention*
- *interaction to support learner control/self-regulation*
- *interaction to increase motivation*
- *interaction for clarification [and negotiation] of understanding*

The message is interaction should be taking place hence the importance of an active learning approach. Again the question of body language arises or the lack of, thus the e-coach is required to facilitate interactivity to provide for its absence.

### 9.7 The Conclusion

Motivation is an important factor in the success of e-learning and requires more research. What has been discovered so far is the tutors and coach's play an important role in the motivation of students and the pedagogical understanding is critical even more so than the technology itself. The technology can be a de-motivating factor particularly when it is used entirely to deliver material. The environment in which the student learns is also crucial to motivation thus the coach has to ensure it is a safe place to learn. Most students that embark on e-learning will participate in the hours proceeding work therefore likely to be tired and less tolerant to technical problems. The coach/tutor also requires good skills in reading a student's language without the normal everyday body language.

The role of a tutor, coach or moderator has an important influence into the success of an e-learning environment as realised in motivational research but it is essential they acquire the skills to perform adequately. The design of materials for e-learning courses plays an important part in keeping students and users motivated it is therefore important that tutors/coaches and material designers understand the approach to instructional design.

# Chapter – 10

## Instructional Design and Learning Theory Application

Instructional design *"refers to the systematic and reflective process of translating principles of learning and instruction into plans for instructional materials, activities, information resources, and evaluation"* (Smith and Ragan, 1999, page 2). The importance of this definition is the relative ease it can be interpreted into online pedagogy yet many designers tend to ignore the pedagogy and produce content in a similar fashion to the traditional didactic approach to teaching and learning. Present e-learning methods give lip service to this approach and can lead to increased attrition rates and have an adverse affect on motivation. To design learning materials, and translate the principles of learning for instructional materials, tutors, designers and moderators are required to understand theories of learning considered applicable to e-learning. In the past traditional teaching methods have been based on objectivism which is very much aligned to the didactic approach. E-learning is deemed suitable to constructivist theory which is closely related to active learning providing a more modern learner centred approach (Nasseh, 2002).

### 10.1 Design of Instructional Material

When designing instructional material the literature refers to *three basic strategies* (Mesher, 1998, pp. 18-20):

- Passive Interactivity – If we consider traditional classroom learning, ambience provides a *contextual presence* which has to be compensated for in the virtual classroom. A constructivism method can help to overcome short comings because the student is more engaged in the learning process.
- Hyperlinked Activity – This is related to asynchronous online learning but can also act as a source for synchronous learning.

- Interpersonal Activity – This relates to the collaborative aspects of both synchronous and asynchronous communication. Communication with both tutor and student creating a collaborative learning environment encouraging deep learning.

Constructivism, engagement, collaboration are all terms pertinent to design methods yet, how many designers incorporate them into their methods. The use of an instructional design process is important to encourage a high level of learning expectations. Ideally instructional design can be aligned to taxonomy such as Bloom or SOLO to ensure the required level of attainment is reached and learning outcomes are met.

## 10.2 Frameworks for Design

A framework for instructional design created by Weston, Gandell, Mcalpine, & Finkelstein (1996) depicted in Figure 16 will aid the thought process when considering or designing content for online learning. It is suggested that there is a distinct lack of consideration given to the pedagogical side of online learning in web design yet the importance is significant. It is necessary to include some of the factors within the framework when instructing either coaches or designers to guide consideration towards a target audience.

Similar for many design forms of online learning, a variety of synonyms are created which makes it difficult to discriminate from its actual contents or meaning. Instructional design for example is associated with multimedia and can be found under the banner of computer-based instruction, computer-assisted instruction, and computer-mediated instruction.

Instructional design for online learning can be based on existing principles and guidelines which can be categorised in four principles; Instructional Design, Subject Matter, Language and Presentation which provides a comprehensive framework for discussion, Weston et al (1996). The framework is portrayed in Figure 16 which provides a method of query for instructional design for online learning.

74

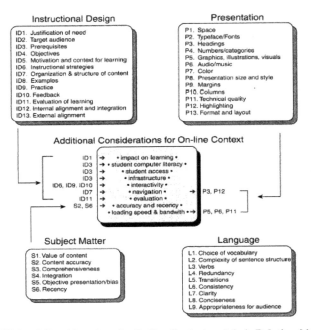

**Instructional Design**

ID1. Justification of need
ID2. Target audience
ID3. Prerequisites
ID4. Objectives
ID5. Motivation and context for learning
ID6. Instructional strategies
ID7. Organization & structure of content
ID8. Examples
ID9. Practice
ID10. Feedback
ID11. Evaluation of learning
ID12. Internal alignment and integration
ID13. External alignment

**Presentation**

P1. Space
P2. Typeface/Fonts
P3. Headings
P4. Numbers/categories
P5. Graphics, illustrations, visuals
P6. Audio/music
P7. Color
P8. Presentation size and style
P9. Margins
P10. Columns
P11. Technical quality
P12. Highlighting
P13. Format and layout

**Additional Considerations for On-line Context**

| ID1 | → | • impact on learning • |
| ID3 | → | • student computer literacy • |
| ID3 | → | • student access • |
| ID3 | → | • infrastructure • |
| ID6, ID9, ID10 | → | • interactivity • |
| ID7 | → | • navigation • | → | P3, P12 |
| ID11 | → | • evaluation • |
| S2, S6 | → | • accuracy and recency • |
| | | • loading speed & bandwith • | → | P5, P6, P11 |

**Subject Matter**

S1. Value of content
S2. Content accuracy
S3. Comprehensiveness
S4. Integration
S5. Objective presentation/bias
S6. Recency

**Language**

L1. Choice of vocabulary
L2. Complexity of sentence structure
L3. Verbs
L4. Redundancy
L5. Transitions
L6. Consistency
L7. Clarity
L8. Conciseness
L9. Appropriateness for audience

**Figure 16 - Additional Considerations for Online Context and their Relationship to Existing Instructional Principles - Weston et al (1996)**

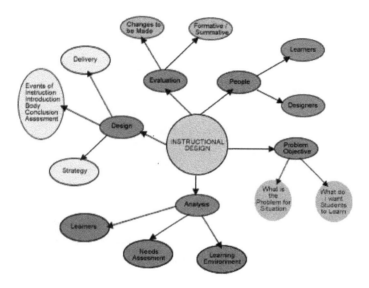

**Figure 17 - Concept Map for Instructional Design - Smith and Hill (1999)**

The framework attributes are suitable to both design and instruction but needs to be considered in categorisation.

Figure 17 provides a concept map based on a less complex perspective for instructional design for which the main attributes are Evaluation, People, Design, Problem Objective and Analysis.

Chapters 11, 12 & 13 will look at a variation of concepts in relation to the framework to produce ideal instruction for improve understanding.

The Analysis focuses on the needs of the learner and the learning environment. The Problem Objective is pertaining to learning outcome and learning objectives. It also addresses the problem and the situation that has caused the problem to occur which aids design strategy highlighting the objectives. The design question should observe certain rules that give guidance to production of material and the learning outcome should be referenced when answering the design question.

76

These frameworks act as a structure to evaluate requirements for the design principles for online learning – Figure 16 has more detailed attributes that cover most of the Figure 17 Model.

## 10.3 Instructional Design

Although all categories have their importance, along with Subject Matter, this is a significant for design pedagogy, and requirements within this category and helps to formulate questioning and reasoning at the planning stage. If you imagine a design cycle for this framework, the aforementioned categories are useful for the initial stages. It begins with the *justification of need* which suggests there must be some justification for the requirement which you can relate to *'What is the Problem of the Situation'* as portrayed in the concept Model. In order for the design to be utilised in the correct manner the target audience must be taken into account for example, age, background, knowledge, abilities. This can relate to *'What do I want the Students to Learn'* as in the concept model. This category is not represented very well amongst web instructional data i.e. pedagogical principles are not well thought out in web design and is therefore not ideally represented in the literature.

Most importantly users have to be motivated;

> *'Students experience the felt need to get there. The art of good teaching is to communicate the need where it is initially lacking. 'Motivation' is a product of good teaching, not it's prerequisite',* (Biggs, 1999).

It is required that when designing instructions and material for online learning this concept of *'communicating the need'* is well thought-out. Motivation is a key issue in online learning therefore 'the art of engagement is the quality of instructional design and learning content'. The learning environment should allow the students who feel the need to get there, to get there.

### 10.3.1 Subject Matter

The problem subject matter poses in Web Design is, it is consistently dated Weston et al (1996) and rarely proven or referenced. It revolves around the content matter and is considered with a number of attributes: Relevancy, timely, value of content, content accuracy and recentness.

Whilst surfing the web for conferences recently it was noticed that many of the conference sites were dated sometimes well over a year. As a provider of information, the web is quite unruly as there are no distinct standards as in publishing or media (Berk & Kanf, 1996).

Accuracy is quite an important attribute as is the objectivity of any presentation. These categories, as are many listed, revolve around the context of the design and are dependent on the subject matter and provision of the learning online. It, for example, can be just as unpleasant for a learner to be lead into a false belief, as it is to provide inaccurate content and bias information.

### 10.3.2 Language

The language again is an important issue but somewhat unconsidered in the design process. Again this is dependent on the target audience. If for example you are designing for a course in many continents of the world, a heterogeneous approach to vocabulary would be required for example; words would be used in a simpler format. Alternatively a variety of different designs could be used, dependent on the audience.

The semantics, syntax, complexity of sentence structure are all-important attributes in design and should be considered in terms of the target audience.

### 10.3.3 Presentation

This category focuses on graphics, format and layout. In general it relates to the variety of common file formats used in the design process which provides a number of attributes that relate to the interface between user and information. The style and such attributes as graphics, illustrations, and audio or music can provide for a rich presentation of content, rich expressive of quality and depth of information content. The presentation content is well represented within the web design world. Berk & Kanfer (1996) suggest, audience & purpose should be considered with the balance between all the presentation attributes. One other important factor when using graphics and audio is the Bandwidth. Use of compact graphics formats such as GIF or JPEG and condensed audio formats e.g. MP3 can considerably reduce bandwidth.

An additional category highlighted for additional consideration projected in Figure 16, Weston et al (1999) takes into account student ability and addresses many of the technical issues.

### 10.3.4 Impact on Learning

Weston et al (1999) question the justification of time against design, meeting the objective which is a valid observation. There is no justification in designing ineffective content or excessive use of resources which is again addressing the issue of '*What is the Problem for the Situation*' in the concept model of Figure 17.

Design of a system and content requires deliberation of both learners and moderators. The role of the moderator requires ease of use to minimise time involved to least possible. The design proposal has to consider the length of time the moderator or tutor spends online. At the same time goals and objectives have to be met and required levels of competency reached.

### 10.3.5 Goals & Objectives

The goals and objectives should be directed towards producing a quality in which users, students and tutors can engage and obtain the level of learning required to foster deep learning. A taxonomy should be considered to determine the levels of competence students are expected to achieve. Constructive alignment should also be considered for a student centred approach. The idea is to align teaching methods and assessments with objectives and goals of the learning activities.

The objectives are addressed in the '*conceptions of phenomena change*' and our world view in which we acquire information as being conducive towards education Biggs, (1999):

*1. It is clear to students and teachers what is appropriate, what the objectives are, where all can see where they are supposed to be going.*

*2. Students experience the felt need to get there. The art of good teaching is to communicate the need where it is initially lacking. 'Motivation' is a product of good teaching, not its prerequisite.*

*3. Students feel free to focus on the task, not on watching their backs. Often attempts to create a felt need to learn, particularly through ill-conceived and urgent assessments, are counter productive. The game then becomes a matter of dealing with the test, not with engaging the task deeply.*

*4. Students can work collaboratively and in dialogue with others, both peers and teachers. Good dialogue elicits those activities that shape, elaborate, and deepen understanding.*

Students can set their goals through clear objectives and the pathway to where they need to get to is uncluttered. Similarly the use of simple instruction can be detrimental i.e. encourage a surface approach. Multiple choice assessments tend to create this environment if not considered carefully. Within an online learning environment the platform exists for peer, teacher and student collaboration, it is the design element that decides how this is done. Once the design principles are in place, the tutor or moderator takes on the role of facilitator and mediator thus '*the premise of good teaching*' takes precedence.

The competency standards of the students are a subject that cannot be ignored in online-learning particularly because it may be relative to attrition rates. More research in this area would help discover if it is a reason for high drop-out rates. It has been noticed on tLB course that some of the students are not as adept as one would expect or they let on to be; Thus a course has to be held up for these students to get on a level plain. Competency standards should be a part function of pre-course evaluation.

### 10.3.6 Technical Issues

The technical issue has been underplayed by Weston et al (1999) who consider the consequences and skills required to operate within a online learning environment: Typing skills, browsing, email, word processing and last but not least technical skills. It is important to bring students of similar technical levels together if possible. It has been stated that technology should not be allowed to dominate the learning but in an online learning environment, during a live session it is of significant importance as a slow student can easily de-motivate others.

### 10.3.7 Access

In order to access online-learning the student requires suitable equipment and must be computer literate. It is important that the student is familiar with the use of IT equipment to keep pace with the course. The general rule is the course can only proceed as fast as the slowest student as with the equipment, the slowest bandwidth will dictate the speed the VLE session takes place.

### 10.3.8 Infrastructure

The infrastructure is the basis for the online-learning system and its efficiency is of significant importance. The technical team takes on the role of insuring the availability of equipment, the availability of the system and users access.

The use of active learning principles online requires the consideration of where the learner is going to be at any point in time (Austin & Mescia, 2002).

### 10.3.9 Conclusion

Instructional design, in the past, has refrained from pedagogical consideration but should be considered to achieve systems that are on par with traditional methods of learning. The principle behind e-learning is not to achieve the traditional methods of learning but to design pedagogy, with constructive alignment and active learning situations. With this in mind two models for consideration of pedagogy in online-learning are investigated.

Both frameworks are a useful tool for instructional design although Figure 16 takes an in depth look and uses attributes which prove to be more comprehensive and can be used relative to the level of requirements. The Figure 17 model has greater emphasis on planning process plus evaluation where the Figure 16 model portrays the internal attributes hence establishing greater emphasis on design pedagogy.

# Chapter – 11

## The Role of the Coach in E-learning

### 11.1 Is traditional coaching style suitable for e-learning?

If technology is not meant to be the dominant factor in a learning environment and the system is learner centred as advocated in constructive alignment Biggs (1999) a simple answer would be 'yes', as traditional coaching skills are suitable any learning environment, but additional skills are required to facilitate and manage the learning environment. The coach for example, would require more technical skills or at least an understanding of problems that can occur as realised whilst coaching on tLB. Skills in motivation, facilitating and moderating in an e-learning environment are also required to keep users engaged. Experiences on the tLB has proven this is the case – To date user motivation as been a significant problem and very few users have taken to the learning environment.

E-learning is presently far from trainer-less training as predicted by Massie (2002) who suggests training portals are the thing of the future. The coach/trainer will always have a role to play. Materials have to be designed and students have to be monitored as assignments and tests have to be set. There is some truth to this statement by way of artificial intelligence where the system takes over the role of the coach but this is a long way from materialisation. Another argument is the e-learning system is designed for a purpose for example tLB is designed for coaching online and it is difficult to see how technology can substitute for this. What can be predicted is that most training will take place online and trainers have to develop new skills to operate within these environments. E-learning has presently resorted to a blended format and future trainers will adapt to the skill sets required to perform this method of delivery as they learn and compress their delivery into shorter sessions to keep the attention span of the learners. The skill sets required for online training are as set out in Massie (2002) 'The Trainer of the Future':

- Shorter events for shorter attention spans and availability of online materials will shorten traditional classroom time.

83

- The use of active learning practices such as case studies, collaborative practices and simulations to *leverage the live environment*.
- The digital surround of events where trainers host materials for pre and post course work.
- VLE support and the use of tracking data to supply information for user's requests.
- Use of tools to transform user requests into asynchronous and synchronous information for learners.
- Become comfortable with sitting in front of microphones, audio video equipment.
- Develop and understand protocol for evaluating learner's moods without body language.

The subject of technical ability has arisen many times in this book and has Massie (2002) suggests, in the above list, it is an important skill set for the trainer. A number of technical difficulties arose from a tLB pilot study as one of the major obstacles. This was unexpected but became one of the major issues requiring attention prior to the start of the course. This has been the bane of the online classroom as the literature highlights; it can act as a de-motivator confirmed by the frustration discharged by users. Technical issues can make or break an online-learning course it is therefore imperative they are addressed early on.

## 11.2 Facilitative and Collaborative Skills

With reference to deep and surface learning the facilitator has a role to play to ensure students engage in deep learning, (Marton & Säljö, 1976; Entwistle 2000; Atherton, 2002) and experience variation in learning, Fazey & Marton (2002). The role of the facilitator when using electronic medium is to provide activities of a nature where students are able to approach the learning form different points of view and to be able to convey that knowledge in a way other than compartmentalising as highlighted by Thomas J. The student must understand *new knowledge* and have the ability to relate it to *existing knowledge*. An existing method for helping students achieve this is to use the student as collectors, evaluators and conduits of information. This method has the act of introduction of variation into the learning emphasised by Fazey & Marton (2002). In order to convey information the student is required to both learn and understand it. To evaluate information the student has to learn, reflect and understand and in order to act as a conduit the student is required to not just understand but have the ability to act on it. In order to achieve this the student has engaged in a number of different learning processes thus seeing the learning outcome from a teaching and learning aspect along with the many other methods used to acquire, understand and convey the knowledge.

*To correctly perform their duties as collectors, evaluators or conduits of information, students must bring to the task information they already have and then use that information in the context of new information to expand existing knowledge structures that become the basis for preparing information for consumption by others. Discussion activities that place students in the roles of collectors, conduits, or evaluators of information have the potential for incorporating the following features of deep learning:*

*--they provide students with practice with open-ended assignments that increase divergent thinking;*

*--they provide students with practice in processing and thinking using real life topics, issues;*

*--they "require" active processing on the parts of the students to do them correctly;*

*--they "require" mental organization, manipulation, and integration of information;*

*--they "require" reflection;*

*--they provide models that could be used for emulation or avoidance; surface learners can use the comments of deep learners as models of cognition;*

*--they produce either dissonance or consistency when processing the information obtained from others (more likely to restructure their own thoughts as a result);*

*--they provide experience with writing-for-the-web or help to improve writing-for-the-web skills;*

*--they provide experience with organizing thoughts for writing online (which takes place at a more rapid rate than the write—review and edit--re-write pattern that has been promoted in composition classes;* Thomas J (2004)[8].

85

These skills you would imagine a good coach to already possess although have to be understood in an e-learning context. The facilitative skills are required to make use of, and enhance the collaboration taking place which is what is being emphasised in the previous paragraph. A good understanding of the theories behind the theory and practice in e-learning will help the facilitator.

With reference to Hootstein (2002), an e-learning facilitator "*'wears four pairs of shoes'--acting as instructor, social director, program manager, and technical assistant*". Hootstein (2002) points out the changes in the education system from instructor-lead to learner-centred and the responsibilities of the facilitator for 'structuring the learning experiences' and emphasises the dependency on them for success in 'delivering and managing instruction'.

Examining the four areas which Hootstein (2002) suggests being requirements in the role of a facilitator:

### 11.2.1 Instructor

The role of the facilitator in this capacity is to use judgement in helping learners to 'acquire knowledge and develop skills' by providing information for learners to develop projects and complete assignments, 'develop strategies for learning' and encourage experiential learning using three main methods:

- o Fostering learner-centeredness
- o Structuring problem-based learning and authentic work
- o Providing informative feedback

The function of the facilitator is to focus on learning and not the technology. They should often participate in the challenge and scaffold learners to achieving a learning outcome. The collaborative environment, in which the learner exists, is guided by the facilitator who should also include the students in setting an agenda and providing learning outcomes. This is best achieved with learning activities, rather than '*didactic approaches*', in which the learner has greater engagement and interaction. An active e-learning environment can help add to the experience and inclusion of asynchronous and synchronous tools can endorse the experience. The facilitator should be familiarised with these tools before engaging in any action as there can be nothing worse than encountering problems based on inexperience, McLoughlin and Oliver (1999).

The importance of providing feedback is all the greater in an e-learning environment because of the isolated situation of the student. Hootstein (2002) suggests informative feedback but encouraging learners to 'evaluate their own responses' through reflection as depicted in 'Kolbs' Learning Cycle' can be advantageous. The use of goal setting, journals and learning logs provide the reflective tools from which the student can judge their learning against objectives or expected learning outcomes.

Hootstein (2002) has again highlighted the importance of constructivism theories in the role of the facilitator. Much of what Hootstein (2002) conveys in his paper falls in line with the *Presage*: student factors and teaching context of Dunken & Biddle's (1974) and 3P Model Biggs (1999).

### 11.2.2 Social Director

This role is about the facilitators function in developing collaborative environments e.g. 'fostering collaborative learning'. The passage below came from Surowiecki (2003) who wrote a book entitled 'The Wisdom of Crowds' that looks at the outcome of collaborative or aggregated decisions:

*There are four key qualities that make a crowd smart. It needs to be diverse, so that people are bringing different pieces of information to the table. It needs to be decentralized, so that no one at the top is dictating the crowd's answer. It needs a way of summarizing people's opinions into one collective verdict. And the people in the crowd need to be independent, so that they pay attention mostly to their own information, and not worrying about      what      everyone      around      them      think.      (Surowiecki, 2003)[7]*

As Mitchell (2002) states there are risks involved in the methods that are portrayed in active learning processes:

> *Essentially, any time most of the people in a group are biased in the same direction, it's probably not going to make good decisions. So when diverse opinions are either frozen out or squelched when they're voiced, groups tend to be dumb. And when people start paying too much attention to what others in the group think, that usually spells disaster, too. For instance, that's how we get stock-market bubbles, which are a classic example of group stupidity: instead of worrying about how much a company is really worth, investors start worrying about how much other people will think the company is worth. The paradox of the wisdom of crowds is that the best group decisions come from lots of independent individual decisions* (Surowiecki, 2003)[7].

The above passage provides evidence that all is not straightforward in collaborative e-learning, facilitators have to work at creating the right settings for learning to take place. Hootstein (2002)[8] states *'Encouraging and ensuring a high degree of interactivity and participation is one of the most important facilitation skills according to e-learning experts'*.    The observation qualities and what could be termed interactive grouping and manipulation skills are essential. For example, there is clear distinction between dialogue and discussion Enoroth (2000). Discussion is based on students taking a stand point for arguments sake and dialogue tends to emerge into a consensus or mutual agreement.    The facilitator's role is to ensure that the environment is adequate for dialogue to take place in the correct manner to achieve an objective.

Collaboration can occur quite naturally amongst users but it is important to ensure none are excluded.    The coach observes and monitors interaction between the users and ensures they

---

[7] http://www.randomhouse.com/features/wisdomofcrowds/Q&A.html
[8] http://www.learningcircuits.org/2002/oct2002/elearn.html

engage in the learning process. The coach will watch to see how users interact and if necessary encourage timid users or dampen dominant action. There exists an abundance of tools for collaborative learning in an e-learning environment which coach/trainer is required to master, as Massie (2002) has indicated, in order to maintain a session. Generally students tend to migrate towards their own corners and form their own groups; it is the up to the coach to make sure that these groups are conforming to learning objectives.

### 11.2.3 Project Manager

The facilitator as a project manager has to deal with many issues and unless preparation is undergone many of the examples in the above chapter can be overlooked. The project manager has to be aware of the many aspects of learning and be able to make correct judgements on different types of learners. Returning to Biggs' (1999) 3 P model, the facilitator can use a model such as this to obtain correct details on students similar to the presage stage in order to design an environment where the learning outcome is not affected by the technology.

This facilitator's role still however involves the administrative and technical skills required if the use of VLE's is to be become part of the learning process. The technical issues have been addressed above and are re-emphasised in other chapters, for example, it is interesting how views on Lotus Learning Space differentiate between those that found the system difficult to use and were being classified as surface learners or lacking time availability where by those that became intrigued were classified as deep learners. This view can easily be regarded as biasness against adult learners. Having worked with Lotus Learning Space it is understandable the difficulty in usability and frustration of users which doesn't equate to surface learning. The interface was not the standardised Web browser that students are familiar with therefore the learning curve is greater. Non-technical aroused students are liable to have problems with such non-standard interface therefore availability of technical support is important. Lack of time to get use to a non-standard interface is more likely to be the correct reason behind criticism of Lotus Learning Space. All coaches should remember they are sometimes dealing with business people and adult learners that have preference for online learning because of the lack of time availability. They are the customers and one should realise this and ensure that the environment is suffice not just to keep them, but for their recommendations to others.

The technical issues must be addressed prior to the start of the course by issuing study guides that includes procedures along with '*guidelines, protocols and netiquette*'. The facilitator must also be equipped to deal with any issues that arise during course.

## 11.3 Designing the Syllabus

According to a Gifford (2002), a Professor of Marketing at Miami University, there are 9 important steps to syllabus design in online learning. His belief is, to ignore these steps will be perilous to any 'e-syllabus' which he equates to only 15% of what is required. The nine steps (see Table 3) serve as a blue print for the trainer to be aware of as they become involved in the syllabus design.

| Step 1: | The first of these nine steps is a clear understanding of your personal and corporate values, attitudes, beliefs, preferences, priorities and philosophy about teaching, e-learning, and assessment. Why should your employees or students complete this learning module? How will it help them succeed? Is it your function to be the sage on the stage or the guide on the side? How much responsibility do you expect the employees or students to take for their learning? What is the intended balance between knowledge acquisition and skills development? What performance standards are appropriate? Until you can answer these questions, you should not move to step two. |
|---|---|

| Step 2: | What is the role of this learning module within the total corporate or university training and development sequence? Is there a minimum knowledge, technology, and skill set required before your employee or students will understand and benefit from this learning module? Are there future modules that depend upon specific e-learning outcomes accomplished in this course? When in their professional career should this learning module be required? |
|---|---|

| Step 3: | Are you constrained by internal and external limitations such as available computer access and broadband, employee or student time, administrative or support parameters, or mandated budgetary or technology standard? Do your employees or students have easy access to computers? Are you constrained by a 28.8 transmission rate or can you use Java and streaming video via broadband? Are there format or content standards set by your corporation or institution? Is this learning module optional or required? |
|---|---|

Step 4: Target market attributes and other relevant stakeholders. What is the educational level of your students? Is English their first language? How motivated are they to complete your learning module? Are they adult learners? Are you also training multiple audiences, such as domestic and international employees, vendors and other supply chain partners? Can this be accomplished in one e-learning experience or will it require a series of courses?

Step 5: Course mission, vision, and values. You must be able to write down the following before you start your courses: the intended operational scope, its sense of social responsibility, and its future direction; the roles, rights, and responsibilities of the intended users; and a general blueprint for accomplishing the organizations missions, goals, and objectives to be accomplished through this e-learning experience.

Step 6: Desired detailed course environment and structure. Will this e-learning experience be highly structured or more informal, and will it contain remedial learning options? Can it be consumed in small "bites" or must it be completed in one sitting? Will you structure the e-learning course as a metaphor, a journey, by difficulty level, from micro to macro ideas or as a sports game?

Step 7: Course learning objectives and a list of what the users must be able to know and be able to do upon completion of the e-learning experience. Based upon the prior six steps, what outcomes are desired and how will you know that they have been accomplished? How will you measure these outcomes?? How can you move your audience from "knowing" to "applying" effectively in their professional behavior?

Step 8: Levels of learning desired. Do you want your audience to memorize certain facts or to translate these facts into information, knowledge, and eventually wisdom? Is it satisfactory to be able to have a certain skill or must they understand why that skill is important and how to make adjustments based up unique situational conditions? Do they need to become experts, or is there a certain level of understanding acceptable?

**Table 3 - Nine Steps to E-learning - Gifford (2002)**

The first step states that to install an e-learning system you must have a clear vision of the corporate values in the same instance these can be substituted for institutional values where again it can be considered consistent with Biggs (1999) constructive alignment. In other words the e-learning system has to be aligned with the strategy. Another important factor is the architectural hardware has to be able to convey and uphold the e-learning system. This gives us a system that users are able to browse without problems and the courses are relevant to career moves or the job in hand. The courses also have to be designed with all the users in mind i.e. the medium mix.

In any environment there has to be a set of rules that govern usage and in learning it is required even more so as discipline can be problematic. A neologism used to express behaviour is 'netiquette' (Dugglby, 2000). When engaging in online communication, common sense should prevail but to be certain, a general set of rules should be written into a course e.g.:

1. Treat people with respect and politeness
2. Awareness of other cultures and what may offend them
3. Don't invade peoples time i.e. Long emails and large files etc
4. Remember that bandwidth is important so large files (above 2.5mb) may cause a strain to 56k modem users
5. Privacy is an important issue and permission should be sought before using other learner's material or e-mail information.
6. Try to avoid provoking or getting into any arguments on the net. Polite disagreement is generally the way.
7. Remember users level of Internet skills may vary so be patient when necessary
8. In a collaborative situation be prepared to share knowledge.
9. Try to avoid using capitals exclusively it is considered bad manners on the internet.

Internet users are developing a language by use of abbreviations and pseudonyms and new recipients may not have developed these skills, it is therefore good practise to send a communiqué before a course, setting the rules or explaining some of the abbreviations or a general ruling on their usage.

# Chapter – 12

## Learning Outcomes Assessment & Learning Objectives

Learning outcomes have transpired from Learning Objectives because the role of the coach or tutor requires a skill set to induce deep learning within students. Learning outcomes are dependent on facilitation and mentoring i.e. what the teacher does Biggs (1999), where as objectives are more pertaining to behaviourism and are based on exacting criteria that has to be assessed. Learning outcomes gives the learner the opportunity to take a journey where skills are utilised from an innate perspective. Objectives on the other hand sets out the journey one has to take by making decisions on a set of criteria met through the process.

*Outcomes can be as good or as better than traditional classes but when individuals are not engaged in higher complex cognitive learning the results can be disappointing* (McCarthy-McGee, 2001, pp 175 - 181).

Lublin (2003)[9] Notes: *Although often used interchangeably, there is a difference between learning objectives and learning outcomes that is to do with level of specificity. Learning objectives are strict behaviourist statements which specify exactly the action that is to be assessed. Compare the following :*

| Learning Outcome | Equivalent Learning Objectives |
|---|---|
| *At the end of this module you will be able to evaluate a course.* | *At the end of this module you will be able to:*<br>• *Select an appropriate method for evaluating a course.*<br>• *Justify the selection of that method by reference to the literature.*<br>• *Collect information in order to evaluate a course.*<br>• *Analyse the information gathered.*<br>• *Report the evaluation findings.* |

**Table 4 - Learning Outcomes and Learning Objectives – (Moon, 2002)**

---

[9] http://www.ucd.ie/~teaching/good/deep.htm

## 12.1 Deep & Surface Learning in an E-Learning Environment

It is generally considered that a coach expects the student to share their enthusiasm in the approach to a subject to gain a deep understanding. A coach delivering a workshop expects some enthusiasm in the subject matter from the student hence they are hoping the student approach to the course is of a deep nature. It helps that students are taking charge of their own subjects and the coach acts a facilitator and mentor has it is the attitude and approach of the coach that helps to create a deeper approach to the learning (Biggs, 1999 & Lublin, 2003). Objectives tend to suggest a fixed and expected outcome where the student is required to follow a pattern of learning and arrive at a pre-determined point, where a more learner centred learning outcome pertains to experiential learning and where formative assessment is the suggested format for measurement of that outcome.

The list given below gives some indication to what is expected in a deep approach to learner (Lublin, 2003):

- *Actively seek to understand the material / the subject*
- *Interact vigorously with the content*
- *Make use of evidence, inquiry and evaluation*
- *Take a broad view and relate ideas to one another*
- *Motivated by interest*
- *Relate new ideas to previous knowledge*
- *Relate concepts to everyday experience*
- *Tend to read and study beyond the course requirements*

The table suggests some general tips to deep learning further to this the use of the taxonomy of learning can provide a measurement of the learner's progress. The use of the taxonomy although can be used to measure objectives; is a good judgment of learning outcomes because it takes a subjective approach to student progress.

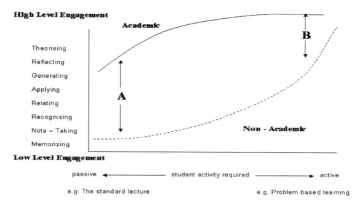

**Figure 18 - Teaching Method – (Biggs, 1999)**

The above graph shows the required activity between a passive student and an active student reaching a particular level of engagement.

The activities of the passive learner can be summarised in the following table (Lublin, 2003 & Entwhistle, 2000):

- Try to learn in order to repeat what they have learned
- Memorise information needed for assessments
- Make use of rote learning
- Take a narrow view and concentrate on detail
- Fail to distinguish principles from examples
- Tend to stick closely to the course requirements
- Are motivated by fear of failure

Students who try to reach the higher order engagement level tend towards what is termed a strategic approach Lubin (2003). This is arguably pertaining to the middle of the table as the general approach is as indicated below according to Lublin (2003):

- Intend to obtain high grades
- Organise their time and distribute their effort to greatest effect
- Ensure that the conditions and materials for studying are appropriate
- Use previous exam papers to predict questions
- Are alert to cues about marking schemes

The above is more indicative of attempting to obtain objectives and would require a similar approach for assessment to obtain the required grades. Past exam papers and to practise objectivity is predictive, although it can be argued that a certain amount of rote learning is required whatever the subject matter, but in order to reach a higher level of engagement theorising, analysing and reflection is required.

Another school of thought but perhaps the most widely used for engagement levels and learning domains is Blooms Taxonomy which includes cognitive (mental skills & knowledge), affective (attitude) and psychomotor (manual or physical skills) skills (Clark, 1999). The attributes that relates to the various skills and activities are listed in Appendix F. Bloom's taxonomy has been used to derive the following list of suggested verbs for engagement levels:

| Level | Suggested Words |
|---|---|
| Evaluation | judge, appraise, evaluate, compare, assess. |
| Synthesis | design, organise, formulate, propose. |
| Analysis | distinguish, analyse, calculate, test, inspect. |
| Application | apply, use, demonstrate, illustrate, practice. |
| Comprehension | describe, explain, discuss, recognise. |
| Knowledge | define, list, name, recall, record. |

**Table 5 - Engagement Levels - (Lublin, 2003)**

The significance of the taxonomy not only give us a dimension into learning categorisation but also take into account organisational requirements and how affective active learning processes can be if such standards are adhered to. Taking a subjective approach into the progression of the student can determine these outcomes and inform us of the level a student has obtained. The use of the taxonomy is an adequate framework for a subjective learner centred approach to online-learning requirements.

## 12.2 Assessment

It is important to know the ability of the students early on in a course because it can determine at what level it should be pitched at. This may seem irrelevant if there is no course assessment but quality of learning is of equal importance and is required to be consistent. In the case of a post grad e-learning course, it should be marked at university level therefore meet that criteria. The assessment criteria require guidelines so not entirely based on subjective judgement. The use of Structure of the Learned Objective Outcome SOLO taxonomy can guide the coach into broad assessment criteria. The SOLO is a taxonomy based on outcome level by consideration of initial quantifiable ability followed by the more distinguishable qualitative which defines the student ability (Biggs, 1999). There are available sophisticated marking systems which makes marking less subjective than it otherwise should be but it is almost impossible to annihilate completely. It can be argued that the judgement of the coach/tutor to analyse assignments on criteria is a part of the skill set acquirement that leads to self improvement. It is also the skill of setting the learning outcomes to achieve a certain criteria level that leads to deep learners therefore agreeable that the coach/tutor should administer a degree of subjective judgment that approaches uniformity with experience and practice.

## 12.3 Tracking progress

Tracking student progress can become an important part of the assessment process in an e-learning situation. The time the students spend online, where they go, there contribution to discussions and chats. LCMS systems have the ability to track students progress but essentially it is part of the facilitators role is to approach a learning environment with the intention of monitoring student activity with a view to assessment. For example students attending an Information Systems course on tLB were marked on their commitment to the course if the subject areas were not applied to the marked assignment. The instructors relationship and involvement in the collaborative aspects of the course e.g. discussion, chats, VLE meetings can prove an indicator of student aptitude.

# Chapter – 13

# Effective Model for E-Learning

## 13.1 The Platform Development Life Cycle

The present dynamism in e-learning is such that development cannot be readily predicted and projects cannot be established easily. The tLB project got on the way very early into this new phase of e-learning and future problems or direction was difficult to forecast. What this suggests is it is unfeasible to set a concrete project plan scope for change and flexibility was crucial because of the rapid changes in technology and consequently specification. The Platform Development Cycle (PDLC) is defined in the diagram below.

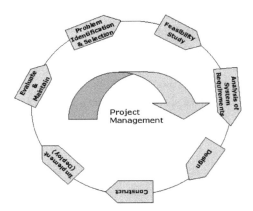

**Figure 19 - Platform Development Life Cycle**

The project was consistently operating at all stages of the life cycle apart from problem identification. Functionality is still essential to the maintenance of the platform therefore difficult to exit from any stage of the life-cycle. The main interest of this study relates to the evaluation and maintenance stage with the view of establishing a good practice model from the

99

existing platform. The evaluation stage allows us to construct models for evaluation in order to improve upon them.

## 13.2 Evolvement of an Effective Model

The effective model was constructed from the result of a variety of sources: review of literature, result of the evaluation, experience of building an e-coaching platform and through feasibility, project design and trial and error. The problem cannot be fully solved until the design has been proven after implementation and to achieve this it is necessary to continuously develop the models. The true model emerged from the design specification and the implemented product in its current form: the content, the learning theories and instructional design. The model is based on the factors affecting the requirements of the learning environment which were evaluated and compared.

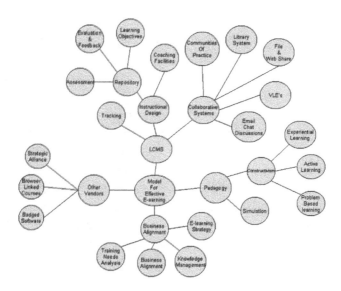

**Figure 20 - Effective E-learning Model**

The model was drawn from a review of the main subject areas and the sub systems that make up requirements for an effective e-learning system which include:

- Business Model
- LCMS Model
- Pedagogical Model

### 13.3 The Business Model

The e-learning market suggests that when designing a system there are a number of factors here that should be considered e.g. feasibility of purchasing on the shelf systems that can easily be re-badged and integrated to an existing system. The cost of design should be the considered matched against the cost of a strategic alliance or buying in of a particular service. The market examination shows a number of alliances have taken place over time and are not many e-learning providers have complete systems. The tLB is itself presently made up of a number of vendor's services such as Live Support, VLE, HTML Marketing, customised syllabus based courses and a survey system. These are all services bought in from other vendors making considerable savings on development costs. Comparing costs to SmartForce who have spent $100 million on a system could possibly have built a system by today's standards for less than one tenth of the sum and produced an equally adequate platform. The likes of Oracle are likely to spend large sums on integrating their e-learning system into distributed networks using their own database and resources available to them but are very unlikely to reach the levels of spending of Smart Force to achieve this level of functionality. The review has shown Oracle are operating on a much larger platform and heavily involved in takeovers of content suppliers for system improvement, the strategic bid for Peoplesoft was a good example. They also had the opportunity to push out e-learning to a huge existing customer base. Similarly on a smaller scale, tLB development has bought in courses from content suppliers that can be seamlessly and simply linked into the platform through a Browser link.

Buildings of bespoke e-learning systems have proven to be resource consuming and problematic which users often find difficult to tolerate. Vendors that concentrate on creating subsystems can manage more robust applications to meet users' needs. This reduces the technical problems users have to encounter leading to a reduction in attrition rates.

The comparison of e-learning systems has proven that tLB was on course to deliver similar systems to the larger existing players and with existing functionality may even surpass some with market share.

The business model is important has to how the e-learning is portrayed to organisations. Many organisations fail to understand the rationale behind an e-learning program simply because they see it as a means to an end. They fail to examine the real need for e-learning and how to sell it to stakeholders. E-learning has to meet the business need i.e. create an environment where staff can make use of it to enhance their ability to provide business needs more efficiently. A shift from trainer centred system to a learner centred system to provide the requirements for life-long learning to increase the flexibility of the organisation and meet the needs of the business objectives. Training organisations use e-learning systems to provide course content but in what context? Generally the context is learning of soft skills where an e-learning system is more than that. For example, to take a supply chain: An e-learning system can reduce the time it takes to become familiar with a product by allowing other organisations access to their e-learning system. E-learning LCMS systems are ideal for providing Enterprise Resource Planning (ERP) and Product Data Planning (PDP) systems with up to date training on new products. It can also provide sales training and keep sales staff informed the on the road reducing the requirement for them to return to the office if a product specification has altered. Imagine the time saved on passing data down through the supply chain before the product is released to the next stage. E-learning and e-coaching is presently contained in delivery of courses but has much more valuable presence if organisations can see the value. The use of e-learning system can provide the means to enable organisations to meet business objectives and become more flexible if consideration is given to these options. There are downsides for the organisational staff one of which is a reduction in social activities due to the provisional elimination of face to face sales meetings which is one of the factors driving the introduction of blended learning into the training world. Blended learning introduces e-learning alongside face to face to act as a support mechanism for training. In time the balance will favour e-learning reducing the face to face contact time as organisations will see this as a way to save on costs. Action learning plays a role in organisational training because staff can continue working as it takes place and it general involves a project relevant to the business objectives. In this context the e-learning system is more favourable has it supports the coach and reduces face to face contact time.

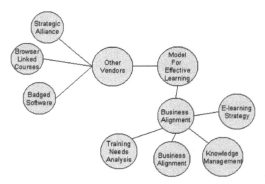

**Figure 21 - Business Model**

### 13.4 Learner Centred LCMS Model

The results of the review was considered an ideal model for a construction of a learner centred e-learning system as in Figure 22, the LCMS model should consider a number of factors in its construction. Essential is the consideration of instructional design factors to include learning theories and repository. These LCMS should consider learning theories i.e. how the courses are to be developed and conveyed within the system. The chapter on instructional design highlights the problem of developing e-learning systems without pedagogical considerations. Constructivist theories include active learning processes such as experiential learning and problem based learning are available to keep users engaged. This repository contains learning objects that are derived with constructivist theories as are the collaborative facilities. Coaching facilities within the LCMS enable the coach to build repositories with pedagogy qualities suitable for learning. Evaluation and feedback and tracking create a system to monitor progress of the learner and help to improve on the system as users sample the facilities. The emphasis should be the student's use of the system and not the technology (MacLoughlin and Oliver, 1999).

A coaching e-learning system should not be afraid of using syllabus based materials on the system as long as they are contained within in a collaborative process. The use of a repository for content is just one of the methods of adding content. As the model portrays the content can arrive via other content providers but within the collaborative environment. The coach and users have the facilities to discuss courses, upload and download relative materials and offer each other advice. It should not be considered that active learning processes should not include syllabus based courses even though it is pertaining to a didactic approach. The emphasis should be on the learning environment that is provided to host and not the course content as this can be just as active. This approach provides motivation for those that are used to a more didactic approach and find it difficult to engage in active learning. In the design construction and selection of LCMS greater consideration should be given to Pedagogy in provision of a learner centred system.

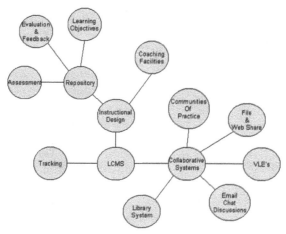

**Figure 22 - LCMS Model**

### 13.5 Pedagogical Model

The review has seen dedicated literature towards the consideration of Pedagogy in e-learning. Learning theories applied in today's modern learning environments should also be incorporated into e-learning. Too many designers are developing systems without much consideration of pedagogy, (Smith and Ragan, 1999). Constructivism is one of the main theories linked to modern teaching and learning and is considered easily adaptable to e-learning by way of active learning processes. Active learning allows learners to call on past experiences and engage in meaningful activities to develop cognitive processes hence greater retention. Action learning extends constructivism into the work place so the skills become relevant.

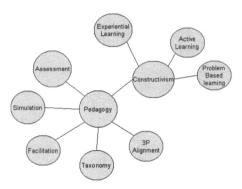

**Figure 23 - Pedagogical Model**

The provision of courses in e-learning environment should not see the falling of standards therefore should be relative to an assessment standards or taxonomy. Using such a method allows the design of courses and assessment to meet the expected education levels thus establishing uniformity of standards. The inclusion of 3P alignment within the model is to create an interactive system (Biggs, 1999). The 3P model brings together the knowledge of the student, the tutor's ability and expertise, and the assessment criteria to provide deep learning environments. The role of the tutor includes that of facilitator in an e-learning environment which requires certain skills that are not applicable to normal learning environments. The skill of the tutor is therefore important if the system is to meet the requirements of the 3P model. Appropriate assessment criteria are also required to test the skill of the learner preventing rote learning and to encourage engagement.

Use of teaching strategies in e-learning is a subject that cannot be ignored if the platform is to meet adequate standards and provide learners with value for money. E-learning can fall from grace in the same way the institutions fail if the learner feels they are not getting the education they have paid for. In time e-learning systems could possibly be graded in the same way has an education establishment by using league tables. If this is to be the case, emphasis is on importance to meet standards from the start. This can only be done by applying learning theories to development producing a learner centred system.

The e-learning model is a subsystem of pedagogy and takes into consideration the technology e.g. LMS and LCMS and looks at how contents can be provided to meet meticulous outcomes from within the learning system. It also incorporates one of the more important aspects of constructivism as a theory in the form of active learning. This is agreed by many theorists to be the best form of learning process to apply to an e-learning environment. It also considers the tLB, the learning platform on which most of this study is based. The importance of pedagogy in e-learning is something that tends to be ignored but is of significant importance and when designing material, there should be greater consideration in incorporating modern methods of teaching and learning. The instructional design methodology is somewhat significant in the way it approaches pedagogical and socio-theoretical aspects.

The Pedagogical model is a framework for good online practice and is derived from many of the top learning theorists.

The shift from traditional learning to e-learning requires research on the differences between objectivism and behaviourism and constructivism in a traditional environment analysis of the differences. It can then be transformed to practice in an e-learning context. Research results in

106

Chapter 15-18 has shown that constructivism lends itself to e-learning and the use of active learning activities produces higher level learning. This replicates changes in traditional learning which are now becoming more focused on the learner.

The model takes the form of active learning in an online process but how is this done? Active learning consists of greater engagement in the learning process which requires a higher skill level from the coach/tutor. The role of the coach/trainer is plays an important role utilising technology to best advantage of the learners; and the application of the learning theory to provide a learner centred system where students can engage. They are required to understand IT at an appropriate level to monitor an online course they are also required to acquire a level of technical skill to solve mediocre problems when they occur. Their ability to coach and facilitate learning also put them in the category of practitioners that requires a skill set not unlike but with slight differences to traditional teaching.

It is good practice to use learning theory as a framework for delivery of a course and Kolb's learning cycle is one that springs to mind although there are many more available. The learning cycle is readily used in coaching on tLB giving consistency to the training process which makes for constant evaluation.

For concrete experience the tLB uses both face to face sessions and collaborative sessions in the live classroom. To use e-coaching course as an example there is a specific learning outcome to be met which students need to practice to become proficient. The purpose of this model is to give students practice to aid the transition to proficiency so what is necessary is to develop a series of learning outcomes to provide this.

The session begins with the student requiring concrete experience. This can be done by creating group sessions where students are separated and given a task or reading or a lecture online. They can even be given tasks to go away and discuss or participate in live sessions to accomplish the task. A typical e-coaching task, as an example, the tutor could ask the students to come up with a suitable learning theory for online learning. Reading list could be supplied otherwise web site locations or no material at all as part of the process of learning is to search for materials. However whichever way it is done the student is gaining concrete experience. The task is established as a learning outcome.

Once the student has gained concrete experience by whatever method, selected reflection can take place within a collaborative session or on a discussion. It might be better to have a live classroom session followed by a continuous discussion. The coach/tutor can direct students to papers or websites on subjects they are unsure about. The session also allows students to see other views which are an essential part of collaborative learning.

Abstract conceptualisation can be the categorising of the learning theories that give themselves readily to e-learning and active experimentation may be writing a course using these principles and concepts. The learning cycle could be followed through to define the findings in greater detail which can be considered as practice. The reality of practice is seeing the subject from a different angle which takes us to the next point of this model.

With reference to Figure 23 that points out requirements to achieve higher level engagement. The theory shows it is the activity of the students that engages them in higher level learning after passing through a number of the active processes where reflection appears high up on the engagement level. Encouragement of students to use learning logs and journals helps to reinforce theses principles

## 13.6 Establishing a Repository

As the Learning Outcomes become established the materials for the repository become available to all coaches/tutors. In the diagram above the point of the repository object storage and management, the learning objects would be replaced by learning outcomes. The substitute of learning outcomes for learning objects supports the active learning methods. At the point where registration takes place, the addition of personal profiling would be appropriate to give the instructor that type of information to aid group dynamics.

# Chapter – 14

## General Study Methodologies

The methodology for the evaluation study is mapped out in Figure 24 and based on a study by Rossi and Freeman (1993) for *conceptualisation, design, implementation, and utility* in online-learning. The framework suits this particular approach in evaluating the tLB platform has it incorporates current stages of development, presently taking place. One addition to the model is to re-evaluate after modifications has taken place. After every evaluation it is necessary to re-measure the effect of changes to ensure a positive effect and therefore becomes a continuous process.

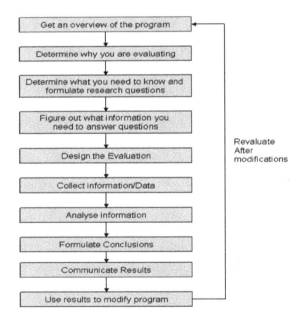

**Figure 24 - Methodology - Rossi and Freeman (1993)**

# Chapter – 15

## Evaluation

### 15.1 Abstract

The basis of this study was inspired through the creation of an online-learning platform ('theLearningBusiness (tLB)') by the BTC Group in co-operation with the Research Institute for the Enhancement of Learning, University of Bangor and The Teaching Company Scheme now known as TTI.

The methodology was based on an e-learning design model made up of a number of sub models created from practical experience, observation plus a review of best practice literature to date within the industry, plus an evaluation study based on existing principles. It took into account consideration of the impact of e-learning and its effectiveness in the commercial world. It considered the many aspects of an e-learning system and measured the system's ability to deal with psychological factors of learning. The intentional outcome was a best practice model for e-learning design and pedagogy.

The tools compared the functionality of the tLB platform in relation to the model to identify any failings for rectification by comparison of the evaluation results matched against current practices and development, concluded by recommendations to close the gap between the existing platform and best practice.

The results showed that in general the development and approach was correct and highlighted gaps in the feedback process.

## 15.2 Introduction

### 15.2.1 Definition for Evaluation

Evaluation is defined in a number of ways but a simple and applicable explanation for this process is *"the systematic application of social research procedures for assessing the conceptualization, design, implementation, and utility of ... programs"* (Quinones & Kirshstein, 1998, Page 6).

The evaluation process is considered in this e-learning context to address implementation and continuous improvement as formative summation whilst summative summation covers the stages between implementation and completion. Summative evaluation determines use of technology, use of technological skills and motivational aspects of the technology pertaining to the student. The evaluation system in question is based on both summative and formative approach in order to establish whether the system meets the demands of constructive alignment to provide a learner centered system.

The provision of evaluation is significant in assessing e-learning platforms and courses as, they add value, improve quality therefore success and has a positive effect on student motivation. (Hazari & Schno, 1999*)*. Gagne and Briggs (1979*)* also place accent on the need to provide feedback and the role of evaluation in the effective learning process. The evaluation and feedback process provides a means of ensuring the learning process meets learner's needs and a measure of whether it satisfies the learning outcome Hazari & Schno (1999). The designer needs to know if the system meets the user's needs i.e. materials and courses, the use of tools for asynchronous and synchronous communication: online testing, discussion groups, conferences, whiteboards, streaming audio and video with supplementary access facilities such as goal setting and file transfer, text, usability, technical aspects and the VLE, are providing a function to teaching and learning?

The extracts of a 2003 survey from HR Zone – Table 6 below shows 39% of users like the virtual learning classroom and those that think it is not ready for the market. 35% of these users

111

believe the technology is not presently good enough. How many of these have had bad experiences with navigational and technical difficulties is anybody's guess, though from experience, the cause could be anything from low bandwidth issues to user application faults. The 'only useful for corporate with deep pockets' is a leading question and will encourage anti VLE attitudes but still acts as an indicator for those liable to despondency. Therefore, indicatory factors suggest from 52% to 60% is likely to become less motivated users when encountering a problem.

| The live virtual classroom is a key part of e-learning, but what are your experiences of it so far? | | |
|---|---|---|
| 98 people have voted | | |
| Like the idea, but my learners would expect a free service | | 12 Votes / 12% |
| Other methods of online learning are more effective | | 8 Votes / 8% |
| Only useful for large corporate with deep pockets | | 18 Votes / 18% |
| Technology not good enough to deliver a proper experience | | 34 Votes / 35% |
| Like it, already using it | | 26 Votes / 27% |

**Table 6 - Virtual Classroom Survey Extract – HR Zone (2003)**

The figures in Table 6 are indicative of the way users feel about experience in e-learning. The rationale behind evaluation was to attempt to remove as many deprecating factors as possible.

Assessment in this context means evaluate interactivity and the ability of the platform to provide a learner centred environment for the users. It is important that users participate in course evaluation assessment to ensure the system has the desired effect of teaching and learning.

The primary reason for evaluation in online-learning was to improve quality Rosenkrans (2000) and McCarthy-McGee (2001) and provide quality assurance with the emphasis on learner centred processes. Online-learning systems were still at the evolutionary stage Hazari & Schno (1999) which therefore requires the input of the learners to provide meaningful tools and processes to construct learning systems fit for purpose. A negative aspect of Web-based courses was, they can engage learners in interactive format but were generally used for delivering *static documents* (syllabus, schedule, announcement and reading lists) how does one ensure this was not the case on tLB platform.

There is much to be said about students who take part in evaluation and feedback where the tutor is assessed through an evaluation process:

> *Students who take part in evaluation assessments reinforce their grasp of course content and strengthen their own skills at self-assessment. And the fact that departments are interested in the outcome has a tendency to motivate* (Hazari & Schno 1999, Page 4).

According to the aforementioned the use of technologies for *'receiving and acting on feedback'* can enhance pedagogical achievements. It is the job of all involved in system/content design and delivery to ensure the learners develop the qualities required e.g. cognitive aspects such as critical thinking. This is achievable through a learner centred approach. *'Evaluation assessment should be a continuous process in an online learning environment'*.

Many of the traditional evaluations and assessments were based on the use of models of objectivism and behavioural science. Cognitive science embraces constructivism and action learning and is based on higher level concepts. This requires different approach to measurement of learning for example a learner centred formative approach assesses the learner's ability to achieve the learning outcome and acts as an indicator to the capacity or implausibility of students and pedagogy (Baie, 1999). According to McCarthy-McGee (2001), measurement of constructivists learning environment require the use of formative evaluation to determine *"the efficiency and performance of the learner"*.

The ex-University of Bangor RIEL department, re-formed from the Centre of Learning and Development, had been involved in a number of online-learning research studies, of which one factor, "Pedagogy in Online Learning" has been of some interest in writing this book similar to their online system learning technology Colloquia pilot study.

The first of these studies has been significant in the design of the test model to measure effective learning. This book includes extracts and facts from both these studies and various e-learning seminars given by the institution.

Pedagogy is an important dimension in this study as e-coaching relies on its intricacies to provide for substance for what is, at the time of writing, an unknown environment. It is important to learn from the aforementioned studies for research pedagogical application. The implications bears hallmark to the starting point of the pedagogy questions for the questionnaire. There needs to be a starting point from which we can make comparisons and to indicate the fact that progress has been made.

There are a number of reasons as to why evaluation is required in online learning. Firstly evaluation is a requirement in any learning system to ensure that learning has taken place and the pedagogy is appropriate to the type of learning. With reference to Biggs (1998) and constructive alignment the student factors and objectives, assessment, climate/ethos and teaching are aligned with activities to provide suitable learning outcomes. To value *the presage process and product* in an online learning environment evaluation has to take place. The fact that most students are likely to be learning at a distant should not dissuade from constructive alignment but all the more reason to ensure it is present.

As highlighted in constructive alignment, the learning outcome has become important and should be measured to ensure learning has taken place. There are available tracking tools incorporated in the LMS and LCMS to measure student progress as they travel through the system but these cannot tell how well the student has learned. The tracking tools however have the functionality to watch student progress by *collection of data and analysis of errors which can determine difficulties students encounter*, Weston et al (1999). Apart from this, the dynamic nature of

114

online requires changes in materials, student's skills, moderators, courses and updating of equipment. Continuous update relies on revision of these factors (Smith and Regan, 1999).

*Constructivist learning environments tend to be collaborative therefore the measurement of prior learning experiences of students with* Pre-Instructional Evaluation *becomes essential. This helps to formulate strategy and acts as an indicator of where the learner is in relation to the learning outcome and what additional abilities a student conveys within the learning environment Baie (1999).*

The use of constructivist theory behind the learning process establishes the use of high level thought processes and collaborative efforts for team building (McCarthy-McGee, 2001). A good evaluation system should provide the tools to measure and ensure that this is taking place.

## 15.3 Overview of the Program

The purpose of this study was to discover the effectiveness of theLearningBusiness platform and its fitness for purpose by evaluation. There are a number of questions that need to be answered in order to determine the platforms success in achieving its learning capabilities:

1. How Should Feedback be Measured on the tLB
2. How effective are the communities on tLB?
3. How to measure the user's level of ability?
4. Will evaluation, feedback and assessment provide improvement to our system if tailored to users through constant feedback?
5. Should the role of the Moderator include obtaining feedback?
6. What Areas of the tLB should be monitored in a feedback process?
   - Collaboration
   - Course and Community Content
   - Usability
   - Technical
   - Functionality

115

- Moderators / Tutors
- Student progress
- Learning Outcomes

7. Is the functionality of the system on average satisfactory to users?
8. Is the look and feel of the system on average satisfactory to users?
9. Are students satisfied with the courses?
10. What collaborative processes are or are not working on the system?

Although it is not possible to cover all of these in this study, carefully selected questions can cover a wide area and provide an assortment of data. The correct approach at this stage is to select some of areas that require immediate attention to improve the functionality, the look and feel and ensure the users are satisfied with the system.

The Validation Criteria for the learner should consist of the following, McCarthy-McGee (2001):

- Knowledge base of the learner
- Usability and Performance of the learners
- Performance
- Instructor Validation (Facilitation of learners)

Presently the tLB administration tools allow physical and statistical monitoring of learner visits to the system and discussion threads. This in any event will play an important role in assessment of an online course. It is essential that students participate in evaluation as an element of collaborative and constructive learning.

### 15.3.1 Participants

The participants consisted of 30 learners who had taken part and completed courses on theLearningBusiness platform. There were difficulties in obtaining the right mix of learners because of problems with system in its early days and the failure of some users to complete courses.

### 15.3.2 Procedures

The evaluation tool was used to test for a number of factors mentioned in the above.

The Pearson's two tailed correlation was used based on variance where significance was used to assess the likelihood of an association. N was = 30 and r based on a scale of +1 to -1, the higher the value of r, the more positive the correlation. The lower the value of r (less than zero), the more negative the correlation.

**Figure 25 - Scale of Correlations - Coolican H. (1999)**

### 15.3.3 Design

The study was originally designed to assess Learndirect courses delivered online and was used to capture the following information on learners:

- The quality of pedagogy
- The skills of the learners
- IT skills capability of the learners
- Assessing quality of computer based training packages
- Establishing feedback on high quality learning
- Is the functionality of the system on average satisfactory to users?
- Is the look and feel of the system on average satisfactory to users?
- Are our courses doing their job or in need of improvement?
- What collaborative processes are working on the system?

This study was important for validating the quality of courses with a view to determining the following factors:

1. User friendliness

2. Match to learner

3. Clarity of aims

4. Structure and content

5. Use of multimedia

6. Engagement

7. Opportunity for active learning

8. Self-reported learning outcomes

## 15.4 Question Selection Process

From Qual IT evaluation tool which has been altered for tLB categorised under the following main subject headings.

1. Technical - T

2. Usability - U

3. Operating System - O

4. Learning – L

5. Engagement for Courses & Communities

6. Motivation - M

Each question under its subject heading was further categorised for suitability for courses or communities.

The questions were filtered for suitability which was listed in the following Tables

In this analysis a further column is added to prioritise the questions in the following manner:-

1 - Very Important

2 – Important

3 – Less Important

4 – Not very important but desirable

| User Friendliness | | | | |
|---|---|---|---|---|
| No | Question | Courses Eval. A<br>Community Eval. B | Subject<br>Category | Priority |
| 1.1 | The course was user-friendly. | A + B | U | 1 |
| 1.2 | I could get support when I needed it | A + B | U | 1 |
| 1.3 | It was easy to start up the course | A + B | O | 3 |
| 1.4 | It was easy to exit the course | A | T/U | 4 |
| 1.5 | I could have completed the course without any outside help. | A | T/U | 2 |
| 1.6 | It was easy to find my way forwards through the course. | A + B | O | 1 |
| 1.7 | It was easy to move backwards through the material | A + B | T/U | 1 |
| 1.8 | I could move around the material with ease. | A + B | T/U | 3 |
| 1.9 | The help/Nav system was easy to understand | A + B | T/U | 1 |
| 1.10 | Technical support was sufficient for the course | A + B | T/U | 1 |
| 1.11 | The start-up and exit of the system was straightforward | B | T | 3 |
| 1.12 | Do you have any comments about the user friendliness of the course? | A + B | T/U | 1 |

**Table 7 - User Friendliness**

119

| Match to Learner | | | | |
|---|---|---|---|---|
| **No** | **Question** | **Courses Eval. A** **Community Eval. B** | **Subject** **Category** | **Priority** |
| 2.1 | The course suited my level of knowledge. | A | L | 1 |
| 2.2 | The course was suitable for me. | A + B | L | 2 |
| 2.3 | The language was the right complexity for me. | A | L | 1 |
| 2.4 | My learning progressed at a suitable rate for me. | A + B | L | 3 |
| 2.5 | The course used an approach that suited my style of learning. | A + B | L | 2 |
| 2.6 | The course allowed me to learn in my own way. | A + B | L | 1 |
| 2.8 | Do you have any comments about how the course matched your needs? | A + B | L | 1 |

**Table 8 - Match to Learner**

| Clarity & Content | | | | |
|---|---|---|---|---|
| **No** | **Question** | **Courses Eval. A** **Community Eval. B** | **Subject** **Category** | **Priority** |
| 3.1 | The course structure was clear. | A | O | 1 |
| 3.2 | The course clearly presented its aims. | A | L | 1 |
| 3.3 | The course clearly explained what I would learn. | A | L | 2 |
| 3.4 | New ideas were explained well. | A | L | 1 |
| 3.5 | The course helped me to plan my learning. | A + B | L | 2 |
| 3.6 | The course gave me all the information I needed. | A + B | L | 1 |
| 3.7 | The course material was error free. | A + B | T/U | 2 |
| 3.8 | Do you have any comments about the clarity of the course or the quality of its content | A + B | | 1 |

**Table 9 - Clarity and Content**

| Quality of Presentation | | | | |
|---|---|---|---|---|
| **No** | **Question** | **Courses Eval. A Community Eval. B** | **Subject Category** | 1 |
| 4.1 | The course made good use of pictures. | A + B | T/U | 3 |
| 4.2 | The print was just the right size. | A + B | T/U | 2 |
| 4.3 | There was an appropriate balance between graphics and text for me. | A + B | T/U | 3 |
| 4.4 | The package made good use of colours. | A + B | T/U | 3 |
| 4.5 | The course made full use of multimedia. | A + B | T/U | 4 |
| 4.6 | Do you have any comments about the quality of multimedia elements in the course? | A + B | T/U | 1 |

**Table 10 - Quality of Presentation**

| Opportunities for Active Learning | | | | |
|---|---|---|---|---|
| **No** | **Question** | **Courses Eval. A Community Eval. B** | **Subject Category** | **Priority** |
| 5.1 | There was appropriate use of examples in the course. | A + B | L | 1 |
| 5.2 | The course gave me lots of chance to practice what I was learning. | A + B | L | 2 |
| 5.3 | The course was interactive. | A + B | L | 1 |
| 5.4 | The course let me experiment with ideas. | A + B | L | 3 |
| 5.5 | The course gave the opportunity for me to reflect on what I was learning. | A + B | L | 2 |
| 5.6 | I could relate the course content to my own personal experience. | A + B | L | 3 |
| 5.7 | The course inspired me to use what I had learnt in the work place | A + B | L | 4 |
| 5.8 | | A + B | L | 1 |
| 5.9 | I felt I needed to practise what I was learning in the workplace | A + B | L | 3 |

**Table 11 - Opportunities for Active Learning**

Opportunities for active learning is an important category, the questions address the reaction of these users to the tLB. The suitability of tLB is important to the distant learners.

| Engagement for Courses & Communities | | | | |
|---|---|---|---|---|
| No | Question | Courses Eval. A Community Eval. B | Subject Category | Priority |
| 6.1 | The course, community material was interesting. | A + B | M | 1 |
| 6.2 | The content motivated me to complete the course or subscribe to the community | A + B | M | 1 |
| 6.3 | The course/community encouraged me to learn. | A + B | M | 1 |
| 6.4 | The course/community helped me to get interested in what I was learning. | A + B | M | 1 |
| 6.5 | The course was about the right length | A | M | 2 |
| 6.7 | I was able to achieve my goals | A + B | M | 1 |
| 6.8 | Do you have any comments about how well the course/community engaged you? | A + B | M | 1 |

**Table 12 - Engagement for Courses and Communities**

| Feedback and Assessment | | | | |
|---|---|---|---|---|
| No | Question | Courses Eval. A Community Eval. B | Subject Category | Priority |
| 7.1 | The course provided me with enough feedback. | A + B | O | 1 |
| 7.2 | The course gave me the chance to assess my progress. | A + B | L | 2 |
| 7.6 | Do you have any comments about the Feedback and Assessment in the course? | A + B | L | 1 |

**Table 13 - Feedback and Assessment**

| Learning Outcomes | | | | |
|---|---|---|---|---|
| No | Question | Courses Eval. A Community Eval. B | Subject Category | Priority |
| 8.1 | The course increased my knowledge of the subject matter. | A + B | L | 1 |
| 8.2 | The course developed my learning skills. | A + B | L | 1 |
| 8.3 | The course improved my learning. | A + B | L | 2 |
| 8.4 | The course made me want to carry on learning. | A + B | M | 1 |
| 8.5 | The learning I gained from the course is relevant to my everyday life. | A + B | L | 3 |
| 8.6 | The things I learnt are going to be very useful. | A + B | L | 2 |
| 8.7 | Do you have any comments about the Learning Outcomes of the course? | | | 1 |

**Table 14 - Learning Outcomes**

### 15.4 .1 Evaluation Gap Analysis

### 15.4.2 Usability

Usability is an important aspect of the system that can easily be ignored yet it is most important for learners because of the demands of system navigation and requirements. This provision of user friendly navigational systems is not always the case for example, a previous survey of 10 web sites showed they were not very successful in facilitating user navigation and were over complex thus the users tend to find navigation systems challenging therefore are reluctant to use them(Alertbox). The other important aspect of this survey was the site maps proved difficult to find. It must be understood that intuition will not tell us if users find it easy to use, this information can only be gained by direct gathering. Having to explain to an experienced IT person how to use the system which is presumed to be navigationally simple suddenly brings home certain facts the system is lacking. Personal ability to use the system clouds judgment in respect to interaction of others which provides empathy for an evaluation questionnaire for highlighting these factors.

*"One of the oldest hypertext usability principles is to visualize the structure of the information space to help users understand where they can go. On today's Web, site maps are a common approach to facilitating navigation. Unfortunately, they are often not very successful at it."* Jakob Nielsen's Alertbox, January 6, 2002

These questions provide ample coverage of usability of the system, if there are some areas which require covering they are likely to appear in operative section. Or it can be inferred from other sections such as motivation and technical

|  |  |  |  | Priority |
|---|---|---|---|---|
| 1.1 | The course was user-friendly. | A + B | U | 1 |
| 1.2 | I could get support when I needed it | A + B | U | 1 |
| 1.4 | It was easy to exit the course | A | T/U | 2 |
| 1.5 | I could have completed the course without any outside help. | A | T/U | 3 |
| 1.7 | It was easy to move backwards through the material | A + B | T/U | 4 |
| 1.8 | I could move around the material with ease. | A + B | T/U | 2 |
| 1.9 | The help/Nav system was easy to understand | A + B | T/U | 1 |
| 1.10 | Technical support was sufficient for the course | A + B | T/U | 1 |
| 1.12 | Do you have any comments about the user friendliness of the course? | A + B | T/U | 1 |
| 3.7 | The course material was error free. | A + B | T/U | 1 |
| 4.1 | The course made good use of pictures. | A + B | T/U | 2 |
| 4.2 | The print was just the right size. | A + B | T/U | 2 |
| 4.3 | There was an appropriate balance between graphics and text for me. | A + B | T/U | 3 |
| 4.4 | The package made good use | A + B | T/U | 3 |

| | | | | |
|---|---|---|---|---|
| | of colours. | | | |
| 4.5 | The course made full use of multimedia. | A + B | T/U | 4 |
| 4.6 | Do you have any comments about the quality of multimedia elements in the course? | A + B | T/U | 1 |
| 3.7 | The course material was error free. | A + B | T/U | 1 |

**Table 15 - Usability**

### 15.4.3 Technical

The Colloquia Online-Learning pilot study at the University of Bangor highlighted a number of technical difficulties as one of the major obstacles that arose. This was unexpected but became one of the major issues and required attention prior to initiation. This has also been the bane of tLB online classroom can act as de-motivator judging by the frustration discharged by users. Technical issues can make or break an online-learning course it is therefore imperative that we address them early on. Although criteria were written into the course joining instructions, and students were selected on their technical ability for the colloquia course, technical issues became one of priority very early on in the study. It is therefore important to try to get to grips with these issues by logging and use of questionnaires such as this. As in every questionnaire we have to place a text box to gain user input, because technical issues vary greatly this is of major importance this section of the questionnaire.

| | | | | Priority |
|---|---|---|---|---|
| 1.4 | It was easy to exit the course | A | T/U | |
| 1.5 | I could have completed the course without any outside help. | A | T/U | |
| 1.7 | It was easy to move backwards through the material | A + B | T/U | |
| 1.8 | I could move around the material with ease. | A + B | T/U | |
| 1.9 | The help/Nav system was easy to understand | A + B | T/U | |
| 1.10 | Technical support was | A + B | T/U | |

| | | | | |
|---|---|---|---|---|
| | sufficient for the course | | | |
| 1.12 | Do you have any comments about the user friendliness of the course? | A + B | T/U | |
| 3.7 | The course material was error free. | A + B | T/U | |
| 4.1 | The course made good use of pictures. | A + B | T/U | |
| 4.2 | The print was just the right size. | A + B | T/U | |
| 4.3 | There was an appropriate balance between graphics and text for me. | A + B | T/U | |
| 4.4 | The package made good use of colours. | A + B | T/U | |
| 4.5 | The course made full use of multimedia. | A + B | T/U | |
| 4.6 | Do you have any comments about the quality of multimedia elements in the course? | A + B | T/U | |
| 3.7 | The course material was error free. | A + B | T/U | |

**Table 16 - Technical**

Some of the likely technical issues which can probably be summed up in one question using a text box – i.e. Do you have any comments on the technical issues during the course or community usage?

Some of the likely issues that we need to address in the questionnaire

- Logging On & Off
- Downloading applets to use in the live classroom
- Machine wouldn't work
- My machine keeps stopping
- Sound card difficulties
- Freezing of the screen

It is predetermined that these issues are going to arise; therefore need to be addressed by summarised comment.

### 15.4.4 Learning

| 2.1 | The course suited my level of knowledge. | A | L |
|-----|------------------------------------------|------|---|
| 2.2 | The course was suitable for me. | A + B | L |
| 2.3 | The language was the right complexity for me. | A | L |
| 2.4 | My learning progressed at a suitable rate for me. | A + B | L |
| 2.5 | The course used an approach that suited my style of learning. | A + B | L |
| 2.6 | The course allowed me to learn in my own way. | A + B | L |
| 2.8 | Do you have any comments about how the course matched your needs? | A + B | L |
| 3.2 | The course clearly presented its aims. | A | L |
| 3.3 | The course clearly explained what I would learn. | A | L |
| 3.4 | New ideas were explained well. | A | L |
| 3.5 | The course helped me to plan my learning. | A + B | L |
| 3.6 | The course gave me all the information I needed. | A + B | L |
| 5.1 | There was appropriate use of examples in the course. | A + B | L |
| 5.2 | The course gave me lots of chance to practice what I was learning. | A + B | L |
| 5.3 | The course was interactive. | A + B | L |
| 5.4 | The course let me experiment with ideas. | A + B | L |
| 5.5 | The course gave the opportunity for me to reflect on what I was learning. | A + B | L |
| 5.6 | I could relate the course content to my own personal experience. | A + B | L |
| 5.7 | The course inspired me to use what I had learnt in the work place | A + B | L |

| 5.8 | | A + B | L |
|---|---|---|---|
| 5.9 | I felt I needed to practise what I was learning in the workplace | A + B | L |
| 7.2 | The course gave me the chance to assess my progress. | A + B | L |
| 7.3 | Do you have any comments about the Feedback and Assessment in the course? | A + B | L |
| 8.1 | The course increased my knowledge of the subject matter. | A + B | L |
| 8.2 | The course developed my learning skills. | A + B | L |
| 8.3 | The course improved my learning. | A + B | L |
| 8.5 | The learning I gained from the course is relevant to my everyday life. | A + B | L |
| 8.6 | The things I learnt are going to be very useful. | A + B | L |

**Table 17 - Learning**

The questions in the above table addresses issues on the course itself, missing is feedback on such things as how the tutor faired during the course did he/she fulfil the role of tutor. How well was the course facilitated? The effects of the collaborative aspects! Some of these I expect can be judged from the level of interaction but it would still be valuable to know what the user actually feels about these subjects. How well did the collaborative aspects influence the user during the course or during a period on the community?

### 15.4.5 Motivation

| 6.1 | The course, community material was interesting. | A + B | M |
|---|---|---|---|
| 6.2 | The content motivated me to complete the course or subscribe to the community | A + B | M |
| 6.3 | The course/community encouraged me to learn. | A + B | M |
| 6.4 | The course/community helped me to get interested in what I was learning. | A + B | M |
| 6.5 | The course was about the right length | A | M |

| 6.7 | I was able to achieve my goals | A + B | M |
|-----|-------------------------------|-------|---|
| 6.8 | Do you have any comments about how well the course/community engaged you? | A + B | M |
| 8.4 | The course made me want to carry on learning. | A + B | M |

**Table 18 - Motivation**

There appears to be gaps in the motivational section. Although the questions address the issue of the level of feelings towards the course it doesn't tell us why they were, or were not motivated. Some of the questions in other categories will provide some of the answers but we need to capture what does or does not motivate users. What are they motivated by or what are the de-motivating factors? I guess another comment box can address this issue!

Many of the technical questions are significant in the motivational factors. Can we assume for example if the user cannot find their way through the course or encounter technical difficulties they become liable to de-motivational factors? Then we have to pose the question aren't users expected to encounter technical difficulties to a certain extent? This is where the original motivation of users becomes an important factor e.g. from studies mature students are more likely to seek solutions to these problems.

### 15.4.6 Operating System

| Operating Systems | | | |
|-----|----------|-------------------------------------------|---------------------|
| **No** | **Question** | **Courses Eval. A Community Eval. B** | **Subject Category** |
| 1.3 | It was easy to start up the course\community | A + B | O |
| 1.6 | It was easy to find my way forwards through the course\community | A + B | O |
| 3.1 | The course\community structure was clear. | A | O |
| 7.1 | The course\community provided me with enough feedback. | A + B | O |

**Table 19 - Operating System**

129

The above table focuses on questions relative to the operating system/application and ask questions of whether they tell users what they want to know about navigating the system? It also looks at the operations of the system.

## 15.5 Results of Analysis

Pearson correlation analysis was conducted to examine Bivariate relationships between user friendliness, match to learner, clarity and content, quality of presentation, active learning, engagement for courses and communities, feedback and assessment and learning outcome. Pearson's correlation was used to measure the extent of related values and to determine if a value on a single variable can be predicted from the other. The correlation was expected increase with a positive value (close to +1) otherwise value is negative (close to -1) and there is a lack of correlation between the variables.

Note cause cannot be inferred from strong correlations and when N is large small correlation coefficients can be significant.

### 15.5.1 Factor Analysis & Correlations

(See Appendix D - Evaluation Factor Analysis)

**Correlations**

|  |  | usermean | matchmean | clmean | presmean | acmean | fbmean | lomean | engmean |
|---|---|---|---|---|---|---|---|---|---|
| usermean | Pearson Correlation | 1 | -.386(*) | .071 | .253 | .134 | .136 | .125 | .110 |
|  | Sig. (2-tailed) | . | .018 | .690 | .148 | .442 | .443 | .481 | .534 |
|  | N | 40 | 37 | 34 | 34 | 35 | 34 | 34 | 34 |
| matchmean | Pearson Correlation | -.386(*) | 1 | .952(**) | .894(**) | .943(**) | .877(**) | .975(**) | .928(**) |
|  | Sig. (2-tailed) | .018 | . | .000 | .000 | .000 | .000 | .000 | .000 |
|  | N | 37 | 37 | 34 | 34 | 35 | 34 | 34 | 34 |
| clmean | Pearson Correlation | .071 | .952(**) | 1 | .863(**) | .935(**) | .893(**) | .953(**) | .946(**) |
|  | Sig. (2-tailed) | .690 | .000 | . | .000 | .000 | .000 | .000 | .000 |
|  | N | 34 | 34 | 34 | 34 | 34 | 34 | 34 | 34 |
| presmean | Pearson Correlation | .253 | .894(**) | .863(**) | 1 | .863(**) | .896(**) | .910(**) | .872(**) |
|  | Sig. (2-tailed) | .148 | .000 | .000 | . | .000 | .000 | .000 | .000 |
|  | N | 34 | 34 | 34 | 34 | 34 | 34 | 34 | 34 |
| acmean | Pearson Correlation | .134 | .943(**) | .935(**) | .863(**) | 1 | .864(**) | .956(**) | .928(**) |
|  | Sig. (2-tailed) | .442 | .000 | .000 | .000 | . | .000 | .000 | .000 |
|  | N | 35 | 35 | 34 | 34 | 35 | 34 | 34 | 34 |
| fbmean | Pearson Correlation | .136 | .877(**) | .893(**) | .896(**) | .864(**) | 1 | .879(**) | .886(**) |
|  | Sig. (2-tailed) | .443 | .000 | .000 | .000 | .000 | . | .000 | .000 |
|  | N | 34 | 34 | 34 | 34 | 34 | 34 | 34 | 34 |
| lomean | Pearson Correlation | .125 | .975(**) | .953(**) | .910(**) | .956(**) | .879(**) | 1 | .934(**) |
|  | Sig. (2-tailed) | .481 | .000 | .000 | .000 | .000 | .000 | . | .000 |
|  | N | 34 | 34 | 34 | 34 | 34 | 34 | 34 | 34 |
| engmean | Pearson Correlation | .110 | .928(**) | .946(**) | .872(**) | .928(**) | .886(**) | .934(**) | 1 |
|  | Sig. (2-tailed) | .534 | .000 | .000 | .000 | .000 | .000 | .000 | . |
|  | N | 34 | 34 | 34 | 34 | 34 | 34 | 34 | 34 |

\* Correlation is significant at the 0.05 level (2-tailed).
\*\* Correlation is significant at the 0.01 level (2-tailed).

**Table 20 - Evaluation Correlations**

### 15.5.2 Analysis of Data

User Friendliness

There proved to be only a negative significant correlation at the 0.05 level with Match to learner ($r=-.386$, $P>0.05$) where there was minor or negative significant relationships between all other variables indicating a lack of relationship between User friendliness and the course suitability and materials.

131

**Match to Learner**

There existed significant correlations (r<0.5) between Match to Learner and Clarity of Content (r=-.386, P>0.01), Match to Learner & User friendliness (r=-.386, P>0.01); Match to Learner & Quality of Presentation (r=.894, P>0.01), Match to Learner & Clarity and Content (r=952, P>0.01), Match to Learner & Opportunities for Active Learning (r=.943, P>0.01) Match to Learner & Feedback and Assessment (r=.877, P>0.01), Match to Learner & Learning Outcomes (r=.975, P>0.01), Match to Learner & Engagement for Courses and Communities (r=.928, P>0.01). The correlations are expected to be significant because all are related to the course response and course content.


There were significant correlations at the 0.01 level (2 tailed) between all variables apart from User friendliness: There is positive significant relationship (r>0.5) between Match to Learner & Clarity and Content (r=952, P>0.01); There is positive significant relationship (r>0.5) between Match to Learner & Quality of Presentation (r=.894, P>0.01); There is positive significant relationship (r>0.5) between Match to Learner & Opportunities for Active Learning; (r=.943, P>0.01); There is positive significant relationship (r>0.5) between Match to Learner & Feedback and Assessment (r=.877, P>0.01); There is positive significant relationship (r>0.5) between Match to Learner & Learning Outcomes (r=.975, P>0.01); There is positive significant relationship (r>0.5) between Match to Learner & Engagement for Courses and Communities (r=.928, P>0.01).

**Clarity and Content**

There existed a negative significant relationship (r<0.5) between Clarity & Content & User friendliness (r=.0.71, P>0.6) as expected all others showed significant at the 0.01 level (2 tailed): There is positive significant relationship (r>0.5) between Clarity and Content & Match to Learner (r=.952, P>0.01); There is positive significant relationship (r>0.5) between Clarity & Content & Quality of Presentation (r=.863 P>0.01), There exists a positive significant relationship (r>0.5) between Clarity & Content & Opportunities for Active Learning (r=.935,

132

P>0.01), There is positive significant relationship (r>0.5) between Clarity & Content & Feedback and Assessment (r=.893, P>0.01), There is positive significant relationship (r>0.5) between Clarity & Content & Learning Outcomes (r=.953, P>0.01), There is positive significant relationship (r>0.5) between Clarity & Content & Engagement for Courses and Communities (r=.946, P>0.01).

**Quality of Presentation**

Quality of presentation showed significant at the 0.01 level (r>0.1) between all variables apart from User friendliness where correlation showed (r<0.5), a negative significant relationship (r=0.253, P>0.1): There is positive significant relationship (r>0.5) between Quality of Presentation & Match to Learner, (r=.894, P>0.01); There is positive significant relationship (r>0.5) between Quality of Presentation & Clarity & Content (r=.863 P>0.01); There is positive significant relationship (r>0.5) between Quality of Presentation & Opportunities for Active Learning (r=.863, P>0.01; There is positive significant relationship (r>0.5) between Quality of Presentation & Feedback and Assessment (r=.896, P>0.01); There is positive significant relationship (r>0.5) between Quality of Presentation & Learning Outcomes (r=.956, P>0.01); There is positive significant relationship (r>0.5) between Quality of Presentation & Engagement for Courses and Communities (r=.872, P>0.01).

**Opportunities for Active Learning**

Opportunities for Active Learning showed significant at the 0.01 level (r>0.1) between all variables apart from the aforementioned user friendliness; There is negative significant relationship (r<0.5) between Opportunities for Active Learning & User friendliness (r=0.134, P>0.4); There is positive significant relationship (r>0.5) between Opportunities for Active Learning & Match to Learner (r=.943, P>0.01); There is positive significant relationship (r>0.5) between Opportunities for Active Learning & Clarity & Content (r=.935 P>0.01); There is positive significant relationship (r>0.5) between Opportunities for Active Learning & Quality of Presentation (r=.863, P>0.01); There is positive significant relationship (r>0.5) between Opportunities for Active Learning & Feedback and Assessment (r=.864, P>0.01); There is positive significant relationship (r>0.5) between Opportunities for Active Learning & Learning

133

Outcomes (r=.956, P>0.01); There is positive significant relationship (r>0.5) between Opportunities for Active Learning & Engagement for Courses and Communities (r=.928, P>0.01).

**Feedback and Assessment**

Feedback and Assessment showed significant at the 0.01 level (r>0.1) between all variables apart from the aforementioned user friendliness; There is negative significant relationship (r<0.5) between Feedback and Assessment & User friendliness (r=0.136, P>0.4); There is positive significant relationship (r>0.5) between Feedback and Assessment & Match to Learner (r=.877, P>0.01); There is positive significant relationship (r>0.5) between Feedback and Assessment & Clarity & Content (r=.893, P>0.01); There is positive significant relationship (r>0.5) between Feedback and Assessment & Quality of Presentation (r=.896, P>0.01); There is positive significant relationship (r>0.5) between Feedback and Assessment & Opportunities for Active Learning (r=.864, P>0.01); There is positive significant relationship (r>0.5) between Feedback and Assessment & Learning Outcome (r=.879, P>0.01); There is positive significant relationship (r>0.5) between Feedback and Assessment & Engagement for Courses and Communities (r=.886, P>0.01).

**Learning Outcomes**

Learning Outcomes showed significant at the 0.01 level (r>0.1) between all variables apart from the aforementioned user friendliness; There is negative significant relationship (r<0.5) between Learning Outcomes & User friendliness (r=0.125, P>0.4); There is positive significant relationship (r>0.5) between Learning Outcomes & Match to Learner (r=.975, P>0.01); There is positive significant relationship (r>0.5) between Learning Outcomes & Clarity & Content (r=.953, P>0.01); There is positive significant relationship (r>0.5) between Learning Outcomes & Quality of Presentation (r=.910, P>0.01); There is positive significant relationship (r>0.5) between Learning Outcomes & Opportunities for Active Learning (r=.956, P>0.01); There is positive significant relationship (r>0.5) between Learning Outcomes & Feedback and Assessment (r=.879, P>0.01); There is positive significant relationship (r>0.5) between Learning Outcomes & Engagement for Courses and Communities (r=.934, P>0.01);

**Engagement for Courses and Communities**

Engagement for Courses and Communities showed significant at the 0.01 level (r>0.1) between all variables apart from the aforementioned user friendliness; There is negative significant relationship (r<0.5) between Engagement for Courses and Communities & User friendliness (r=0.110, P>0.5); There is positive significant relationship (r>0.5) between Engagement for Courses and Communities & Match to Learner (r=.928, P>0.01); There is positive significant relationship (r>0.5) between Engagement for Courses and Communities & Clarity & Content(r=.946, P>0.01);

There is positive significant relationship (r>0.5) between Engagement for Courses and Communities & Quality of Presentation (r=.872, P>0.01); There is positive significant relationship (r>0.5) between Engagement for Courses and Communities & Opportunities for Active Learning (r=.928, P>0.01); There is positive significant relationship (r>0.5) between Engagement for Courses and Communities & Feedback and Assessment (r=.886, P>0.01); There is positive significant relationship (r>0.5) between Engagement for Courses and Communities & Learning Outcomes (r=.934, P>0.01).

## 15.6 Discussion

### 15.6.1 User Friendliness

The tLB platform was designed to be user friendly in order to appeal to a wide range of users. Almost 42 % of users agreed the system was user friendly 21% strongly agreed and 17% very strongly agreed. 5% thought it was not applicable 4% neither agreed, nor disagreed. 4% of users strongly disagreed whilst 4% disagreed and 1% very strongly disagreed. There were some negative responses due to user's belief that they could not have completed the course without the technical help and some felt the help navigation system was not easy to understand and requires re-designing which will be undertaken in the next stage of implementation.

### 15.6.2 Match to Learner

The overall results of Match to Learner showed in all aspects to be satisfactory to students where from the first set of results 26% strongly agreed and 31% agreed overall although there was a high percentage of response (35%) that neither agreed or disagreed which led to the conclusion that some of the questions were difficult to respond to because of the nature of the wording.

The results where 35% neither agreed nor disagreed and none very strongly agreed whilst 27% strongly agreed and 31% agreed. The 3% that strongly disagreed and 6% that disagreed believed the course was not suited to their style. This may have been to due to students not being used to the active learning style has McLoughlin and Oliver, (1999) have signified, there are risks to this style of learning. Few users would have preferred to learn in their own way and a small minority thought they couldn't learn new things in small steps. There were no users that strongly disagreed.

### 15.6.3 Clarity and Content

Clarity and Content was satisfactory to the users with 40% of results centred on agreement whilst 15% strongly agreed and 20% very strongly agreed where 15% of users were disillusioned with the course not helping them to plan their learning and not being able to get the information they needed. tLB houses facilities for learning goals and learning logs this therefore must revolve around the coach or facilitator not encouraging users to fill in the learning logs.

The learning log reader on tLB actually shows very few users filling in their learning logs. As for users not being able to obtain the information required is an expectation. Most didactic based courses offer a pre-course package containing handouts therefore users expect this. A solution to this is to explain to users the principle behind action learning prior to the course.

### 15.6.4 Quality of Presentation

Response for Quality of presentation proved to be quite positive with a 30% of users agreed, 13% very strongly agreed, 13% agreed whilst 17% disapproved. One user felt it gave them some 'idea about how various ways of communication can be put together to convey meaning (live sessions). Many of the delegates failed to experience the full use of graphics in particular within the live session it is therefore understandable why some disagreed. It has been agreed amongst tLB developers that some areas on the site required better presentation. The site does lack images particularly within the courses which are due to be addressed. The demand for use of colours is very subjective and again some users would have experienced brainstorming sessions where colour was the key to identification. This question is slightly ambiguous e.g. what presentation quality are the disagreeable users objecting to. Multimedia is presently being incorporated into the course as and when it is required more consideration is presently being given to appropriate multimedia material and colour.

### 15.6.5 Active Learning

Active learning results indicated a normal distribution where 39% agreed 11%strongly agreed and 14% very strongly agreed. 13% disagreed whilst 2% strongly disagreed and none strongly disagreed which is constant with the literature. It is to be expected that some users are unlikely to adapt to this system ordinarily as the literature instigates. The users disagreed with appropriate use of examples and not having the option to practice what they learnt. This is quite unusual because the majority of the courses were linked to a project within the organisation; apart from the e-coaching courses. In order to improve on e-coaching a user is required to practice what they have learnt.

### 15.6.6 Engagement for Courses and Communities

87% of responses demonstrate engagement where 53% agreed, 17% strongly agreed and 17% very strongly agreed which is to be expected regardless of any negative response in active learning. Whatever the 17% of users felt about active learning it is considered engaging. The rejection against active learning however appears unjust as engagement shows very positive result apart from 6% of users who thought the course did not help them to get interested in what they was learning and disputed the length of the course. 6% of users neither agreed nor disagreed and 3% thought the question was not applicable.

### 15.6.7 Feedback and Assessment

As expected, 37% of users disagreed with feedback and assessment. Users expect feedback in their courses as the literature suggests. Formative feedback is of particular importance as users need to know if they are doing well. tLB lacks feedback resources where the trainer/coach can gain immediate response from user. There exists implements for polling and application for

137

developing surveys which are open to administrators, consideration should be given to developing feedback systems for coaches. 27% of users agreed overall and 20% very strongly agreed whilst 7% thought it was not applicable.

### 15.6.8 Learning Outcomes

The response from learning outcomes approached a normal distribution showing the perceptions were consistent with expectations. 44% of users agreed whilst 15% strongly agreed and 13% very strongly agreed with the learning outcome but 9% did not understand what the course was trying to teach and believed it never helped them to develop learning skills or improve their learning. This again is a part of the active learning risk factor hence the users thought the course did not inspire them to carry on learning. The majority of courses were not qualification based although some were based on degree level qualifications. The 9% of users who thought that learning outcome was not applicable to them may have left the course early or were observers and coaches.

### 15.7 Conclusion

The categorisation of the evaluation questions proved difficult to draw conclusions from the correlation in hindsight fewer questions and less categories might have been more successful. One of the main problems encountered whilst attempting to obtain responses from the survey was the lack application from users. It has taken almost 2 years to provide the required data. This is partially due to the lack of robustness on the system which has the tendency to de-motivate users. It has only been since 2003 - 2004 the system has proved to be robust where failures were few and far between. The problem this poses is the data for the evaluation has been obtained from students who have had a positive time on the platform and students who are generally doing the same course.

The correlation means proved to be significant in all respects where the relationships were significant at the 0.01 level apart from user friendliness which expected. This does not prove however that the responses and relationships were wholly correct but it provides favourable argument for response to the evaluation results.

The results of the evaluation studies showed most of the responses favourable to system satisfaction from user friendly, usability, technical and teaching /learning. The collaborative aspects of connectedness and learning also proved favourable. Some of the more positive comments ' *a very good chance to improve computer literacy and knowledge about how e-communities work*' , '*I got an idea about how various ways of communication can be put together to convey meaning (live sessions)*' or '*a very good chance to improve computer literacy and knowledge about how e-communities work*'. This is indicative of learners being focused on technology or can be considered as deep learners however the novelty factor does have an effect on judgment and that can only be eliminated when learners are no longer overawed by the technology.

There were some negative aspects within connectedness and there was much criticism against the feedback Comments such as '*just me I think!!*' and '*the menu system on the side seemed to conflict with selecting options from drop down menus*' and '*for ages I hadn't realised that after selecting from a drop down that it did not redirect automatically and I had to press OK*' are indicative of navigational problems.

Some of the text responses were ambiguous for example the response to the question, '*1.10 Do you have any comments about the user friendliness of the course? (Usability)*', were 'discussion boards' and 'face-to-face'. These responses are meaningless and un-interpretable.

There was an air of mixed feelings amongst the active learning processes e.g. negative response '*felt the need for a moderators presence to give feedback and set a pace for discussion*' and positive response, 'again *the nature of degree dictates that you find your own example thrown in the deep a bit but felt good when you got to the other side through your own research*'. This particular response shows flashes of a learner whom had initial disillusion but had come round in the end which could be construed as a 'surface learner' come out of the other end of the course as a 'deep learner'. These are positive signs for both course tutor course and system. This particular comment endorses the active learning process *'Good pointers the main gain was acquiring the reflective dimension of thinking and practice'*. A statement for active learning was reinforced by *'It was a shock to realise I was going to have to think for myself throughout! Most courses I have attended/worked through recently have been mere box-ticking exercises designed to keep the training providers' numbers up and get me through as quickly as possible. This one has actually made me think about marketing'*. This text response shows the course is working for some and judging from other statements the motivational factors are coming into play and the deep and surface learners become apparent.

The feedback system has taken not 'quite a bashing' but very close although the proved to be contradiction in the text response *'concise and gave useful feedback'* and *'more continual feedback needed'*. The last remark was reinforced by the graphical response on feedback and assessment proved to be the only positively skewed response to a positive question output in a graph. A denotation of a negative response to the quality of feedback and assessment as proven by a learners reply to 'Learner Outcome,' *I feel a bit arrogant saying agree to this one! I think I got it all.* The feedback system again has not worked for this learner otherwise he would have realised is position in relation to the learning outcome.

Arguments to the validity of the evaluation study 1 response could render it unacceptable because of various factors influencing the response from learners: The evaluation survey for example contained too many questions and should have been broken into various sections and issued at intervals throughout the course. To expect users to answer too many questions from two extensive and demanding surveys was asking a lot from them. The timescale and number of users on the system was the main factors preventing this. Judging by the response the users become listless has they continued through each section and some did not get through them all. The way the surveys were separated into different sections where users had to click on each one to respond was a disincentive factor although many of the respondents that completed the survey managed to get through them all. It may be necessary to carry out a second survey to get an improved response hence a better picture of the tLB system. A second argument is the value of

140

the questions and learners perceptions of reference. How many of the users understood the meaning of active learning? This could explain the many not applicable and neither response.

The use of feedback and surveys is crucial to bring e-Learning forward. It is not evident what people want in e-Learning systems although it is well known it can provide huge savings for organisations and reduce the size of learning institutions. It has implications for UK Universities and Colleges in overseas markets by reducing the costly necessity for the student to attend for the whole of the course. It is taking the a leaf out of the Open University book using the distant learning approach where the students attend workshops and summer camps a few times during a course depending on duration which tends to be sufficient in this case. Face to face contact with learners is essential to ascertain competence. Communication over a medium does not establish learner competence because it is very subjective. The conception of learners has to competence can vary according to background and peer group realisation which is not always consistent. A learner might consider themselves competent amongst a low level intelligence group but will feel out of place amongst deep thinkers. The subject of different levels of expectance and competency can reflect in the response of the questionnaire for example the disagreement against colours is a subjective area and this type of question should elicit more of an individual response. Communication language is also important where vocabulary level should also be considered. Generally this is determined by the level of the course but when dealing with communities of learners from different cultures, backgrounds and countries the level of it becomes an issue.

Evaluating learners through the system will lead to a failure to get the bigger picture because learners who have been disgruntled may not contribute to response. The result of this is not getting the complete picture of why, or if, the system is failing a number of learners. It is useful to create specific worded surveys to canvas response from this group to provide the necessary data.

The overall response was a positive indication towards tLB system design and courses and the general approach to learning and development was approaching the right direction. However

141

there were minor problems especially concerned with Feedback and the Help/Navigation system and Active Learning processes.

The response proved the need for feedback from users to help develop the system for the future and it is of significant importance to continue receiving feedback from users. The survey has given us food for thought in future design although the surveys could have been slightly more direct. There are significant relationships between the questions and responses but this survey in itself requires a more focussed approach to deliver more sophisticated answers in particular to the answer the questions of attrition and motivation. On this basis it is imperative to include students who drop out of courses whom can provide information on factors essential to the success of e-learning.

# Chapter – 16

## Study of Effective Communities

### 16.1 Abstract

This study was devised to measure the sense of community within an e-learning collaborative environment. Data was collected from delegates enrolled in an online course from 16 countries.

The 20 item Classroom Community Scale has been validated and established has a *reliable measure of classroom community* which yields two interpretable factors, *Connectedness* and *Learning*. It was used to establish whether the communities on theLearningBusiness e-learning platform provided a sense of community amongst learners using the system.

The conclusion was there was a sense of community amongst learners but some of the sense of community amongst learners was lacking.

### 16.2 Introduction

The use of e-learning platforms is on the increase and increasingly being used as a means to provide distant learning medium via the Internet. One area in e-learning in which very little research has materialised is classroom communities. The significance of community's have risen in online learning since it was discovered that dropout rates are 10% to 20% higher in online learning than traditional learning Rovai (2002). Suggestions for this are the lack of sense of community through separation which facilitates the feeling of isolation. Social integration plays an important part in traditional learning of which communities are a substitute in distance learning. This helps to reduce dropout rates *'social integration has had a significant positive effect on retention in an higher education business program'* according to Ashar & Skenes (1993) although attrition is not always viable according to (Ewell, 1984, Page 7):

143

*"It is often observed that retaining students is not in itself an appropriate goal for an educational institution. There are many reasons, for example, why a given student ought not to continue to be enrolled in a particular institution. Among these are lack of academic skill, lack of motivation, and attainment of the student's own educational goals ..... "*

E-learning within communities is more than just provision of space to learners it also an environment where students have a sense of belonging and commitment, Bellah, Madsen, Sullivan, Swidler, and Tipton (1985). A strong sense of community involves commitment therefore *a feeling of connectedness* based on obligations towards one another which will affect the learning outcome, Rovai (2002).

The building of communities in distance education programs requires 'proper attention' because it is the sense of belonging to which learners are initially attracted based on their world view, Asher & Skenes (1993). Rovai (2002) based a study of communities on three research questions in provision of a conceptual framework to enable the *understanding of a sense of community* termed the 'classroom community scale' that included online community's using the Blackboard system. Rovai (2002) developed the Classroom Community Scale to measure this sense of Community based on a number of research questions:

1. How Valid is the classroom community scale?
2. How reliable is the classroom community scale?
3. Is there a single dimension or are these multiple dimensions underlying the items that make up the classroom community scale?

Rovai (2002) concluded the 20-Item Classroom Community Scale is effective tool for measurement of the sense of classroom community to produce two interpretable factors, *connectedness* and *learning*. However all students belong to a single institution therefore may have become part of, or enrolled in similar peer groups prior to the e-learning experience which is pointed out in the study. The 'Classroom Community Scale' is validated to be an adequate tool for measuring the sense of community and is to be used and monitored as such for the tLB study.

Given the emphasis on communities within the tLB platform, it is imperative that its effectiveness is realised by measurement of activity. Rovai (2002, Page 198) suggests '*elements of community are spirit, trust, mutual interdependence among members, interactivity, shared values and beliefs and common expectations*', developed an instrument to measure feeling of connectedness and learning within a classroom community. To achieve high activity within a community these factors should exist at least within a majority of the group members.

### 16.3 Methodology

The Classroom Community Scale Test Instrument has gone through a validation procedure that has provided evidence to prove it an '*efficient instrument*' for '*measuring the extent of the classroom community*'. This instrument has been used to test the effectiveness of communities of practice on tLB and is used to provide data for analysis.

### 16.4 Participants

Participants consisted of 30 students enrolled in a British Council learner support course from 16 countries across the world. There was no Demographic information taken from the participant because of the nature of their work, but they were all adult learners of whom 1/3 had an educational background and fewer than 10% had a qualification in an educational field.

### 16.5 Setting

This study was based on an Active Learning course provided by theLearningBusiness e-learning platform developed by BTC Group training and learning organisation in relationship with University of Wales Bangor. The students were selected from a group of British Council learners with a ratio of students to tutors from a low of 1:8 and a high of 1: 15. The courses were delivered to students over 8 weeks with 7 weeks of learning taking place on a platform based on asynchronous and synchronous learning tools consisting of:

- Asynchronous Tools (Chat facilities, File Share and Web Share, Profiles, Discussion Boards, Editing Facilities, Material Library, E-mail, Learning Logs, Goal Setting.
- Synchronous Tools (White Board, Audio and Video Facilities, Application Sharing, Web Follow Me, Polling.

The learners were separated into 3 separate communities but were allowed to interact between each both asynchronously and synchronously. Courses content was similar throughout but delivered through groups of 6 to 8 students.

## 16.6 Procedures

The Classroom Community Scale Test Instrument has gone through a validation procedure by a panel of experts that has provided evidence to prove it an *'efficient instrument'* for *'measuring the extent of the classroom community'*.

- Validity Analysis

*An examination of the 20 Classroom Community Scale items reveals that on face value they appeared to measure what was needed to measure classroom community. Additionally, the procedures used to develop the Classroom Community Scale provide high confidence that the test instrument also possesses high content and construct validities. Considerable effort was expended to ensure that the concept of classroom community was based on the concept of community as contained in the professional literature (e.g., Bellah et al., 1985; McMillan & Chavis, 1986) as applied to an educational setting. Additionally, all 20 final Classroom Community Scale items were rated as totally relevant to sense of community in a classroom setting by three university professors who taught educational psychology* (Rovai, 2002, Page 204).

This instrument was used to test the effectiveness of communities of practice on theLearningBusiness and is used to provide data for analysis from 20 questions based on a 7 point Likert Scale: Very Strongly Agree, Strongly, Disagree, Neither, Agree, Strongly Disagree, Very Strongly Disagree. An 8th point 'Not Applicable' was added to allow for non-relevant response.

**Table 21 - Classroom Community Scale Items Connectedness**

| |
|---|
| 1. I felt that students on the course cared about each other |
| 2. I felt encouraged to ask questions |
| 3. I felt connected to others in this course |
| 4. I felt that it was hard to get help when I had a question |
| 5. The course gave the opportunity for me to reflect on what I was learning. |
| 6. I could relate the course content to my own personal experience. |
| 7. The course inspired me to use what I had learnt in the work place |
| 8. I felt I needed to practise what I was learning in the workplace |
| 9. I felt isolated in the course |
| 10. I trusted others in the course |

**Table 22 - Classroom Community Scale Items Learning**

| |
|---|
| 11. I felt reluctant to speak openly |
| 12. I did not trust others in this course |
| 13. I felt that I could rely on others in the course |
| 14. I feel that other students do not help me learn |
| 15. I felt that members of this course depended on me |
| 16. I felt that I was given ample opportunities to learn |
| 17. I felt uncertain about others in this course |
| 18. I felt that my educational needs were not being met |
| 19. I felt confident with the support from others |
| 20. I felt that the course did not promote a desire to learn |

Each of the students was e-mailed a post course questionnaire from which they were asked to respond via an online survey application. The responses were aggregated within the application and downloaded for analysis.

The community scale tests the overall score and two subscales based on:

- Connectedness – cohesion, spirit, trust, and interdependence
- Learning – feelings of community, interaction with each other, shared values and beliefs

## 16.7 Design

The respondents data was measured quantitatively using statistical correlation methods to measure the sense of connectedness and learning taken place within each community.

## 16.8 Results Analysis

Pearson's analysis was conducted to examine Bivariate relationships for connectedness and learning. Pearson's correlation was used to measure the extent of related values and to determine if a value on a single variable can be predicted from the other. The correlation was expected increase with a positive value (close to +1) otherwise value is negative (close to -1) and there is a lack of correlation between the variables (see Figure 25 Chapter 15).

Note: cause cannot be inferred from strong correlations and when N is large small correlation coefficients can be significant. In this case N = 12.
The classroom is a validated instrument proven to identify the sensitivity between internet courses.

## Connectedness

|  |  | Com1 | Com2 | Com3 | Com4 | Com5 | Com6 | Com7 | Com8 | Com9 | Com10 |
|---|---|---|---|---|---|---|---|---|---|---|---|
| Com1 | Pearson Correlation | 1 | .775(**) | .976(**) | .980(**) | .810(**) | .881(**) | .832(**) | .841(**) | .898(**) | .941(**) |
|  | Sig. (2-tailed) | . | .003 | .000 | .000 | .001 | .000 | .001 | .002 | .000 | .000 |
|  | N | 12 | 12 | 12 | 12 | 12 | 12 | 12 | 10 | 12 | 12 |
| Com2 | Pearson Correlation | .775(**) | 1 | .838(**) | .786(**) | .941(**) | .912(**) | .851(**) | .868(**) | .908(**) | .846(**) |
|  | Sig. (2-tailed) | .003 | . | .001 | .002 | .000 | .000 | .000 | .001 | .000 | .001 |
|  | N | 12 | 12 | 12 | 12 | 12 | 12 | 12 | 10 | 12 | 12 |
| Com3 | Pearson Correlation | .976(**) | .838(**) | 1 | .939(**) | .836(**) | .889(**) | .880(**) | .841(**) | .892(**) | .938(**) |
|  | Sig. (2-tailed) | .000 | .001 | . | .000 | .001 | .000 | .000 | .002 | .000 | .000 |
|  | N | 12 | 12 | 12 | 12 | 12 | 12 | 12 | 10 | 12 | 12 |
| Com4 | Pearson Correlation | .980(**) | .786(**) | .939(**) | 1 | .825(**) | .885(**) | .800(**) | .905(**) | .923(**) | .940(**) |
|  | Sig. (2-tailed) | .000 | .002 | .000 | . | .001 | .000 | .002 | .000 | .000 | .000 |
|  | N | 12 | 12 | 12 | 12 | 12 | 12 | 12 | 10 | 12 | 12 |
| Com5 | Pearson Correlation | .810(**) | .941(**) | .836(**) | .825(**) | 1 | .964(**) | .904(**) | .917(**) | .895(**) | .896(**) |
|  | Sig. (2-tailed) | .001 | .000 | .001 | .001 | . | .000 | .000 | .000 | .000 | .000 |
|  | N | 12 | 12 | 12 | 12 | 12 | 12 | 12 | 10 | 12 | 12 |
| Com6 | Pearson Correlation | .881(**) | .912(**) | .889(**) | .885(**) | .964(**) | 1 | .938(**) | .982(**) | .897(**) | .905(**) |
|  | Sig. (2-tailed) | .000 | .000 | .000 | .000 | .000 | . | .000 | .000 | .000 | .000 |
|  | N | 12 | 12 | 12 | 12 | 12 | 12 | 12 | 10 | 12 | 12 |
| Com7 | Pearson Correlation | .832(**) | .851(**) | .880(**) | .800(**) | .904(**) | .938(**) | 1 | .905(**) | .841(**) | .849(**) |
|  | Sig. (2-tailed) | .001 | .000 | .000 | .002 | .000 | .000 | . | .000 | .001 | .000 |
|  | N | 12 | 12 | 12 | 12 | 12 | 12 | 12 | 10 | 12 | 12 |
| Com8 | Pearson Correlation | .841(**) | .868(**) | .841(**) | .905(**) | .917(**) | .982(**) | .905(**) | 1 | .883(**) | .894(**) |
|  | Sig. (2-tailed) | .002 | .001 | .002 | .000 | .000 | .000 | .000 | . | .001 | .000 |
|  | N | 10 | 10 | 10 | 10 | 10 | 10 | 10 | 10 | 10 | 10 |
| Com9 | Pearson Correlation | .898(**) | .908(**) | .892(**) | .923(**) | .895(**) | .897(**) | .841(**) | .883(**) | 1 | .901(**) |
|  | Sig. (2-tailed) | .000 | .000 | .000 | .000 | .000 | .000 | .001 | .001 | . | .000 |
|  | N | 12 | 12 | 12 | 12 | 12 | 12 | 12 | 10 | 12 | 12 |
| Com10 | Pearson Correlation | .941(**) | .846(**) | .938(**) | .940(**) | .896(**) | .905(**) | .849(**) | .894(**) | .901(**) | 1 |
|  | Sig. (2-tailed) | .000 | .001 | .000 | .000 | .000 | .000 | .000 | .000 | .000 | . |
|  | N | 12 | 12 | 12 | 12 | 12 | 12 | 12 | 10 | 12 | 12 |

** Correlation is significant at the 0.01 level (2-tailed).

**Table 23 - Correlation Classroom Community Scale Items Connectedness 1-10**

This list of items is expected to determine whether there exists a sense of connectedness within the community. This is an important concept on the basis of several theories e.g. Laurillard (1999) conversational further expanded by Pask (1985) whom signify the relationships have a significant factor in the learning process particularly in making knowledge explicit through. Overall the relationships were significant at the 0.01 level (2 tailed) where (R>0.05). In order to see the existence of connectedness relationships are expected to be significant between Q1 & Q3 where there is positive significant relationship (r>0.5), (r=.976, P>0.01), Q 5 & Q6, where there is positive significant relationship (r>0.5), (r=.964, P>0.01), Q6 & Q7 where there is positive significant relationship (r>0.5) between, (r=.938, P>0.01), Q1 & Q2 where there is positive significant relationship (r>0.5), (r=0.775, P>0.01) and Q4 and Q9 where there is positive significant relationship (r>0.5) between Q4 & Q10, (r=.940, P>0.01). The fact that correlations between these relationships were significant indicated a tLB platform and course capable of providing a sense of community an opportunity for connectedness.

## Learning

| | | Com11 | Com12 | Com13 | Com14 | Com15 | Com16 | Com17 | Com18 | Com19 | Com20 |
|---|---|---|---|---|---|---|---|---|---|---|---|
| Com11 | Pearson Correlation | 1 | .877(**) | .676(*) | .878(**) | .800(**) | .671(*) | .453 | .383 | .319 | .735(**) |
| | Sig. (2-tailed) | . | .000 | .016 | .000 | .002 | .017 | .162 | .245 | .338 | .006 |
| | N | 12 | 12 | 12 | 12 | 12 | 12 | 11 | 11 | 11 | 12 |
| Com12 | Pearson Correlation | .877(**) | 1 | .815(**) | .899(**) | .833(**) | .784(**) | .650(*) | .731(*) | .539 | .872(**) |
| | Sig. (2-tailed) | .000 | | .001 | .000 | .001 | .003 | .030 | .011 | .087 | .000 |
| | N | 12 | 12 | 12 | 12 | 12 | 12 | 11 | 11 | 11 | 12 |
| Com13 | Pearson Correlation | .676(*) | .815(**) | 1 | .825(**) | .930(**) | .945(**) | .930(**) | .825(**) | .954(**) | .840(**) |
| | Sig. (2-tailed) | .016 | .001 | . | .001 | .000 | .000 | .000 | .002 | .000 | .001 |
| | N | 12 | 12 | 12 | 12 | 12 | 12 | 11 | 11 | 11 | 12 |
| Com14 | Pearson Correlation | .878(**) | .899(**) | .825(**) | 1 | .878(**) | .873(**) | .651(*) | .686(*) | .571 | .949(**) |
| | Sig. (2-tailed) | .000 | .000 | .001 | . | .000 | .000 | .030 | .020 | .066 | .000 |
| | N | 12 | 12 | 12 | 12 | 12 | 12 | 11 | 11 | 11 | 12 |
| Com15 | Pearson Correlation | .800(**) | .833(**) | .930(**) | .878(**) | 1 | .894(**) | .802(**) | .700(*) | .840(**) | .821(**) |
| | Sig. (2-tailed) | .002 | .001 | .000 | .000 | | .000 | .003 | .016 | .001 | .001 |
| | N | 12 | 12 | 12 | 12 | 12 | 12 | 11 | 11 | 11 | 12 |
| Com16 | Pearson Correlation | .671(*) | .784(**) | .945(**) | .873(**) | .894(**) | 1 | .854(**) | .827(**) | .871(**) | .870(**) |
| | Sig. (2-tailed) | .017 | .003 | .000 | .000 | .000 | . | .001 | .002 | .000 | .000 |
| | N | 12 | 12 | 12 | 12 | 12 | 12 | 11 | 11 | 11 | 12 |
| Com17 | Pearson Correlation | .453 | .650(*) | .930(**) | .651(*) | .802(**) | .854(**) | 1 | .879(**) | .941(**) | .636(*) |
| | Sig. (2-tailed) | .162 | .030 | .000 | .030 | .003 | .001 | . | .000 | .000 | .035 |
| | N | 11 | 11 | 11 | 11 | 11 | 11 | 11 | 11 | 11 | 11 |
| Com18 | Pearson Correlation | .383 | .731(*) | .825(**) | .686(*) | .700(*) | .827(**) | .879(**) | 1 | .796(**) | .705(*) |
| | Sig. (2-tailed) | .245 | .011 | .002 | .020 | .016 | .002 | .000 | . | .003 | .015 |
| | N | 11 | 11 | 11 | 11 | 11 | 11 | 11 | 11 | 11 | 11 |
| Com19 | Pearson Correlation | .319 | .539 | .954(**) | .571 | .840(**) | .871(**) | .941(**) | .796(**) | 1 | .587 |
| | Sig. (2-tailed) | .338 | .087 | .000 | .066 | .001 | .000 | .000 | .003 | . | .058 |
| | N | 11 | 11 | 11 | 11 | 11 | 11 | 11 | 11 | 11 | 11 |
| Com20 | Pearson Correlation | .735(**) | .872(**) | .840(**) | .949(**) | .821(**) | .870(**) | .636(*) | .705(*) | .587 | 1 |
| | Sig. (2-tailed) | .006 | .000 | .001 | .000 | .001 | .000 | .035 | .015 | .058 | . |
| | N | 12 | 12 | 12 | 12 | 12 | 12 | 11 | 11 | 11 | 12 |

** Correlation is significant at the 0.01 level (2-tailed).
* Correlation is significant at the 0.05 level (2-tailed).

**Table 24 - Correlation Classroom Community Scale Items Connectedness 11-20**

The learning proved to have 2 positively led question (13 & 19) which both referred to others on the course and also showed a sense of connectedness and the theoretical relationships on conversational and cognitive learning depicted by Laurillard (1999) and Pask (1975). The results showed a positive significant relationship (r>0.5) between Q13 & Q19, (r=.954, P>0.01). Questions 12 & 14 & 12 & 17 showed very negative aspects towards learning and were expected to yield similar factors, The results indicated positive significant relationship (r>0.5) between Q12 & Q14

(r=.899, P>0.01) and positive significant relationship (r>0.5) between Q12 & Q17 (r=.650, P>0.01). Questions 18 & 20 also was expected to yield a similar response which proved a positive significant relationship (r>0.5) where (r=0.705, P>0.01). Finally, There showed to be a positive significant relationship (r>0.5) between Q15 & Q13 where (r=.930, P>0.01). In general, the relationship between variables in learning proved to be significant in response therefore the discussions were taken as relative.

## 16.9 Discussion

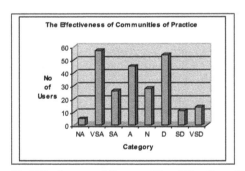

**Figure 26 - Effectiveness of Communities of Practice – Category**

The above graph is the overall results of returns on the evaluation survey. The distributions of the results lean towards a twin peak which suggests there is a mixture of different elements of respondents. The variance and standard deviation endorse this but there are a number of reason why this should be the case. Firstly there were both negatively and positively lead questions

151

which would give a wider spread within the results of the survey. Secondly the respondents come from variety backgrounds and were of different levels of ability from graduates to non-graduates with a low technical ability. This would account for a wider variance due to the high level of subjectivity in responses.

The 19% of users agreed, 11% of users strongly agreed and 24% of users very strongly agreed that there a sense of connectedness existed and the users were able to learn. 23% of users disagreed whilst 5% strongly disagreed and 6% very strongly disagreed. 12% neither agreed nor disagreed and 2% thought the question was not applicable. The response shows 34 % of users disagreed on the appropriateness of connectedness and learning. The variation in results requires individual consideration of questions which are divided into connectedness and learning.

### 16.9.1 Connectedness:

The overall results were a significant indication that users felt the sense of connectedness to the community which Rovai (2002) advocated was necessary for 'community commitment'. Only 2% disagreed and felt they were not connected to the course. This reflects the active learning risks suggested by Mitchell (2002) and an element of the respondents who found it difficult to work in an active learning environment.

The indication was users were able to reflect on what they learnt and felt they could use it in the work place. This is also an indication of active learning processes coming into play and the fact that most courses were based on action learning gave an expected result. Only 1% of users disagreed with this result again reflecting the negative aspects of active learning.

The response to questions '*I felt that I could rely on others in the course*' and '*I felt that members of this course depended on me*' again shows a sense of connectedness with a negative a skewed response to a negatively lead question. However there was no sense of trust between the users with a positive response to a positive lead question. This could reflect a lack of facilitative interactivity within the community. '*I felt uncertain about others in this course*', indicates a positive response reflecting the fact they could rely on each other which in some ways negates the response in Question 15 & Question 12 also questions this response showing the users on average disagreed with the lack of trust within the community. There appears to be a high number of users in the evaluation study whom responded with very strong disagreement overall. The lack of dependency endorses the fact that the facilitative processes were lacking as response to question 15 indicates but it seems that many users were relying on others to lead as question 17 shows by the number of users that felt they could rely on others.

The sense of community is questioned by the response in Question 17 judging by level of uncertainty felt by users but it seems again the active learning processes were in play as the confidence felt by users was very significant indicating a positive response as shown in Question 19.

In general there was a very high sense of connectedness within communities but there was in some cases a lack of trust and a great deal of uncertainty towards other users. It appeared that the users were waiting for others to act or looking for guidance and togetherness from the facilitator. It could be put down to a number of reasons one of which could be the lack of a moderator to permanently monitor the community and the lack of material change. On a positive note the active learning processes appeared to be working within the communities, users gave a positive response to the course activity.

### 16.9.2 Learning

The results of connectedness provide some indicators toward a positive response in learning. The response to the question '*I felt encouraged to ask questions*' indicated a climate within the community where students felt they were able to participate and '*I felt that it was hard to get help when I had a question*' partially endorses this providing evidence that help was available. It seems that a number of them could not get help when they needed it. This may have been due to a number of them residing in a different time zone. A number of facilities are available for users to pose questions it is difficult understand why this was so.

It could possibly relate to the technical failings where there was no access to the tLB platform or with some of a course run by a trained moderator lacking in these skills. There was no indication of what these questions were in this response but the problem can be addressed in the other survey which applies to more technical issues.

Question 6 & Question 8 relate to the active learning processes and both proved a positive response to the questions. There was an element of experiential learning applied to action learning which users related to. A number of users disagreed with the relationship between the course and the work place but this is to be expected because as Mitchell (2002) advocates there is a certain element of risk and not everyone can respond to this method.

Almost all the respondents in Question 10 felt they were able to speak openly which is good sign for course design. It reduces the number of 'lurkers' and shows that the facilitator was able to get users engaged.

The collaborative aspects of the community appears to be working quite adequately as the response to Question 14 shows a very significant response indicating users were able to learn from each other. Question 16 is also a positive endorsement to the active learning processes as a positive response shows there was ample opportunity to learn. Question 18 and Question 20 further promotes the learning processes as the educational needs of the users were met and the communities promoted a desire to learn.

### 16.9.3 Conclusion

The overall conclusion is that active learning has a role to play within communities and users showed a very positive response to the type of learning available within a community. The community however lacked in the sense of community portrayed by Rovai (2002) and McLoughlin and Oliver (1999). The result show that scaffolding or '*supporting others in a zone of proximal development*' was promoting the cognitive development of users but the sense of belonging which is referred to was lacking.

# Chapter – 17

# Learner Facilitators Study

## 17.1 Abstract

The British Council have endeavoured to deliver training to English Language Teachers overseas and are investigating the use of Collaborative learning systems to provide this training. They have a view of developing Knowledge Learning Centres in virtual and physical environments to provide continuous learning systems with the intention of developing staff worldwide, by providing facilitative and moderating skills to enhance learner support, within the individual countries.

An e-learning platform was used to deliver training to delegates in 16 different countries consisting of a module based on project work using asynchronous and synchronous collaborative systems.

This study was designed to investigate whether variation in learning has an effect on *levels of understanding and provision* amongst participant in the British Council over distant learning provided through tLB platform. This concluded that using a varied method of delivery allowed students to encounter different learning styles and were able to reflect on elements of their learning experiences leading to the outcome of provision of training to British Council *Front of House Staff in Learner Support Skills*.

## 17.2 Introduction

One of the main roles of the facilitator is to foster deep learning in an e-learning environment and try to discourage compartmentalized deep learning (Thomas J.). The argument for deep learning is students are able to *understand, apply and use information learned*, Entwistle 2000 & Atherton 2002. The understanding portrayed by Thomas J. is although students are of deep learning ability they are able to compartmentalise knowledge when it '*is isolated within the knowledge framework*' as the student has failed to understand how it can be applied and its

155

usefulness within existing knowledge frameworks. The challenge of the facilitator is practice learning strategies that are able to provoke cognitive skills. Facilitators have the opportunity to construct strategies via electronic mediums of which one method highlighted by

Thomas J. and used successfully amongst psychology classes is 'to have students *act as collectors, discussants, or conduits of information* and the fact that they convey this information in an e-learning set via activities which promote *motivational aspects of deep-learning and critical thinking*. The varied activity available in collaborative e-learning, provide participants with ideas of new activities to convey to learners within their own environment. In this case the students report results of activities back to the class via electronic medium e.g. Discussion Boards. Thomas J.[10] has delivered objectives for designing roles that allows students to achieve this:

- *To structure activities that have the potential to negate student tendencies to adopt surface strategies;*
- *To require students to perform activities that serve to "shape" the mental behaviours that are required of deep learning (active manipulation of information, incorporate information into knowledge structures, use of high level meta-cognition, reflection disequilibrium, evidence collection);*
- *To choose topics and activities that have the effect of creating intrinsic and extrinsic motivations (e.g., disequilibrium, emotion) that will "force" the student to reflect on the information while it is being collected or during its evaluation or to struggle with the explanation or synthesis of information.*

An important factor in student attainment is cultural background. Students of certain cultures have to forgo some of their norms and values gained within their peer group and even refrain from participation in order to participate in a learning process. Distant learning requires a different type of discipline to traditional learning because peer groups that are derived from

---

[10] http://www.celt.lsu.edu/CFD/E-Proceedings/Facilitation%20of%20Critical%20Thinking%20and%20Deep%20Cognitive%20Processing.htm

social integration are established in a longer time. It is between this time and the time it takes to establish social groups online that students tend to drop out. The fact is they may have decided that online learning is not for them and have not necessarily dropped out, but sought a different approach. Tinto (1993) suggests that lack of challenge (academic boredom) or the student is reluctant to invest resources into achieving required grades. The objective of those setting the studies for the students is to improve the system in order to increase student-retention of which an evaluation system plays a significant role in identifying shortfalls in the system. The provision of a student centred environment with the necessary support services is obligatory in distant educational services. An evaluation system serves to fine-tune the learning process with stakeholder input. It is required that students and moderators understand the competency factors and find ways of early establishment.

The British Council in consideration of facilitative and supportive systems for learners are presently biased towards Library systems and information services. They need to examine other methods of supportive systems. In considering the need for Staff training the approach to learning in which the learners are engaged should give consideration to the level of learning aspired to. A good example would be, setting learning goals and objectives to allow reflection thus valuing their efforts.

Higher level education establishments have now adopted a theory on deep and surface learning developed by Entwistle and Ramsden, (1983) which is questioned in terms of social background and culture (critical notes in deep and surface learning). The concept of deep learning regardless, is one adopted by many institutions (see chapter 12.1) and used as means of measuring learning outcome.

### 17.3 Methodology

### Module 1

Learners starting point was determined by use of Baseline Survey based on initial understanding of learning and learner support based on the following questions:

- Why did you sign up to do this course?

- What do you want to be able to do by the end of this course?
- Give an example of a memorable learning experience.
- What made the experience memorable?
- What is the best support you can give a learner?

## 17.4 Participants

The participants for this study consisted of 30 British Council respondents all enrolled on Leaner Support Project using theLearningBusiness platform. The respondents came from information management or the knowledge centre based in 25 countries. The majority of respondents were of an educational background from either:

- Diploma in Library Science
- MPhil
- MSc in Management
- MA
- BA
- Advanced Diploma in Business Administration
- MBA
- Teacher Training Certificate

The respondents either offered or managed services from the table below:

| Individual | | | | Centre | | |
|---|---|---|---|---|---|---|
| Always | Never | S'times | | Always | Never | S'times |
| 55% | 13% | 29% | **Information for Prospective Students** | 13% | 0% | 84% |
| 26% | 45% | 23% | **Application to Institutions** | 36% | 20% | 42% |
| 35% | 48% | 13% | **Registration on Courses** | 29% | 19% | 48% |
| 39% | 20% | 39% | **Induction & Orientation to BC** | 29% | 13% | 55% |
| 45% | 23% | 29% | **English Language Learning Support** | 10% | 10% | 76% |
| 39% | 23% | 45% | **English Language** | 23% | 10% | 65% |

| | | | Teacher Training | | | |
|---|---|---|---|---|---|---|
| 6% | 71% | 19% | **Academic Tutoring** | 26% | 64% | 6% |
| 16% | 36% | 45% | **Personal Counselling/Welfare** | 42% | 36% | 19% |
| 32% | 36% | 29% | **Technical Support** | 29% | 26% | 42% |
| 19% | 42% | 35% | **Study Skills** | 35% | 29% | 26% |
| 68% | 7% | 29% | **Library/Information Services** | 16% | 3% | 77% |
| 26% | 32% | 29% | **Information Literary Skills** | 42% | 29% | 10% |
| 19% | 39% | 39% | **Learner Communities** | 58% | 32% | 19% |
| 0% | 45% | 10% | **Students with Disabilities** | 48% | 36% | 0% |
| 6% | 36% | 55% | **Careers Advice** | 48% | 32% | 16% |
| 3% | 45% | 36% | **Alumni** | 39% | 26% | 32% |

**Table 25 - Learner Support Services Offered**

## 17.5 Setting

A learner support programme was developed to deliver 3 modules to British Council staff.

Module 1 consisted of 12 – 15 hours of online learning examine:

- Use of collaborative learning
- Individual needs analysis
- Initial concepts of learning

Module 2

A five-day face-to-face programme of seminars, workshops and visits studying:

- Learning
- Coaching
- Learning Design
- Evaluation

Module 3

Online project work using community support and individual tutorials, over a four week period immediately following the face to face event.

## 17.6 The response

Module 1

*What is your perception of learning?*

- Learning is the best investment in life
- Learning is obtaining knowledge or/and new skills via investigating.
- Learning is a knowledge that you acquire and is on-going
- I think learning is a process of acquiring new knowledge which encourage learners to feel more confident

*What is the best support you can give a learner?*

- To help a learner overcome initial shock which everyone experiences when in a new situation
- To put learner in the right learning track
- To give the right advice at the right time
- To help them in their learning process
- Regardless of the contents of the learner support, I think we need to provide a support which is very easy for our learner-customers to access whenever they need to.

Using the scale developed by Marton, Dall & Beaty (1993) which categorises learning by *interviewing students about their perceptions*, which categorised learning in the following;

| Level | Description |
|-------|-------------|
| 1 | Increasing own knowledge |
| 2 | Memorising and reproducing |
| 3 | Applying |
| 4 | Understanding |
| 5 | Getting perspectives on things |
| 6 | Changing as a person |

**Table 26 - Learning Categories – Marton et al (1993)**

160

| Levels | Description |
|--------|-------------|
| 1 & 2 | Learning for purposes of reproduction i.e. not applied an no deeper understanding gained |
| 3 & 4 | Deeper understanding gained |
| 5 | Learner can consider subject matter from a variety of angles |
| 6 | Learner gains belief and understanding in the learning |

**Table 27 - Category Levels**

## Module 2

Participants were examined on perception of learning based on experience of collaborative and online-experience of which the following quotes were given:

- Conscious process of obtaining information in order to be able to apply it.
- Learning is not always individual
- It is not about being given information, it can be about finding the information yourself, developing your ideas through discussion.

The above statements show participants have developed higher level of understanding about learning. The following statements show participants have identified the advantages of shared learning experiences i.e. use of e-learning and collaborative learning and *sharing of cultural learning*:

- Sharing learning experiences with people from six countries was amazing
- Having a person coaching us rather than teaching made the experience more attractive
- Gave time for reflection
- It was an enhancing experience providing a wealth of material for me to decide which to interact with.
- Feedback was continuous and peer feedback was less daunting
- Answers do not always have to be from the teacher
- Using a combination of learning styles, for example, visual, kinaesthetic, discussion gave you an opportunity to look at material from different perspectives.

161

- The variation kept me on the edge, it spurred me on.
- It was not linear like listening and reading, it made me think differently
- It allowed me to choose, be in control of my learning.

Participants were asked to develop a skills matrix containing elements of *Skill, Knowledge and Understanding* which on examination provided significant increase in competency scores in relation to those taken at the beginning of the course, following module 1, and following module 2.

## 17.7 Discussion

The program achieved its aims by allowing individuals to explore new ideas of learner support delivery and action plan for supporting learners within their individual centres. Although as a consequence of the survey in module 1 students response were based around categories 1 & 2 in Table 26 & Table 27 – They understood learning as a means of gaining knowledge and memorisation and reproduction but not in the higher level learning categories. The above has shown participants have a different viewpoint based on reflection of the program of learning and now see things from a different perspective. The participants have altered a surface view of learning and adopted a deeper approach as they proceeded through the module reflected by the significant change from the skills matrix.

For further discussion it would be useful to provide a further survey for a quantitative measure of the significance of the changes and the extent to which the ability is retained and used.

## 17.8 Conclusion

The programme based on varied methods of course delivery proved to develop the understanding of learning of the participants. Participants on reflection were able to identify these changes.

# Chapter – 18

# Discussion Conclusion & Future Recommendations

## 18.1 Platform Construction

Many organisations are still in the investigative stage of e-learning and exploration has revealed that future prospects find it difficult to identify needs. The e-learning market has changed quite drastically over a short space of time leaving those considering e-learning systems in a state of uncertainty. The PDLC is a tool designed to address e-learning system feasibility on a holistic basis. To design an e-learning system for an organisation; or to implement an existing e-learning system warrants holistic consideration in order to embrace all influential processes and factors. These include stakeholders (users, owners, designers, administrators, legislators, coach's, moderators, trainers, human resources, theorists) business strategy, learning outcomes, courses, etc. A realistic approach would involve stakeholder input on relevant subsystems and processes. For example using a project management framework where the coach would oversee material elements and functionality in design relevant to teaching/ and learning, where the administrator would oversee the functionality required for set up and monitoring. Inclusion of stakeholders is a means of ensuring pedagogy consideration within the project which acts as an advantage when seeking agreement from the hierarchy. Following such a process also would prevent project drift and provide a learner centred user friendly platform

The design process of e-learning projects should be placed under constant revue because the e-learning environment is changing constantly as more research data becomes available. E-learning systems are impending thus the project scope requires flexibility. Specification and requirements will constantly change and important to prevent having an out of date system. This would be considered bad practice in under normal project management circumstances but, important relative technology such as Bandwidth, and video and audio streaming, is improving faster than the pace of development.

E-learning developers can find a solution to project drift in alliances and consideration in purchase off the shelf products that meet the requirement. The increase in strategic alliances and mutual agreements between content providers and system providers has helped to consolidate the e-learning market allowing more resources to be allocated to pedagogical aspects and standardisation. It is important to compare costs against building bespoke components and buying in of the shelf packages that are more than capable of meeting specification as SmartForce has realised to its cost in its $100 million outlay, which is likely to be one of the more expensive e-learning systems built in early 2000, which by today's standards is very expensive. Unfortunately the revenue returns did not meet expectations and by 2003 SmartForce had layed off staff. Far too many e-learning producers have made the mistake of bespoke building components only to find the costs are escalating where providers can meet the need at a fraction of the cost. This has been the case to some extent with the design of tLB. tLB was designed as a bespoke system for specific purpose namely training and coaching using active learning principles within the work place where in the early stages there were very few vendors that could provide anything like it. Today this may not be the case but content providers; VLE providers and commerce system providers all can play a part in construction of the tLB platform, by freeing up resources to be allocated elsewhere.

## 18.2 tLB Requirements

The tLB was devised for organisational training needs and functioned to meet the requirements and demands of coaches and trainers working within action learning principles. It therefore had to be user friendly, simple to navigate, and capable of engaging users. The evaluation survey has to some extent agreed with a number of these points and proved the system is on course to achieving its specified outcome. However to compare with some of the top e-learning systems a comparison (see Chapter 5.3 & Appendix B) has shown it requires:

- Course catalogue
- LCMS, IMS compliant,
- VLE that can run on any platform
- Crash recovery

Data

- Marking on-line
- Managing records
- Analysing and tracking

Web Browsing

- Bookmarks,
- Multimedia,
- Recovery and security,
- Newsgroups.

Student tools

- Self-assessing
- Progress tracking
- Searching
- Motivation building
- Study skill building

Support Tools

- Course planning
- Course managing
- Course customizing
- Course monitoring
- Evaluation & Feedback

The above points are taken from a comparison between many of today's leading market systems and tLB, what it does not tell us is which of these components are relevant. tLB is built on the basis functionality is included through stakeholder demand. Can the same be said for other e-learning vendors?    Some of the components listed in the comparison are useful for administrative purposes particularly the support tools.  Student tools can also help the learner to reflect on course work which acts as a feedback process.  Most important is an evaluation and feedback process which is not listed in Table - Appendix B although an evaluation framework is used to establish the position of the existing system; it is not suffice for the needs of moderators and coaches.  An evaluation system should be incorporated into the platform for easy coach and moderator access.

### 18.3 E-Learning Models

The review has covered a number of subjects within the context of e-learning to provide a framework to enable the analysis of any gaps between the existing model tLB platform, best practice, design and user satisfaction.  The evaluation studies presents the stakeholders view which is mapped against the existing tLB platform and the framework devised through a phenomenological approach in parallel with a review of the literature.

The e-learning model takes into consideration many of the subject areas provided covering in particular, the technology e.g. LMS and LCMS and looks at how contents can be provided to meet meticulous outcomes from within the learning system.  It also incorporates one of the more important aspects of constructivism as a theory in the form of active learning.  This is agreed by many theorists to be the best form of learning process to apply to an e-learning environment.  It also considers the tLB which is the learning platform used in the test and on which most of this study is based.  The importance of pedagogy in e-learning is something that tends to be ignored but is of significant importance when designing material, and should be considered greatly to incorporate modern methods of teaching and learning.  The instructional design methodology is somewhat significant in this respect as it incorporates the pedagogical and socio-theoretical aspects into e-learning.

The e-learning evaluation system was based on Qual IT an evaluation model used in a Bangor University project.  This was adopted for the tLB and a further system was developed for pre-course evaluation and collaborative sessions

166

The Pedagogical model is a framework for good online practise and is derived from many of the top learning theorists.

The shift from traditional learning to online learning requires that we look at the differences between the many different theorists in a traditional environment and try to analyse the differences and adopt them to e-learning environments. It can then be transformed to create practice in e-learning context. Research has shown that a number of theories lend themselves to e-learning, conversational, constructive alignment, variation, constructivism. Constructivism readily lends itself to e-learning and is considered perhaps the most important although the other theories such as conversational and variation are also significant. Learning bytes for instance is based on Miller 7+-1 theory. Adopting these theories in the form of learning activities produces higher level learning. This replicates changes in traditional learning which are now becoming more focused on learner centred processes.

The model takes the form of active learning in an online process but how is this done? Active learning consists of greater engagement in the learning process which requires a higher skill level from the coach/tutor. The role of the coach/trainer is plays an important role utilising technology to best advantage of the learners; and the application of the learning theory to provide a learner centred system where students can engage. They are required to understand IT at an appropriate level to monitor an online course; they are also required to acquire a level of technical skill to solve mediocre problems when they occur. Their ability to coach and facilitate learning and take on new theories also put them in the category of practitioners; that requires a skill-set not unlike but with slight differences to traditional teaching.

Active learning can be delivered in a variety of methods e.g. e-mail, discussion boards chat lines, live classrooms, bulletin boards. It is the method that becomes important i.e. the engagement of the learner into a higher level process. Theorists such has Laurillard and Pask have created modern theories to enhance the experience of active learning whereby students become conveyors of information. The student collaboration, facilitated by the tutor becomes a rich area of experience from which positive significant conclusions can be drawn using instruments such as the Classroom Community Scale. However, Mitchell (2002) suggests using active learning theories in any context can be high risk particularly if students fail to respond to the task expected of them. Contingency within the armour of a tutor/coach in the case of failure is good practice.

It is also good practice to use learning theory as a framework for delivery of a course and Kolb's learning cycle is ideal although there are many others available. The learning cycle is readily used in coaching on tLB giving consistency to the training process which makes for constant evaluation. The process of evaluation and feedback is essential in establishing the course. It allows the designers the scope to reflect on quality of the materials and how well the online learning environment is utilised.

## 18.4 Monitoring and Evaluation Response

Developing and evaluation tool had two distinctive outcomes: It gave us a means of quickly devising evaluation tools for learning environments and it gave us the tool to monitor and evaluate the courses, the learning, and the learning environment.

It was quickly established that formative assessment required more than just an evaluation tool and the use of stats from system files was also deemed important. The engagement of students and their input to courses on the system is significant. It is essential that for continuous improvement these tools are used. It allows us develop and improve a learner centred system which is necessary for innovation to gain competitive advantage. Evaluation is an ongoing process as a factor of continuous development where data analysis points to more targeting and further evaluation tools and refinement to provide a more accurate picture of learners within, and passing through the system.

## 18.5 Competency Profiles

The standards and literacy of students are relative to the course and competency requirements of the course. Online tests are indispensable in determination of competency as standards are based on level of validation. Validated courses will generally have set criteria which students have to meet to proceed. Some courses have precursors to determine capability to continue onto the main course. The level the course is set, should be clear within objectives.

The goals and objectives revolve around producing a quality in which users and students' tutors can engage and obtain the level of learning required to create deep learners. Consideration of taxonomy to determine the levels of competence students are expected to achieve is not unusual. The use of SOLO taxonomy is one method of setting standards of competency. Constructive alignment with a student centred approach is the best way forward. The principle method is to align teaching methods and assessments with objectives and goals of the learning activities.

Biggs (1999) articulates *'conceptions of phenomena change'* and our world view in which we acquire information as being conducive towards education and lists the changes that take place:

*1. It is clear to students and teachers what is appropriate, what the objectives are, where all can see where they are supposed to be going.*

*2. Students experience the felt need to get there. The art of good teaching is to communicate the need where it is initially lacking. 'Motivation' is a product of good teaching, not its prerequisite.*

*3. Students feel free to focus on the task, not on watching their backs. Often attempts to create a felt need to learn, particularly through ill-conceived and urgent assessments, are counter productive. The game then becomes a matter of dealing with the test, not with engaging the task deeply.*

*4. Students can work collaboratively and in dialogue with others, both peers and teachers. Good dialogue elicits those activities that shape, elaborate, and deepen understanding.*

The issues Biggs (1999) addresses can be identified within an e-learning context, and within asynchronous and synchronous communications. The competency standard of the student is a subject that cannot be ignored in e-learning particularly because it may be related to motivation. More research in this area would determine relativity to attrition.

## 18.6 Motivational Factors

Motivation has proved to be a decisive factor to the success of e-learning. The motivational factors of intrinsic and extrinsic learners emerge in observational studies on tLB platform. A number of learners from the British Council who were highly motivated showed many of the intrinsic factor highlighted in Chapter 11. The levels of facilitation relative to this group compared to other less motivated groups were far less. A fact that comes to light questions the use of the word motivation in an online learning context. Sometimes the term is abused in inclusion of learners who are not inclined towards e-learning. This group is very often placed in an extrinsically motivated class whereby, they have genuine reasons for not using the system in a way seen fit. In fact, many of the local tLB users have completed the course without using the VLE. In the case of the British Council learners, the only means of collaborative real-time communication was through conference calling and VLE whiteboard. It is difficult to avoid a VLE when it is a subject of the course. What is clear is level of participation is related to motivational factors and the British Council group was highly motivated. Level of education also has an effect on motivational factors but to what extent cannot be proven within this study has some of the more qualified learners appeared to lack motivation. Again the argument for some of the members for this particular group of users, who were practising chemists, was their lack of technical knowledge. It is difficult to distinguish between motivational factors and technical ability as a rationale for lack of participation.

Some of the main issues involve study skills where students claimed they have a level of competence which is later discovered not fitting. Results from the review showed a similar case in tLB courses. Some of the students did not have the skills to proceed on the course. It is important that competency profiles are put in place to establish learner's capabilities before embarking upon a course. Technical issues can be a de-motivator and it is important that the tutor is able to deal with these very quickly. The competency of the tutor is essential in keeping users motivated. As a facilitator it is important how the course is run! How the facilitator allots time and how the student manages time. If the student spends a great deal of time solving technical issues it is time not being applied to the learning and loss of interaction time with tutor. The technology should not demand such importance because that is not the essence of e-learning.

Kolb's learning cycle could also be utilised in the coaching process but other factors of the model is yet to be implemented and require collaborative effort from coaches to build and catalogue the learning outcomes and effort from the web designers and programmers to build in personal profiling tools to utilise the likes of Belbin's curve and various others.

It is doubtless the tLB has advanced over the project period but still has quite a way to go to meet the demands of today's market. In time it may compete on product quality but presently, methods of teaching and learning is what differentiates it from competitors. It is essential the tLB keeps in touch with users and continues to develop a learner centred user friendly system that coach's, tutors and learners can enjoy using. The challenge is to discover how to break down the gap between the virtual classroom and the traditional classroom as highlighted by Karesenti.

> *Karesenti (1999) from a study argues the point that students may not be ready for autonomy of self-determination when it comes to the 'virtual classroom' and there is a marked decline in student motivation after only four weeks of an online-course. The perceived gap between the university classroom and the virtual classroom is difficult to bridge.*

Finally, the e-learning platform had in some ways given the green light as a method for actively encouraging deep learning in distant learning. Such methods as chats, discussions, web conferencing under the banner of synchronous learning can encourage deep learning given correct facilitation. In some cases moderation is adequate depending of the quality of the students, as is the case in study 3 were British Council students are keen to learn and tend to be proactive. The conversational theorists suggest e-learning as an ideal platform as it encourages the type of learning it advocates. The theory of different varieties of learning is slightly more difficult to provide or at least monitor but good facilitation will ensure that this takes place. Experiential learning can provide for variation in an online context as long as students are engaged and encouraged to participate. One should remember it is the quality of the learning and not the platform for learning that is important although it can play an important part. The technology is not the source of the learning it is only a means to allow it to take place over distance. It is vital that students are not mesmerised by the technology and drawn away by bright lights. Contingencies should be in place to replace the technology if need be.

Used correctly e-learning can be a useful form of distant learning removing the barriers of space and time. Global learning is on our doorstep where courses will be run from any institution from any continent or country anywhere in the world. The reviews have suggested the social aspects of learning can improve with e-learning but it shouldn't be forgotten that face to face meetings also has a role to play in e-learning.

# References

Alertbox - http://www.useit.com    Jan. 2002 Site Map Usability

Argyris, C. (1976). Increasing Leadership Effectiveness. New York: Wiley

Argyris, C. (1993). On Organisational Learning. MA: Blackwell

Atherton, J. S. (2002) Learning and Teaching: Deep and Surface Learning [On-line]: UK:
Available: http://www.dmu.ac.uk/~jamesa/learning/deepsurf.htm

Atherton J. S. (2003) Learning and Teaching: Pask and Laurillard [On-line] UK: Available:
http://www.dmu.ac.uk/~jamesa/learning/pask.htm#Conversational Accessed: 16 December 2004

Austin Diane; Mescia Nadine D.; Strategies to Incorporate Active Learning into Online
Teaching; http://www.cas.usf.edu/lis/presentation

Arle John (2002)
http://www.elearnmag.org/subpage/sub_page.cfm?article_pk=1301&page_number_nb=1&title=
FEATURE%20STORY

Asher, H and Skenes, R. (1993). Can Tinto's Model be Applied to Non-Traditional Students?
Adult Education Quarterly, 43(2), 90-100.

Bengamin S. Bloom, Bertram B. Mesia, and David R. Krathwohl (1964). Taxonomy of
Educational Objectives (two vols: The Affective Domain & The Cognitive Domain). New York.
David McKay.

Baie Verte; Student Assessment, Evaluation and Reporting Policy (1999) DRAFT Central,
Connaigre School District 5

Bellah, R. N., Madsen, R., Sullivan, W. M., Swidler, A., & Tipton, S. M. (1985). Habits of the
heart: individualism and commitment in American life. New York: Harper and Row.

Biggs, J.B., and Collis, K.F. (1982) Evaluating the Quality of Learning-the SOLO Taxonomy (1st ed.). New York: Academic Press. xii + 245 pp.

Biggs J. (1999), Teaching for Quality Learning at University. Buckingham Society for Research into Higher Education, Open University Press.

Bloom, B.S. (Ed.) (1956) Taxonomy of educational objectives: The classification of educational goals: Handbook I, cognitive domain. New York ; Toronto: Longmans, Green.

Bloom Bengamin S., Mesia Bertram B., and Krathwohl David R. (1964). *Taxonomy of Educational Objectives* (two vols: The Affective Domain & The Cognitive Domain). New York. David McKay. Copyright 1999 by Donald Clark; Created June 5, 1999. Updated May 21, 2000, http://www.nwlink.com/~donclark/hrd/bloom.html

Blue Website, http://www.blueu.com; e-learning market growing and maturing
Boatman Andrew Mclain A Collection of Theories and Theorists: an aid to the student of educational theory 1998
http://www.google.com/search?hl=en&ie=UTF8&q=Entwistle+%26+Ramsden&btn

Bodomo A, Luke K. K. and Anttila A. - Evaluating Interactivity in Web-Based Learning; University of Hong Kong,Hong Kong, SAR. http://www.ignou.ac.in/e-journal/ContentIII/Adamsbodomo.htm

Brennan Michael, Funke Susan, and Anderson Cushing, The Learning Content Management System, A New eLearning Market Segment Emerges, *An IDC White Paper*

Brooks, J and Brooks, M (1993) In Search of Understanding: The Case for Constructivist Classrooms

Brophy, J, (1986) Motivating Students to Learn

Bryan Chapman's e-Learning Stock Tracker Year 2002 updated: January 25, 2002
http://www.brandonhall.com/public/ticker/index.htm.

Campbell Elizebeth & Piccinin Sergio, Centre for Univesity Teaching;
http://www.education.mcgill.ca/cutl/default.html

Centre for Teaching & Learning, Good Practises in Teaching & Learning – University College
Dublin
http://www.ucd.ie/~teaching/good/deep.htm

Chickering, A. and Ehrmann, S 1996  Implementing the seven principles: Technology as a lever;
Origin - Seven Principles Resource Center, Winona State University, PO Box 5838, Winona,
MN 55987-5838; ph 507/457-5020.) — Eds.

Chickering, A and Gamson, Z (1987) "Seven Principles for Good Practice' in AAHE Bulletin
39: 3-7

Closing the Gap -
http://www.elearnmag.org/subpage/sub_page.cfm?article_pk=2761&page_number_nb=1&title=
FEATURE%20STORY

Comeaux, P. 1995; The impact of an Interactive Distance Learning Network on Classroom
Communication;  Communication Education 44: 355-361

Coolican H.; Research Methods and Statistics in Psychology, 1999

Cornell, R and Martin, B 1997.

Davies Mathew L. & Crowther David E.A. (1996); The Benefits of Using Multimedia in Higher Education

Deci, E.L., & Ryan, R.M. (1991). A Motivational Approach to Self: Integration in Personality. Dans R.A. Dientsbier (Ed.), Perspectives on Motivation: Nebraska Symposium on Motivation. Lincoln, NE: University of Nebraska Press.

Deci Edward L. and Ryan Richard M. - Intrinsic and Extrinsic Motivations: Classic Definitions and New Directions; Contemporary Educational Psychology 25, 54–67 (2000) doi:10.1006/ceps.1999.1020, available online at http://www.idealibrary.com on; University of Rochester

Deci Edward L., Connell James E, and Ryan Richard M.; Self-Determination in a Work Organisation Journal of Applied Psychology; Copyright 1989 by the American Psychological Association, Inc. 1989, Vol. 74, No. 4, 580-590 0021-9010/89/$00.75; University of Rochester

Dodge, M. (1998). An Atlas of Cyberspaces (http://www.cybergeography.org/).

Donald Clark (Copyright 1999), Created June 5, 1999. Updated May 21, 2000. http://www.nwlink.com/~donclark/hrd/bloom.html.

Dugglby Julia, 2000, How to be an Online Tutor. P48.

Dddr. Sunil Hazari, University of Maryland, Dr. Donna Schno; Leveraging Student Feedback to Improve Teaching in Web-based Courses, June 1999; The Journal Online; Technological Horizons in Education.

Effective Learning and Teaching , Principles of Learning Teaching Science, Mathematics, and Technology.

Elizabeth Goodridge 2001, Consolidation Continues In E-Learning Market
April 9, 2001, InformationWeek.

Enoroth Carl (2000); E_learning for Environment; Improve E-learning as a Tool for Cleaner
Production Education, Lund University Sweden, Licentiate Dissertation.

Entwhistle, N. Promoting deep learning through teaching and assessment. Paper presented at
AAHE conference, June 14-18, 2000.

Eunice A., Kimball L., Silber T. and Weinstein N.; Maximizing Team Learning Through
Boundary less Facilitation 2001; (c) Catalyst Consulting Team and Caucus Systems, Inc.

Ewell, Peter T. 1984. Conducting Student Retention Studies. Boulder, CO: National Center for
Higher Education Management Systems.

Fazey John A. & Marton Ference (2002); Understanding the space of experiential variation
active learning in higher education, The Institute for Learning and Teaching in Higher Education
and SAGE Publications (London, Thousand Oaks, CA and New Delhi) Vol 3(3): 234–250
[1469-7874 (200211) 3:3;234–250;028179] ARTICLE.

Fisher Andrew, Financial Times; Apr 4, 2002.

Franzoi, S. L. (1996) Social Psychology. Chicago: Brown & Benchmark.

Gifford Jack B., Ph.D. a Professor of Marketing at Miami University November 29, 2001,
http://www.elearningmag.com/elearning/article/articleDetail.jsp?id=2763.

Harkus Susan – Seven Plus or Minus Two, What's the Relevance for Web Design 1990.

Hazari Sunil, Schno Donna – Levering Student Feedback to Improve teaching in Web-Based Courses – The Journal Online; Technological Horizons in Education.

Hill W.L. & Jones G. R. – Strategic Management an Integrated Approach. 1998.

HR Zone - http://www.hrzone.co.uk/poll/poll112.html, 2003.

Hootstein Ed; Wearing Four Pairs of Shoes: The Roles of E-Learning Facilitators 2002 - http://www.learningcircuits.org/2002/oct2002/elearn.html.

Honey Peter et al- A Declaration on Learning.

Huitt W.: Last modified: December, 1998
http://www.valdosta.edu/~whuitt/psy702/motivation/motivate.html.

Jeffrey R. Krackhardt Davidhanson, Informal Networks: The Company Behind The Chart, Harvard Business Review, January 1993.

Kaminski J.; BellaOnline's Distance Learning Editor; Learning Theory in Cyberspace.
http://www.bellaonline.com/about/distancelearning.

Kearsley, G. (2000) Explorations in Learning & Instruction: Theory in Practice Database.

Larson Kevin and Czerwinski's - Web Page Design: Implications of Memory, Structure and Scent for Information Retrieval http://www.research.microsoft.com/users/marycz/chi981.htm

Lawson, R.J. - Research Institute for Enhancing Learning, UWB E Coaching & British Learning Facilitators.

Laura Smith,  Dr. Janette Hill,
http://216.239.39.100/search?q=cache:zkOehGWe4IsC:www.arches.uga.edu/~ldsmith/midterm.
doc+Smith+%26+Ragan+1999&hl=en&ie=UTF-8.

Laurillard, D. (1999). A conversational framework for individual learning applied to the
"learning organization" and "learning society." *Systems Research and Behavioural Science, 16*
(2).

Lepper, Mark R. "Motivational Considerations in the Study of Instruction." Cognition and
Instruction 5, 4 (1988): 289-309.

Leiner Barry M., Cerf Vinton G., Clark David D., Kahn Robert E., Kleinrock Leonard, Lynch,
Daniel C Jon Postel., Roberts Larry G., Wolff Stephen. A Brief History of the Internet version
3.31 Last revised 4 Aug 2000.

Lieblein Edward (2001) Critical Factors for Successful Delivery of Online Programs; Internet
and Higher Education 2(2000) 161-174.

Lepper, Mark R. "Motivational Considerations in the Study of Instruction." Cognition and
Instruction 5, 4 (1988): 289-309.

Lublin, Jackie et al, Good Practises in Teaching & Learning – University College Dublin
http://www.ucd.ie/~teaching/good/deep.htm.

McCarthy-McGee Anita F.: Addressing Evaluation and Assessment While Delivering Online
Learning for the Army 2001; The Internet & Higher Education 3(2000) 175-181.

Masie Elliott The Trainer of the Future - e-learning Magazine, January 1, 2002
http://www.elearningmag.com/elearning/article/articleDetail.jsp?id=6714.

Marton, F. & Säljö, R. (976) On qualitative differences in learning I. Outcome and Process. British Journal of Educational Psychology, 46:4-11.

McLoughlin, C and Oliver, R; Pedagogic Roles and Dynamics in Telematics Environments; Telematics in Education: Trends and Issues Edited by: Sillenger, M Pearson, J, (1999), P 33.

Mantyla, Karen (1999). Interactive distance learning exercises that really work! Turn classroom exercises into effective and enjoyable distance learning activities. Alexandria, VA: ASTD. http://opencampus.com/faculty/summaries/INTERACTIVE_DL_EXERCISES.htm.

(M.Mentis@massey.ac.nz). Analysing the Effectiveness of On-line Learning Communities.

Miller George A. - The Magical Number Seven, Plus or Minus Two: Some Limits on our Capacity for Processing Information (1956) Harvard University First published in Psychological Review, 63, 81-97. http://psychclassics.yorku.ca/Miller/.

Mitchell Lynette (2002), Active Learning and Reflection, Department of Classics and Ancient History, University College Exeter, http://hca.htsn.ac.uk/.

Moon, J; Centre for Teaching & Learning, Good Practises in Teaching & Learning, Learning Journals and Logs, Reflective Diaries – University College Dublin http://www.ucd.ie/~teaching/good/deep.htm.

Morton F. Hounsell & Entwistle N. - Phenomenography Understanding Student Learning. London: Croom Helm 1983.

Marton F. & Säljö, R. (976) On qualitative differences in learning I. Outcome and Process. British Journal of Educational Psychology, 46:4-11.

Marton, F. & Säljö, R. (976) On qualitative differences in learning I. Outcome and Process. British Journal of Educational Psychology, 46:4-11.

Narushige Shiode (n.shiode@ucl.ac.uk) A Brief History of Cyberspace: Evolution of Information Spaces Centre for Advanced Spatial Analysis, University College London, United Kingdom.

Nasseh Bizhan Dr., Search for New Pedagogy Teacher Survey, Internet Based Distant Education Research, Ball State University,

National Board for Professional Teaching Standards. (1998). Washington, DC: Author. Available: http://www.nbpts.org/nbpts/.

Nielsen Jakob; Alertbox  Jan 6, 2002 Site Map Usability, www.useit.com.

New Teacher Toolkit; http://cie.ci.swt.edu/newteacher/section3-13.htm.

Pask, G. (1975). Conversation Cognition and Learning. Amsterdam, Elsevier.

Papert, 1993, p. 135, http://pdts.uh.edu/~ichen/ebook/ET-IT/dirty.htm.

Phillips Stephanie' Training Trends 2002, commissioned by TrainingZone, www.trainingzone.co.uk.

Programme for Industry; Dr Jake Reynolds (General Editor) · Dr Lynne Caley · Prof. Robin Mason 2002.

Quinones, S & Kirshstein, R; An Educator's Guide to Evaluating the Use of Technology in Schools & Classrooms 1998.

Reddy Arjun - Is a cost/benefit analysis a better approach?    e-learning Magazine January 1, 2002.

Reynold Jake PHd. Caley Lynne PHd and Professor Robin Mason; How do people learn? Research Report for CIPD Prepared by the University of Cambridge .

Ryann Ellis, 2005, E-learning Standards Update, Learning Circuits and E-Learning Network News; (rellis@astd.org) http://www.learningcircuits.org/2005/jul2005/ellis.htm.

Ryba Ken; Massey University, Auckland, New Zealand (K.Ryba@massey.ac.nz).

Rovai A. P.; Development of an Instrument to Measure Classroom Community; Internet & Higher Education 5 (2002) 197-211.

Rossi and Freeman - An Educator's Guide to Evaluating the Use of Technology in Schools and Classrooms - December 1993.

Schermerhorn, John R. et al. Organizational Behavior 2000,p.101 – 121.

Scigliano John A., Dringus Laurie P., A lifecycle model for online learning management, 21 critical metrics for the 21st century, School of Computer and Information Sciences, Nova Southeastern University,  November 2000.

Scigliano John A., Miller Inabeth , An Internet Higher Education Special Issue on the History of Online Learning, School of Computer and Information Sciences, Nova South Eastern University, November 2000; Internet and Higher Education 3(2000) 1-5.

Seale Jane K. PhD.; Using Learning Technologies in Psychology Education to Encourage Reflection, Technology Psychology and Reflection.

Selby Linda Auckland College of Education, Auckland, New Zealand (l.selby@ace.ac.nz)
Mentis Mandia  Massey University, Auckland, New Zealand.

Shepherd Clive, A day in the life of a learning management system, http://www.fastrak-consulting.co.uk/tactix/features/lms/lms.htm.

Sharp, J,  Communities of Practice: A Review of the Literature, 12 March 1997 Background: Informal Networks are Ubiquitous.

Silbeman, M; Active Learning:101 Strategies to Teach Active Learning, 1996.

Sillenger, M Pearson, J, (1999); Telematics in Education: Trends and Issues.
Skinner, B. F.  *Science and Human Behavior* . New York: Macmillan, 1953.
Skinner, B. F.  1987.  "Behaviourism, Skinner On."  *Oxford Companion to the Mind*.  New York: Oxford University Press.
Smith, P. and Ragan, T. (1999). *Instructional design* (2nd ed.). New York: John Wiley & Sons, Inc.; http://classweb.gmu.edu/ndabbagh/Resources/IDKB/evaluation.htm.

Sterling B Short History of the Internet by  bruces@well.sf.ca.us F&SF Science Column #5.

Strategic Visions International, 2002, E-Learning Market Segments
http://www.stratvisions.com/e-learning-bytes/05-market-segments.html.

Surowiecki, James (jamessuro@aol.com) is The New Yorker's financial columnist and the author of The Wisdom of Crowds. - http://www.wired.com/wired/archive/12.06/view_pr.html.

Surowiecki, J - Q & A session - http://www.wired.com/wired/archive/12.06/view_pr.html.

The development, 2 implementation and valuation of Internet-based undergraduate materials for the teaching of key skills, active learning in higher education; The Institute for Learning and Teaching in Higher Education and SAGE Publications (London, Thousand Oaks, CA and New Delhi) Vol 3(1): 40–53 [1469-7874 (200203) 3:1;40–53;021784].

Thomas Jocelyn 2004 - Facilitation of Critical Thinking and Deep Cognitive Processing by Structured Discussion Board Activities. Department of Psychology, University of New Orleans. http://www.celt.lsu.edu/CFD/E-Proceedings/Facilitation of Critical Thinking and Deep Cognitive Processing.htm.

Tinto V. (1993); Leaving College: rethinking the causes and cures of student attrition. (2nd ed.) Chicago: University of Chicago Press.

University for Industry Collaborative Project between The Centre for Learning and Innovations in Organisations University College Northampton & The Centre for Learning Development University of Wales Bangor, September 2001.

Vallerand, R. J. (1997). Towards a hierarchical model of intrinsic and extrinsic motivation. In M. P. Zanna (Ed.), Advances in experimental social psychology (pp. 271-359). New York: Academic Press.

Vygotsky, L. S. (1962) Thought and Language. Cambridge, MA:Harvard MIT Press.

Vygotsky, L. S. (1978) Mind in Society. Cambridge, MA:Harvard University Press.
Wagner, E. D. (1997). Interactivity: From agents to outcomes. New Directions for Teaching & Learning, 71, 19-26. San Francisco: Jossey Bass.

Warner Doug, 2000, Right Know Technologies White Paper, The Insiders Guide to Building an Effective Knowledge Base.

Welsh Assembly strategy 'A Winning Wales 'Wales Management Council report 2002.

Weston Cynthia, Gandell Terry, Mcalpine Lynn, Finkelstein Adam; 1996 - McGill University, Montreal, Quebec, Canada; Design Instruction for the Context of Online Learning; The Internet and Higher Education 2(1): 35-44.

Williams Peter, 2000, The learning Web.

Young C. Methods of Motivation: Yesterday and Today; November 30, 2000.

**Bibliography**

Beaudoin Michael F. 2002; Learning or lurking? Tracking the "Invisible" Online Student University of New England, Hills Beach Road, Biddeford, ME 04005, 13 March 2002; Internet and Higher Education 5 (2002) 147–155.

Critical Notes on 'Deep' and 'Surface' Approaches - http://www.arasite.org/critdeep&surf.htm.

Cunningham Mary Kay; Engaging Our Visitors: The Value of Conversational Interpretation and Interpretive Training. contact at interpretation@earthlink.net.

Ismail Johan; The design of an e-learning system, Beyond the hype; Patimas Technology Centre, Patimas Computers Berhad, Technology Park Malaysia, Internet and Higher Education, 4 (2002) 329–336.

Draper Stephen W., 1997; The relationship of the Perry, Deep & Shallow learning, and Laurillard models. Department of Psychology; Triggered by students' questions in a class (Nov 1997).

Piaget, J. (1973) To Understand is to Invent, New York: Grossman.

http://www.elearnmag.org/subpage/sub_page.cfm?article_pk=2761&page_number_nb=1&title= FEATURE%20STORY.

http://www.trainingzone.co.uk/zones/elearningzone/.

http://www.project2061.org/tools/sfaaol/Chap13.htm#1.

http://www.utm.edu/research/iep/.

http://www.ucalgary.ca/~iejll/

http://www.utm.edu/research/iep/b/behavior.htm

http://www.utm.edu/research/iep/

http://pdts.uh.edu/~ichen/ebook/ET-IT/cognitiv.htm.

http://pratt.edu/~arch543p/help/phenomenology.htm.

http://www.randomhouse.com/features/wisdomofcrowds/Q&A.html, Q & A with James Surowiecki

# Appendix - A

# Glossary

# Glossary

| | |
|---|---|
| **ADLNet** | **Advanced Distributed Learning Network** |
| **AICC** | **Aviation Industry CBT Committee** |
| **AI** | **Artificial Intelligence** |
| **ARPA** | **Advanced Research Projects Agency** |
| **CBA** | **Cost Benefit Analysis** |
| **CoPs** | **Communities of Practice** |
| **ERP** | **Enterprise Resource Planning** |
| **HTML** | **Hyper Text Mark-up Language** |
| **IEEE** | **Institute of Electrical and Electronics Engineers** |
| **IMS** | **Instructional Management System Global Learning Consortium** |
| **ISP** | **Internet Service Provider** |
| **LMS** | **Learning Management System** |
| **LCMS** | **Learning Content Management System** |
| **LOR** | **Learning Object Repository** |
| **PDLC** | **Platform Development Life Cycle** |
| **NASDAQ** | |
| **PDP** | **Product Data Planning** |
| **PESTLE** | **Political, Economical, Social, ,Legislation, Environmental** |
| **RIEL** | **Research Institute for Enhancement of Learning** |
| **ROI** | **Return on Investment** |
| **SCORM** | **Sharable Content Object Reference Model** |
| **tLB** | **theLearningBusiness** |
| **UCLA** | **University of California** |
| **UFi** | **University for Industry** |
| **VLE** | **Virtual Learning Environment** |

# Appendix – B

# Comparison of E-learning Systems

# Appendix B - Table of Comparisons

| Application home page | CT | BB | LS | TC | TB | MA | FC | EM | tLB |
|---|---|---|---|---|---|---|---|---|---|
| **Features/Tools** | WebCT | BlackBoard | Learning Space | TopClass | Click2learn ToolBook | Authorware | FirstClass | Saba Learning Enterprise | the Learning Bus |

## Learner Tools

| Web Browsing | CT | BB | LS | TC | TB | EM | MP | ES | tLB |
|---|---|---|---|---|---|---|---|---|---|
| Accessibility | yes | yes | | | | | | | yes |
| Bookmarks | yes | yes | yes | yes | yes | yes | yes | | |
| Multimedia | yes | yes | yes | yes | yes | yes | yes | yes | |
| Security | yes | yes | yes | yes | yes | yes | yes | | |

| Asynchronous Sharing | CT | BB | LS | TC | TB | EM | MP | ES | |
|---|---|---|---|---|---|---|---|---|---|
| E-mail | yes | yes | yes | yes | yes | yes | yes | yes | yes |
| BBS file exchange | yes | yes | yes | yes | | yes | | yes | |
| Newsgroups | yes | yes | yes | yes | yes | | yes | yes | |

| Synchronous Sharing | CT | BB | LS | TC | TB | EM | MP | ES | tLB |
|---|---|---|---|---|---|---|---|---|---|
| Chat | yes | yes | yes | | yes | yes | | yes | yes |
| Voice Chat | | yes | | | | | | | yes |
| Whiteboard | yes | yes | yes | | yes | | | yes | yes |
| Application sharing | yes | yes | yes | | yes | | | yes | yes |
| Virtual space | | yes | | | | | | | |
| Group browsing | | yes | | | yes | | | | yes |
| Teleconferencing | | | yes | | yes | | | | yes |
| Videoconferencing | | | yes | | yes | | | yes | yes |

| **Student tools** | CT | BB | LS | TC | TB | EM | MP | ES | tLB |
|---|---|---|---|---|---|---|---|---|---|
| Self-assessing | yes | yes | yes | yes | | yes | | yes | |
| Progress tracking | yes | yes | yes | yes | yes | yes | yes | yes | |

190

| | CT | BB | LS | TC | TB | EM | MP | ES | tLB |
|---|---|---|---|---|---|---|---|---|---|
| Searching | yes | yes | yes | | | yes | | yes | |
| Motivation building | yes | yes | yes | yes | | yes | | | |
| Study skill building | yes | yes | yes | yes | yes | yes | | | |

## Support Tools

| Course | CT | BB | LS | TC | TB | EM | MP | ES | tLB |
|---|---|---|---|---|---|---|---|---|---|
| Course planning | yes | yes | yes | yes | yes | yes | yes | | yes |
| Course managing | yes | yes | yes | yes | yes | yes | yes | yes | yes |
| Course customizing | yes | yes | yes | yes | yes | | yes | | yes |
| Course monitoring | yes | yes | yes | yes | yes | yes | yes | yes | |

| Lesson | CT | BB | LS | TC | TB | EM | MP | ES | |
|---|---|---|---|---|---|---|---|---|---|
| Instructional designing | yes | yes | yes | yes | yes | | yes | yes | yes |
| Presenting information | yes | yes | yes | yes | yes | | yes | yes | yes |
| Testing | yes | yes | yes | yes | yes | yes | | yes | yes |

| Data | CT | BB | LS | TC | TB | EM | MP | ES | tLB |
|---|---|---|---|---|---|---|---|---|---|
| Marking on-line | yes | yes | yes | yes | yes | yes | | yes | |
| Managing records | yes | yes | yes | yes | yes | yes | | yes | |
| Analyzing and tracking | yes | yes | yes | yes | yes | yes | | | |

| Resource | CT | BB | LS | TC | TB | EM | MP | ES | tLB |
|---|---|---|---|---|---|---|---|---|---|
| Curriculum Managing | | yes | yes | | | yes | | | yes |
| Building knowledge | yes | yes | yes | yes | | yes | | yes | yes |
| Team Building | yes | yes | yes | yes | | yes | | yes | yes |
| Building motivation | | yes | yes | yes | | yes | | yes | yes |

| Administration | CT | BB | LS | TC | TB | EM | MP | ES | tLB |
|---|---|---|---|---|---|---|---|---|---|
| Installation | yes | yes | yes | yes | yes | yes | | yes | |
| Authorization | yes | yes | yes | yes | yes | yes | | yes | yes |
| Registering | yes | yes | yes | | yes | yes | yes | yes | yes |
| On-line fees handling | | yes | | | | yes | | | yes |
| Server security | yes | yes | yes | yes | yes | yes | yes | yes | yes |
| Resource monitoring | yes | yes | yes | yes | yes | | yes | yes | yes |
| Remote access | yes | yes | yes | yes | yes | yes | | yes | yes |
| Crash recovery | yes | yes | yes | | | | | | |

| Help desk | CT | BB | LS | TC | TB | EM | MP | ES | tLB |
|---|---|---|---|---|---|---|---|---|---|
| Student support | yes | yes | yes | yes | yes | yes | | yes | yes |
| Instructor support | yes | yes | yes | yes | yes | yes | | yes | yes |

| Server Platform | CT | BB | LS | TC | TB | EM | MP | ES | tLB |
|---|---|---|---|---|---|---|---|---|---|
| RAM | yes | yes | yes | yes | yes | yes | yes | yes | yes |
| Disk Space | yes | yes | yes | | yes | yes | | yes | yes |
| Windows Server | yes | yes | yes | yes | yes | yes | yes | yes | yes |
| Apple Server | | | | yes | | | | | |
| Unix Server | yes | yes | yes | yes | yes | yes | | | |

| Client Platform | CT | BB | LS | TC | TB | EM | MP | ES | tLB |
|---|---|---|---|---|---|---|---|---|---|

| | CT | BB | LS | TC | TB | EM | MP | ES | tLB |
|---|---|---|---|---|---|---|---|---|---|
| Minimum Level | yes | yes | yes | yes | yes | | | yes | yes |
| Target Level | yes | yes | yes | yes | yes | | | yes | yes |
| | | | | | | | | | |
| **Pricing** | **CT** | **BB** | **LS** | **TC** | **TB** | **EM** | **MP** | **ES** | **tLB** |
| Start-up Cost | yes | yes | | yes | | | | yes | |
| On-going Cost | yes | yes | | yes | | | | yes | |
| Technical Support | yes | yes | | | | yes | | yes | |
| | | | | | | | | | |
| **Limitations of package** | **CT** | **BB** | **LS** | **TC** | **TB** | **EM** | **MP** | **ES** | **tLB** |
| IMS Compliance | yes | | yes | | | yes | | | |
| Number of courses | yes | yes | | | | yes | | yes | |
| Number of students | yes | yes | | | | yes | | yes | |
| Number of connections | yes | yes | | yes | | yes | | yes | |
| Number of instructors | yes | yes | | | | yes | | yes | |
| Other Limitations | yes | yes | yes | yes | yes | | | yes | |
| | | | | | | | | | |
| **Extra Considerations** | **CT** | **BB** | **LS** | **TC** | **TB** | **EM** | **MP** | **ES** | **tLB** |
| Options | yes | yes | yes | | yes | | | yes | yes |
| Exit Considerations | | | yes | yes | | | | | yes |

# Appendix – C

# Data Effectiveness of Communities of Practice

## The Effectiveness of Communities of Practice

| Not Applicable | NA |
|---|---|
| Very Strongly Agree | VSA |
| Strongly Agree | SA |
| Agree | A |
| Neither | N |
| Disagree | D |
| Strongly Disagree | SD |
| Very Strongly Disagree | VSD |

| | | NA | VSA | SA | A | N | D | SD | VSD | Mean | Median | Mode | Variance | SD |
|---|---|---|---|---|---|---|---|---|---|---|---|---|---|---|
| 1. I felt that students on the course cared about ea | 12 | 0 | 3 | 2 | 5 | 2 | 0 | 0 | 0 | 1.714286 | 2 | 0 | 3.571429 | 1.889822 |
| | 100.00 | 0 | 25 | 17 | 42 | 17 | 0 | 0 | 0 | | | | | |
| 2. I felt encouraged to ask questions | 12 | 0 | 7 | 1 | 2 | 2 | 0 | 0 | 0 | 1.714286 | 1 | 0 | 6.238095 | 2.497618 |
| | 100.00 | 0 | 58 | 8 | 17 | 17 | 0 | 0 | 0 | | | | | |
| 3. I felt connected to others in this course | 12 | 0 | 3 | 2 | 5 | 0 | 2 | 0 | 0 | 1.714286 | 2 | 0 | 3.571429 | 1.889822 |
| | 100.00 | 0 | 25 | 17 | 42 | 0 | 17 | 0 | 0 | | | | | |
| 4. I felt that it was hard to get help when I had a qu | 12 | 0 | 3 | 0 | 1 | 1 | 3 | 2 | 2 | 1.714286 | 2 | 3 | 1.238095 | 1.112697 |
| | 100.00 | 0 | 25 | 0 | 8 | 8 | 25 | 17 | 17 | | | | | |
| 5. The course gave the opportunity for me to reflect | 12 | 0 | 6 | 2 | 3 | 1 | 0 | 0 | 0 | 1.714286 | 1 | 0 | 4.904762 | 2.21467 |
| | 100.00 | 0 | 50 | 17 | 25 | 8 | 0 | 0 | 0 | | | | | |
| 6. I could relate the course content to my own pers | 12 | 0 | 5 | 3 | 3 | 1 | 0 | 0 | 0 | 1.714286 | 1 | 0 | 3.904762 | 1.976047 |
| | 100.00 | 0 | 42 | 25 | 25 | 8 | 0 | 0 | 0 | | | | | |
| 7. The course inspired me to use what I had learnt | 12 | 0 | 5 | 4 | 2 | 0 | 1 | 0 | 0 | 1.714286 | 1 | 0 | 4.238095 | 2.058663 |
| | 100.00 | 0 | 42 | 33 | 17 | 0 | 8 | 0 | 0 | | | | | |
| 8. I felt I needed to practise what I was learning in t | 12 | 2 | 4 | 1 | 3 | 0 | 2 | 0 | 0 | 1.428571 | 1 | 0 | 2.619048 | 1.618347 |
| | 100.00 | 17 | 33 | 8 | 25 | 0 | 17 | 0 | 0 | | | | | |
| 9. I felt isolated in the course | 12 | 0 | 0 | 0 | 0 | 3 | 4 | 2 | 3 | 1.714286 | 2 | 0 | 2.904762 | 1.704336 |
| | 100.00 | 0 | 0 | 0 | 0 | 25 | 33 | 17 | 25 | | | | | |
| 10. I trusted others in the course | 12 | 0 | 4 | 2 | 4 | 2 | 0 | 0 | 0 | 1.714286 | 2 | 0 | 3.238095 | 1.799471 |
| | 100.00 | 0 | 33 | 17 | 33 | 17 | 0 | 0 | 0 | | | | | |
| 11. I felt reluctant to speak openly | 12 | 0 | 0 | 0 | 0 | 0 | 10 | 0 | 2 | 1.714286 | 0 | 0 | 13.90476 | 3.729909 |
| | 100.00 | 0 | 0 | 0 | 0 | 0 | 83 | 0 | 17 | | | | | |
| 12. I did not trust others in this course | 12 | 0 | 0 | 0 | 0 | 1 | 8 | 1 | 2 | 1.714286 | 1 | 0 | 8.238095 | 2.870208 |
| | 100.00 | 0 | 0 | 0 | 0 | 8 | 67 | 8 | 17 | | | | | |
| 13. I felt that I could rely on others in the course | 12 | 0 | 4 | 2 | 3 | 2 | 1 | 0 | 0 | 1.714286 | 2 | 2 | 2.238095 | 1.496026 |
| | 100.00 | 0 | 33 | 17 | 25 | 17 | 8 | 0 | 0 | | | | | |
| 14. I feel that other students do not help me learn | 12 | 0 | 0 | 0 | 0 | 0 | 8 | 2 | 2 | 1.714286 | 0 | 0 | 8.571429 | 2.9277 |
| | 100.00 | 0 | 0 | 0 | 0 | 0 | 67 | 17 | 17 | | | | | |
| 15. I felt that members of this course depended on | 12 | 0 | 0 | 0 | 0 | 6 | 4 | 2 | 0 | 1.714286 | 0 | 0 | 5.904762 | 2.429972 |
| | 100.00 | 0 | 0 | 0 | 0 | 50 | 33 | 17 | 0 | | | | | |
| 16. I felt that I was given ample opportunities to lea | 12 | 0 | 5 | 3 | 3 | 1 | 0 | 0 | 0 | 1.714286 | 1 | 0 | 3.904762 | 1.976047 |
| | 100.00 | 0 | 42 | 25 | 25 | 8 | 0 | 0 | 0 | | | | | |
| 17. I felt uncertain about others in this course | 12 | 1 | 3 | 0 | 1 | 3 | 3 | 1 | 9 | 1.571429 | 1 | 3 | 1.952381 | 1.397276 |
| | 100.00 | 8 | 25 | 0 | 8 | 26 | 26 | 8 | 0 | | | | | |
| 18. I felt that my educational needs were not being | 12 | 1 | 1 | 2 | 5 | 3 | 0 | 0 | 9 | 1.571429 | 1 | 0 | 3.619048 | 1.902379 |
| | 100.00 | 8 | 8 | 17 | 42 | 26 | 0 | 0 | 0 | | | | | |
| 19. I felt confident with the support from others | 12 | 1 | 4 | 2 | 5 | 0 | 0 | 0 | 0 | 1.571429 | 0 | 4 | 4.619048 | 2.149197 |
| | 100.00 | 8 | 33 | 17 | 42 | 0 | 0 | 0 | 0 | | | | | |
| 20. I felt that the course did not promote a desire to learn | 12 | 0 | 0 | 0 | 0 | 0 | 8 | 1 | 3 | 1.714286 | 0 | 0 | 8.904762 | 192.4344 |
| | | 2140 | 46.66667 | | 532 | 242.6667 | | 420 | 261.3333 | 437.3333 | 94.33333 | 105.6667 | 299.0476 | 261.3333 | 20664.09 | 169.2752 |
| | 100.00 | 2 | 25 | 11 | 20 | 12 | 20 | 4 | 5 | | | | | |

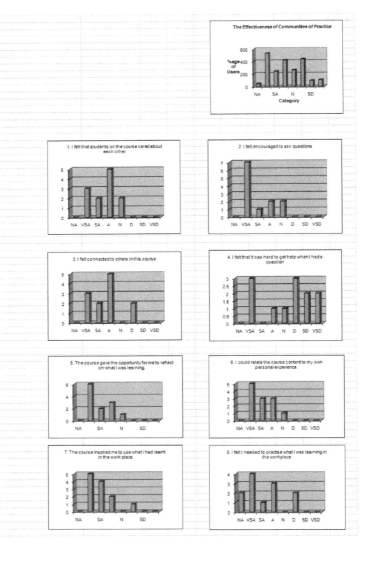

195

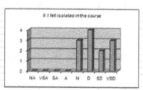

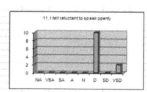

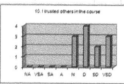

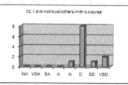

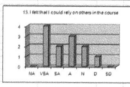

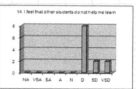

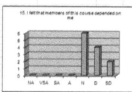

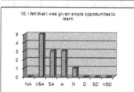

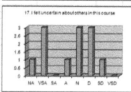

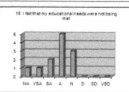

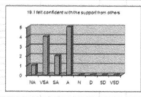

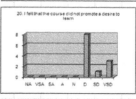

# Appendix - D

# Evaluation Factor Analysis & Correlations

# Factor Analysis

| | | |
|---|---|---|
| Output Created | | 16-DEC-2004 13:43:46 |
| Comments | | |
| Input | Data | E:\louis.sav |
| | Filter | <none> |
| | Weight | <none> |
| | Split File | <none> |
| | N of Rows in Working Data File | 40 |
| Missing Value Handling | Definition of Missing | MISSING=EXCLUDE: User-defined missing values are treated as missing. |
| | Cases Used | LISTWISE: Statistics are based on cases with no missing values for any variable used. |
| Syntax | | FACTOR /VARIABLES user1 user2 user3 user4 user5 user6 user7 user8 user9 match1 match2 match3 match4 match5 match6 match7 match8 cl1 cl2 cl3 cl4 cl5 cl6 cl7 cl8 cl9 pres1 pres2 pres3 pres4 pres5 ac1 ac2 ac3 ac4 ac5 ac6 ac7 ac8 eng1 eng2 eng3 eng4 eng5 eng6 fb1 fb2 fb3 fb4 fb5 lo1 lo2 lo3 lo4 lo5 lo6 lo7 lo8 lo9 /MISSING LISTWISE /ANALYSIS user1 user2 user3 user4 user5 user6 user7 user8 user9 match1 match2 match3 match4 match5 match6 match7 match8 cl1 cl2 cl3 cl4 cl5 cl6 cl7 cl8 cl9 pres1 pres2 pres3 pres4 pres5 ac1 ac2 ac3 ac4 ac5 ac6 ac7 ac8 eng1 eng2 eng3 eng4 eng5 eng6 fb1 fb2 fb3 fb4 fb5 lo1 lo2 lo3 lo4 lo5 lo6 lo7 lo8 lo9 /PRINT INITIAL EXTRACTION /CRITERIA MINEIGEN(1) ITERATE(25) /EXTRACTION PC /ROTATION NOROTATE /METHOD=CORRELATION . |
| Resources | Elapsed Time | 0:00:00.20 |
| | Maximum Memory Required | 391172 (382.004K) bytes |

**Communalities**

|        | Initial | Extraction |
|--------|---------|------------|
| user1  | 1.000   | .837       |
| user2  | 1.000   | .862       |
| user3  | 1.000   | .809       |
| user4  | 1.000   | .912       |
| user5  | 1.000   | .872       |
| user6  | 1.000   | .870       |
| user7  | 1.000   | .933       |
| user8  | 1.000   | .947       |
| user9  | 1.000   | .836       |
| match1 | 1.000   | .947       |
| match2 | 1.000   | .851       |
| match3 | 1.000   | .961       |
| match4 | 1.000   | .881       |
| match5 | 1.000   | .960       |
| match6 | 1.000   | .922       |
| match7 | 1.000   | .808       |
| match8 | 1.000   | .924       |
| cl1    | 1.000   | .921       |
| cl2    | 1.000   | .912       |
| cl3    | 1.000   | .912       |
| cl4    | 1.000   | .966       |
| cl5    | 1.000   | .938       |
| cl6    | 1.000   | .946       |
| cl7    | 1.000   | .951       |
| cl8    | 1.000   | .878       |
| cl9    | 1.000   | .895       |
| pres1  | 1.000   | .923       |
| pres2  | 1.000   | .875       |
| pres3  | 1.000   | .926       |
| pres4  | 1.000   | .934       |
| pres5  | 1.000   | .895       |
| ac1    | 1.000   | .897       |
| ac2    | 1.000   | .912       |
| ac3    | 1.000   | .938       |
| ac4    | 1.000   | .869       |
| ac5    | 1.000   | .901       |
| ac6    | 1.000   | .917       |
| ac7    | 1.000   | .969       |

199

| | | |
|---|---|---|
| ac8 | 1.000 | .959 |
| eng1 | 1.000 | .898 |
| eng2 | 1.000 | .901 |
| eng3 | 1.000 | .928 |
| eng4 | 1.000 | .951 |
| eng5 | 1.000 | .932 |
| eng6 | 1.000 | .956 |
| fb1 | 1.000 | .867 |
| fb2 | 1.000 | .956 |
| fb3 | 1.000 | .944 |
| fb4 | 1.000 | .885 |
| fb5 | 1.000 | .974 |
| lo1 | 1.000 | .932 |
| lo2 | 1.000 | .912 |
| lo3 | 1.000 | .945 |
| lo4 | 1.000 | .970 |
| lo5 | 1.000 | .870 |
| lo6 | 1.000 | .942 |
| lo7 | 1.000 | .932 |
| lo8 | 1.000 | .922 |
| lo9 | 1.000 | .962 |

Extraction Method: Principal Component Analysis.

**Total Variance Explained**

| Component | Initial Eigenvalues | | | Extraction Sums of Squared Loadings | | |
|---|---|---|---|---|---|---|
| | Total | % of Variance | Cumulative % | Total | % of Variance | Cumulative % |
| 1 | 38.299 | 64.914 | 64.914 | 38.299 | 64.914 | 64.914 |
| 2 | 3.239 | 5.489 | 70.403 | 3.239 | 5.489 | 70.403 |
| 3 | 2.900 | 4.915 | 75.318 | 2.900 | 4.915 | 75.318 |
| 4 | 2.340 | 3.966 | 79.283 | 2.340 | 3.966 | 79.283 |
| 5 | 1.919 | 3.253 | 82.536 | 1.919 | 3.253 | 82.536 |
| 6 | 1.557 | 2.640 | 85.176 | 1.557 | 2.640 | 85.176 |
| 7 | 1.380 | 2.339 | 87.514 | 1.380 | 2.339 | 87.514 |
| 8 | 1.259 | 2.135 | 89.649 | 1.259 | 2.135 | 89.649 |
| 9 | 1.053 | 1.786 | 91.434 | 1.053 | 1.786 | 91.434 |
| 10 | .950 | 1.610 | 93.045 | | | |
| 11 | .661 | 1.120 | 94.165 | | | |
| 12 | .543 | .921 | 95.086 | | | |
| 13 | .502 | .851 | 95.937 | | | |
| 14 | .466 | .790 | 96.727 | | | |
| 15 | .393 | .666 | 97.392 | | | |
| 16 | .319 | .540 | 97.932 | | | |
| 17 | .229 | .389 | 98.321 | | | |
| 18 | .196 | .332 | 98.653 | | | |

| | | | |
|---|---|---|---|
| 19 | .185 | .313 | 98.966 |
| 20 | .158 | .267 | 99.233 |
| 21 | .142 | .241 | 99.474 |
| 22 | .108 | .183 | 99.657 |
| 23 | .091 | .155 | 99.812 |
| 24 | .070 | .118 | 99.930 |
| 25 | .041 | .070 | 100.000 |
| 26 | .000 | .000 | 100.000 |
| 27 | .000 | .000 | 100.000 |
| 28 | .000 | .000 | 100.000 |
| 29 | .000 | .000 | 100.000 |
| 30 | .000 | .000 | 100.000 |
| 31 | .000 | .000 | 100.000 |
| 32 | .000 | .000 | 100.000 |
| 33 | .000 | .000 | 100.000 |
| 34 | .000 | .000 | 100.000 |
| 35 | .000 | .000 | 100.000 |
| 36 | .000 | .000 | 100.000 |
| 37 | .000 | .000 | 100.000 |
| 38 | .000 | .000 | 100.000 |
| 39 | .000 | .000 | 100.000 |
| 40 | .000 | .000 | 100.000 |
| 41 | .000 | .000 | 100.000 |
| 42 | .000 | .000 | 100.000 |
| 43 | .000 | .000 | 100.000 |
| 44 | .000 | .000 | 100.000 |
| 45 | .000 | .000 | 100.000 |
| 46 | .000 | .000 | 100.000 |
| 47 | .000 | .000 | 100.000 |
| 48 | .000 | .000 | 100.000 |
| 49 | .000 | .000 | 100.000 |
| 50 | .000 | .000 | 100.000 |
| 51 | .000 | .000 | 100.000 |
| 52 | .000 | .000 | 100.000 |
| 53 | .000 | .000 | 100.000 |
| 54 | .000 | .000 | 100.000 |
| 55 | .000 | .000 | 100.000 |
| 56 | .000 | .000 | 100.000 |
| 57 | .000 | .000 | 100.000 |
| 58 | .000 | .000 | 100.000 |
| 59 | .000 | .000 | 100.000 |

Extraction Method: Principal Component Analysis

201

## Component Matrix(a)

| | Component | | | | | | | | |
|---|---|---|---|---|---|---|---|---|---|
| | 1 | 2 | 3 | 4 | 5 | 6 | 7 | 8 | 9 |
| user1 | .614 | -.016 | .311 | .306 | .137 | -.257 | .248 | .150 | .319 |
| user2 | .321 | -.092 | .793 | -.141 | .024 | -.221 | .123 | .191 | .041 |
| user3 | .659 | .296 | -.197 | -.149 | .181 | -.228 | .156 | .182 | -.291 |
| user4 | .488 | .734 | -.020 | .216 | -.125 | .021 | .214 | -.058 | -.152 |
| user5 | .663 | -.487 | -.062 | -.073 | .171 | -.179 | -.314 | -.147 | .073 |
| user6 | .773 | -.256 | .124 | .033 | .282 | .247 | -.007 | -.161 | -.155 |
| user7 | .650 | -.350 | .260 | .012 | .360 | .340 | .227 | -.038 | -.150 |
| user8 | .843 | .282 | -.129 | .194 | -.203 | .104 | -.161 | -.054 | -.147 |
| user9 | .523 | .202 | .399 | -.272 | .214 | .343 | .261 | .012 | .239 |
| match1 | .871 | -.220 | .077 | -.049 | -.006 | .222 | -.083 | -.090 | .259 |
| match2 | .871 | .157 | -.049 | -.155 | -.014 | -.035 | -.134 | .129 | -.074 |
| match3 | .865 | -.264 | .066 | -.173 | .104 | -.077 | -.099 | .058 | -.282 |
| match4 | .900 | .100 | -.128 | .064 | .089 | .061 | .033 | .014 | -.163 |
| match5 | .956 | .113 | .000 | -.019 | .053 | -.035 | -.069 | -.072 | -.138 |
| match6 | .894 | -.114 | .179 | -.192 | -.099 | .114 | -.101 | .069 | -.048 |
| match7 | .777 | -.088 | -.024 | -.212 | -.169 | -.145 | -.245 | .204 | .014 |
| match8 | .806 | -.219 | .111 | .047 | -.016 | -.210 | .356 | -.177 | -.098 |
| cl1 | .843 | .003 | .185 | -.323 | -.120 | -.024 | .181 | .156 | -.016 |
| cl2 | .737 | .388 | -.213 | -.258 | .216 | -.128 | .075 | -.131 | .146 |
| cl3 | .784 | .354 | -.055 | -.166 | .360 | -.090 | -.037 | -.035 | -.011 |
| cl4 | .716 | .460 | -.066 | -.251 | .344 | .005 | -.115 | .198 | .057 |
| cl5 | .880 | .152 | -.036 | -.217 | -.017 | -.226 | .119 | -.091 | -.134 |
| cl6 | .884 | -.259 | .182 | -.160 | .070 | -.044 | .162 | .027 | .074 |
| cl7 | .933 | -.129 | .108 | .189 | .121 | .008 | -.020 | .047 | .011 |
| cl8 | .815 | -.244 | -.013 | .322 | -.082 | -.190 | .023 | .079 | .021 |
| cl9 | .907 | -.198 | .041 | -.164 | .023 | -.046 | -.011 | -.011 | .043 |
| pres1 | .744 | -.307 | -.309 | .061 | -.189 | -.248 | .051 | -.030 | .276 |
| pres2 | .863 | -.276 | .069 | .123 | -.083 | -.082 | -.020 | .142 | .009 |
| pres3 | .703 | -.319 | -.414 | -.055 | -.174 | .150 | .134 | .238 | -.169 |
| pres4 | .877 | -.080 | -.024 | .141 | -.295 | .149 | -.029 | .134 | .106 |
| pres5 | .709 | -.398 | -.314 | -.042 | -.023 | .176 | .092 | -.304 | -.032 |
| ac1 | .766 | -.035 | .070 | .342 | .111 | -.230 | -.173 | .293 | -.075 |
| ac2 | .698 | .206 | .075 | .388 | .241 | -.281 | -.220 | -.196 | -.046 |
| ac3 | .726 | .277 | .361 | .112 | .057 | .409 | -.134 | -.038 | -.034 |
| ac4 | .869 | -.118 | .081 | .045 | .075 | .071 | -.023 | -.282 | -.014 |
| ac5 | .894 | .023 | .172 | .014 | -.151 | .139 | -.043 | .013 | .166 |
| ac6 | .893 | .108 | .052 | -.015 | -.246 | .109 | .131 | .045 | .115 |
| ac7 | .812 | .459 | .040 | .081 | -.048 | .084 | .041 | -.250 | .132 |
| ac8 | .847 | .163 | .137 | .188 | -.263 | -.025 | -.111 | -.279 | .015 |
| eng1 | .745 | .184 | -.174 | -.448 | -.031 | .103 | -.172 | .151 | .123 |

| | 1 | 2 | 3 | 4 | 5 | 6 | 7 | 8 | 9 |
|---|---|---|---|---|---|---|---|---|---|
| eng2 | .785 | .182 | -.297 | -.155 | -.175 | .039 | .013 | .316 | .092 |
| eng3 | .861 | .165 | -.223 | -.175 | -.152 | -.142 | .060 | -.180 | -.006 |
| eng4 | .909 | .030 | .002 | -.296 | -.099 | .033 | .028 | -.048 | .149 |
| eng5 | .678 | .182 | -.015 | .559 | .018 | .125 | -.252 | .155 | .153 |
| eng6 | .936 | .127 | .100 | .050 | .018 | -.121 | -.062 | -.079 | .165 |
| fb1 | .818 | .113 | .035 | .251 | -.032 | -.035 | .276 | .036 | -.204 |
| fb2 | .738 | -.018 | -.518 | .158 | .091 | .114 | .289 | -.035 | .107 |
| fb3 | .834 | .034 | -.262 | .152 | .334 | .012 | -.031 | .167 | .123 |
| fb4 | .777 | -.229 | -.311 | .116 | .302 | .036 | .048 | .087 | .126 |
| fb5 | .750 | -.085 | -.587 | .097 | .156 | .138 | .079 | -.028 | .033 |
| lo1 | .795 | -.039 | .151 | .034 | -.349 | .283 | -.072 | .157 | -.205 |
| lo2 | .789 | -.153 | .119 | -.041 | .358 | .112 | -.298 | .067 | -.132 |
| lo3 | .933 | .019 | .089 | -.138 | -.117 | -.109 | .035 | -.096 | -.106 |
| lo4 | .910 | -.090 | .071 | -.177 | .042 | -.187 | -.148 | -.188 | -.055 |
| lo5 | .806 | -.130 | -.026 | -.264 | -.289 | -.170 | -.065 | -.130 | .000 |
| lo6 | .911 | -.077 | -.111 | .129 | -.194 | .177 | -.021 | .045 | -.084 |
| lo7 | .838 | -.073 | .159 | .281 | -.036 | -.100 | .292 | .140 | -.065 |
| lo8 | .932 | -.048 | .113 | .057 | -.122 | -.025 | -.030 | -.138 | -.004 |
| lo9 | .908 | .174 | .188 | .115 | -.180 | -.026 | -.136 | -.086 | .010 |

Extraction Method: Principal Component Analysis.
a  9 components extracted.

# Factor Analysis

**Notes**

| Output Created | | 16-DEC-2004 13:48:11 |
|---|---|---|
| Comments | | |
| Input | Data | E:\louis.sav |
| | Filter | <none> |
| | Weight | <none> |
| | Split File | <none> |
| | N of Rows in Working Data File | 40 |
| Missing Value Handling | Definition of Missing | MISSING=EXCLUDE: User-defined missing values are treated as missing. |
| | Cases Used | LISTWISE: Statistics are based on cases with no missing values for any variable used. |

| Syntax | | |
|---|---|---|
| | | FACTOR /VARIABLES user1 user2 user3 user4 user5 user6 user7 user8 user9 /MISSING LISTWISE /ANALYSIS user1 user2 user3 user4 user5 user6 user7 user8 user9 /PRINT INITIAL EXTRACTION /CRITERIA MINEIGEN(1) ITERATE(25) /EXTRACTION PC /ROTATION NOROTATE /METHOD=CORRELATION . |
| Resources | Elapsed Time | 0:00:00.05 |
| | Maximum Memory Required | 11172 (10.910K) bytes |

**Communalities**

| | Initial | Extraction |
|---|---|---|
| user1 | 1.000 | .742 |
| user2 | 1.000 | .603 |
| user3 | 1.000 | .711 |
| user4 | 1.000 | .854 |
| user5 | 1.000 | .682 |
| user6 | 1.000 | .844 |
| user7 | 1.000 | .779 |
| user8 | 1.000 | .775 |
| user9 | 1.000 | .509 |

Extraction Method: Principal Component Analysis.

**Total Variance Explained**

| Component | Initial Eigenvalues | | | Extraction Sums of Squared Loadings | | |
|---|---|---|---|---|---|---|
| | Total | % of Variance | Cumulative % | Total | % of Variance | Cumulative % |
| 1 | 5.401 | 60.013 | 60.013 | 5.401 | 60.013 | 60.013 |
| 2 | 1.097 | 12.188 | 72.201 | 1.097 | 12.188 | 72.201 |
| 3 | .803 | 8.918 | 81.120 | | | |
| 4 | .558 | 6.197 | 87.317 | | | |
| 5 | .359 | 3.990 | 91.306 | | | |
| 6 | .291 | 3.237 | 94.543 | | | |
| 7 | .275 | 3.056 | 97.600 | | | |
| 8 | .162 | 1.805 | 99.404 | | | |
| 9 | .054 | .596 | 100.000 | | | |

Extraction Method: Principal Component Analysis.

**Component Matrix(a)**

|  | Component | |
|---|---|---|
|  | 1 | 2 |
| user1 | .860 | -.035 |
| user2 | .618 | -.471 |
| user3 | .781 | .317 |
| user4 | .633 | .673 |
| user5 | .800 | -.205 |
| user6 | .910 | -.124 |
| user7 | .836 | -.284 |
| user8 | .796 | .377 |
| user9 | .684 | -.203 |

Extraction Method: Principal Component Analysis.
a  2 components extracted.

# Factor Analysis

**Notes**

| Output Created | | 16-DEC-2004 13:48:39 |
|---|---|---|
| Comments | | |
| Input | Data | E:\louis.sav |
|  | Filter | <none> |
|  | Weight | <none> |
|  | Split File | <none> |
|  | N of Rows in Working Data File | 40 |
| Missing Value Handling | Definition of Missing | MISSING=EXCLUDE: User-defined missing values are treated as missing. |
|  | Cases Used | LISTWISE: Statistics are based on cases with no missing values for any variable used. |
| Syntax | | FACTOR /VARIABLES match1 match2 match3 match4 match5 match6 match7 match8 /MISSING LISTWISE /ANALYSIS match1 match2 match3 match4  match5 match6 match7 match8 /PRINT INITIAL EXTRACTION /CRITERIA MINEIGEN(1) ITERATE(25) /EXTRACTION PC /ROTATION NOROTATE /METHOD=CORRELATION . |
| Resources | Elapsed Time | 0:00:00.02 |

| | Maximum Memory Required | 9080 (8.867K) bytes |
|---|---|---|

**Communalities**

| | Initial | Extraction |
|---|---|---|
| match1 | 1.000 | .879 |
| match2 | 1.000 | .907 |
| match3 | 1.000 | .936 |
| match4 | 1.000 | .907 |
| match5 | 1.000 | .954 |
| match6 | 1.000 | .946 |
| match7 | 1.000 | .857 |
| match8 | 1.000 | .867 |

Extraction Method: Principal Component Analysis.

**Total Variance Explained**

| Component | Initial Eigenvalues | | | Extraction Sums of Squared Loadings | | |
|---|---|---|---|---|---|---|
| | Total | % of Variance | Cumulative % | Total | % of Variance | Cumulative % |
| 1 | 7.253 | 90.658 | 90.658 | 7.253 | 90.658 | 90.658 |
| 2 | .203 | 2.535 | 93.193 | | | |
| 3 | .177 | 2.215 | 95.407 | | | |
| 4 | .147 | 1.832 | 97.240 | | | |
| 5 | .095 | 1.190 | 98.430 | | | |
| 6 | .066 | .826 | 99.256 | | | |
| 7 | .036 | .449 | 99.705 | | | |
| 8 | .024 | .295 | 100.000 | | | |

Extraction Method: Principal Component Analysis.

**Component Matrix(a)**

| | Component |
|---|---|
| | 1 |
| match1 | .937 |
| match2 | .952 |
| match3 | .967 |
| match4 | .953 |
| match5 | .977 |
| match6 | .972 |
| match7 | .926 |
| match8 | .931 |

Extraction Method: Principal Component Analysis.
a 1 components extracted.

206

# Factor Analysis

**Notes**

| | | |
|---|---|---|
| Output Created | | 16-DEC-2004 13:49:01 |
| Comments | | |
| Input | Data | E:\louis.sav |
| | Filter | <none> |
| | Weight | <none> |
| | Split File | <none> |
| | N of Rows in Working Data File | 40 |
| Missing Value Handling | Definition of Missing | MISSING=EXCLUDE: User-defined missing values are treated as missing. |
| | Cases Used | LISTWISE: Statistics are based on cases with no missing values for any variable used. |
| Syntax | | FACTOR /VARIABLES cl1 cl2 cl3 cl4 cl5 cl6 cl7 cl8 cl9 /MISSING LISTWISE /ANALYSIS cl1 cl2 cl3 cl4 cl5 cl6 cl7 cl8 cl9 /PRINT INITIAL EXTRACTION /CRITERIA MINEIGEN(1) ITERATE(25) /EXTRACTION PC /ROTATION NOROTATE /METHOD=CORRELATION . |
| Resources | Elapsed Time | 0:00:00.02 |
| | Maximum Memory Required | 11172 (10.910K) bytes |

**Communalities**

| | Initial | Extraction |
|---|---|---|
| cl1 | 1.000 | .779 |
| cl2 | 1.000 | .720 |
| cl3 | 1.000 | .775 |
| cl4 | 1.000 | .722 |
| cl5 | 1.000 | .861 |
| cl6 | 1.000 | .829 |
| cl7 | 1.000 | .831 |
| cl8 | 1.000 | .620 |

207

| cl9 | 1.000 | .814 |

Extraction Method: Principal Component Analysis.

**Total Variance Explained**

| Component | Initial Eigenvalues | | | Extraction Sums of Squared Loadings | | |
|---|---|---|---|---|---|---|
| | Total | % of Variance | Cumulative % | Total | % of Variance | Cumulative % |
| 1 | 6.950 | 77.221 | 77.221 | 6.950 | 77.221 | 77.221 |
| 2 | .837 | 9.297 | 86.518 | | | |
| 3 | .366 | 4.064 | 90.582 | | | |
| 4 | .254 | 2.827 | 93.409 | | | |
| 5 | .187 | 2.073 | 95.482 | | | |
| 6 | .148 | 1.649 | 97.131 | | | |
| 7 | .114 | 1.264 | 98.395 | | | |
| 8 | .088 | .978 | 99.373 | | | |
| 9 | .056 | .627 | 100.000 | | | |

Extraction Method: Principal Component Analysis.

**Component Matrix(a)**

| | Component |
|---|---|
| | 1 |
| cl1 | .883 |
| cl2 | .849 |
| cl3 | .880 |
| cl4 | .850 |
| cl5 | .928 |
| cl6 | .910 |
| cl7 | .911 |
| cl8 | .788 |
| cl9 | .902 |

Extraction Method: Principal Component Analysis.
a  1 components extracted.

# Factor Analysis

**Notes**

| Output Created | 16-DEC-2004 13:49:17 |
|---|---|
| Comments | |

208

| Input | Data | E:\louis.sav |
|---|---|---|
| | Filter | <none> |
| | Weight | <none> |
| | Split File | <none> |
| | N of Rows in Working Data File | 40 |
| Missing Value Handling | Definition of Missing | MISSING=EXCLUDE: User-defined missing values are treated as missing. |
| | Cases Used | LISTWISE: Statistics are based on cases with no missing values for any variable used. |
| Syntax | | |
| | | FACTOR /VARIABLES pres1 pres2 pres3 pres4 pres5 /MISSING LISTWISE /ANALYSIS pres1 pres2 pres3 pres4 pres5 /PRINT INITIAL EXTRACTION /CRITERIA MINEIGEN(1) ITERATE(25) /EXTRACTION PC /ROTATION NOROTATE /METHOD=CORRELATION . |
| Resources | Elapsed Time | 0:00:00.01 |
| | Maximum Memory Required | 4100 (4.004K) bytes |

**Communalities**

| | Initial | Extraction |
|---|---|---|
| pres1 | 1.000 | .766 |
| pres2 | 1.000 | .774 |
| pres3 | 1.000 | .800 |
| pres4 | 1.000 | .819 |
| pres5 | 1.000 | .754 |

Extraction Method: Principal Component Analysis.

**Total Variance Explained**

| Component | Initial Eigenvalues | | | Extraction Sums of Squared Loadings | | |
|---|---|---|---|---|---|---|
| | Total | % of Variance | Cumulative % | Total | % of Variance | Cumulative % |
| 1 | 3.913 | 78.260 | 78.260 | 3.913 | 78.260 | 78.260 |
| 2 | .385 | 7.693 | 85.953 | | | |
| 3 | .303 | 6.059 | 92.012 | | | |
| 4 | .227 | 4.533 | 96.545 | | | |
| 5 | .173 | 3.455 | 100.000 | | | |

Extraction Method: Principal Component Analysis.

**Component Matrix(a)**

| | Component 1 |
|---|---|
| pres1 | .875 |
| pres2 | .880 |
| pres3 | .894 |
| pres4 | .905 |
| pres5 | .868 |

Extraction Method: Principal Component Analysis.
a 1 components extracted.

# Factor Analysis

**Notes**

| Output Created | | 16-DEC-2004 13:49:36 |
|---|---|---|
| Comments | | |
| Input | Data | E:\louis.sav |
| | Filter | <none> |
| | Weight | <none> |
| | Split File | <none> |
| | N of Rows in Working Data File | 40 |
| Missing Value Handling | Definition of Missing | MISSING=EXCLUDE: User-defined missing values are treated as missing. |
| | Cases Used | LISTWISE: Statistics are based on cases with no missing values for any variable used. |
| Syntax | | FACTOR /VARIABLES ac1 ac2 ac3 ac4 ac5 ac6 ac7 ac8 /MISSING LISTWISE /ANALYSIS ac1 ac2 ac3 ac4 ac5 ac6 ac7 ac8 /PRINT INITIAL EXTRACTION /CRITERIA MINEIGEN(1) ITERATE(25) /EXTRACTION PC /ROTATION NOROTATE /METHOD=CORRELATION . |
| Resources | Elapsed Time | 0:00:00.02 |
| | Maximum Memory Required | 9080 (8.867K) bytes |

**Communalities**

|     | Initial | Extraction |
| --- | --- | --- |
| ac1 | 1.000 | .660 |
| ac2 | 1.000 | .728 |
| ac3 | 1.000 | .761 |
| ac4 | 1.000 | .806 |
| ac5 | 1.000 | .848 |
| ac6 | 1.000 | .800 |
| ac7 | 1.000 | .850 |
| ac8 | 1.000 | .866 |

Extraction Method: Principal Component Analysis.

**Total Variance Explained**

| Component | Initial Eigenvalues | | | Extraction Sums of Squared Loadings | | |
| --- | --- | --- | --- | --- | --- | --- |
| | Total | % of Variance | Cumulative % | Total | % of Variance | Cumulative % |
| 1 | 6.319 | 78.992 | 78.992 | 6.319 | 78.992 | 78.992 |
| 2 | .593 | 7.409 | 86.401 | | | |
| 3 | .356 | 4.446 | 90.846 | | | |
| 4 | .250 | 3.124 | 93.970 | | | |
| 5 | .232 | 2.898 | 96.868 | | | |
| 6 | .121 | 1.509 | 98.377 | | | |
| 7 | .100 | 1.246 | 99.623 | | | |
| 8 | .030 | .377 | 100.000 | | | |

Extraction Method: Principal Component Analysis.

**Component Matrix(a)**

|     | Component |
| --- | --- |
|     | 1 |
| ac1 | .812 |
| ac2 | .853 |
| ac3 | .872 |
| ac4 | .898 |
| ac5 | .921 |
| ac6 | .895 |
| ac7 | .922 |
| ac8 | .931 |

Extraction Method: Principal Component Analysis.
a  1 components extracted.

211

# Factor Analysis

| Output Created | | 16-DEC-2004 13:49:55 |
|---|---|---|
| Comments | | |
| Input | Data | E:\louis.sav |
| | Filter | <none> |
| | Weight | <none> |
| | Split File | <none> |
| | N of Rows in Working Data File | 40 |
| Missing Value Handling | Definition of Missing | MISSING=EXCLUDE: User-defined missing values are treated as missing. |
| | Cases Used | LISTWISE: Statistics are based on cases with no missing values for any variable used. |
| Syntax | | FACTOR /VARIABLES eng1 eng2 eng3 eng4 eng5 eng6 /MISSING LISTWISE /ANALYSIS eng1 eng2 eng3 eng4 eng5 eng6 /PRINT INITIAL EXTRACTION /CRITERIA MINEIGEN(1) ITERATE(25) /EXTRACTION PC /ROTATION NOROTATE /METHOD=CORRELATION . |
| Resources | Elapsed Time | 0:00:00.02 |
| | Maximum Memory Required | 5544 (5.414K) bytes |

## Communalities

| | Initial | Extraction |
|---|---|---|
| eng1 | 1.000 | .769 |
| eng2 | 1.000 | .784 |
| eng3 | 1.000 | .864 |
| eng4 | 1.000 | .898 |
| eng5 | 1.000 | .534 |
| eng6 | 1.000 | .840 |

Extraction Method: Principal Component Analysis.

**Total Variance Explained**

| Component | Initial Eigenvalues | | | Extraction Sums of Squared Loadings | | |
|---|---|---|---|---|---|---|
| | Total | % of Variance | Cumulative % | Total | % of Variance | Cumulative % |
| 1 | 4.689 | 78.151 | 78.151 | 4.689 | 78.151 | 78.151 |
| 2 | .629 | 10.476 | 88.627 | | | |
| 3 | .287 | 4.790 | 93.417 | | | |
| 4 | .199 | 3.321 | 96.737 | | | |
| 5 | .123 | 2.052 | 98.789 | | | |
| 6 | .073 | 1.211 | 100.000 | | | |

Extraction Method: Principal Component Analysis.

**Component Matrix(a)**

| | Component |
|---|---|
| | 1 |
| eng1 | .877 |
| eng2 | .885 |
| eng3 | .930 |
| eng4 | .947 |
| eng5 | .731 |
| eng6 | .916 |

Extraction Method: Principal Component Analysis.
a 1 components extracted.

# Factor Analysis

**Notes**

| Output Created | | 16-DEC-2004 13:50:10 |
|---|---|---|
| Comments | | |
| Input | Data | E:\louis.sav |
| | Filter | <none> |
| | Weight | <none> |
| | Split File | <none> |
| | N of Rows in Working Data File | 40 |
| Missing Value Handling | Definition of Missing | MISSING=EXCLUDE: User-defined missing values are treated as missing. |

**Communalities**

| | Initial | Extraction |
|---|---|---|
| fb1 | 1.000 | .736 |
| fb2 | 1.000 | .898 |
| fb3 | 1.000 | .869 |
| fb4 | 1.000 | .902 |
| fb5 | 1.000 | .904 |

Extraction Method: Principal Component Analysis.

**Total Variance Explained**

| Component | Initial Eigenvalues | | | Extraction Sums of Squared Loadings | | |
|---|---|---|---|---|---|---|
| | Total | % of Variance | Cumulative % | Total | % of Variance | Cumulative % |
| 1 | 4.309 | 86.185 | 86.185 | 4.309 | 86.185 | 86.185 |
| 2 | .324 | 6.472 | 92.657 | | | |
| 3 | .230 | 4.597 | 97.254 | | | |
| 4 | .092 | 1.832 | 99.086 | | | |
| 5 | .046 | .914 | 100.000 | | | |

Extraction Method: Principal Component Analysis.

**Component Matrix(a)**

| | Component |
|---|---|
| | 1 |
| fb1 | .858 |
| fb2 | .948 |
| fb3 | .932 |

214

| | | |
|---|---|---|
| fb4 | .950 | |
| fb5 | .951 | |

Extraction Method: Principal Component Analysis.
a 1 components extracted.

# Factor Analysis

**Notes**

| | | |
|---|---|---|
| Output Created | | 16-DEC-2004 13:50:35 |
| Comments | | |
| Input | Data | E:\louis.sav |
| | Filter | <none> |
| | Weight | <none> |
| | Split File | <none> |
| | N of Rows in Working Data File | 40 |
| Missing Value Handling | Definition of Missing | MISSING=EXCLUDE: User-defined missing values are treated as missing. |
| | Cases Used | LISTWISE: Statistics are based on cases with no missing values for any variable used. |
| Syntax | | FACTOR /VARIABLES lo1 lo2 lo3 lo4 lo5 lo6 lo7 lo8 lo9 /MISSING LISTWISE /ANALYSIS lo1 lo2 lo3 lo4 lo5 lo6 lo7 lo8 lo9 /PRINT INITIAL EXTRACTION /CRITERIA MINEIGEN(1) ITERATE(25) /EXTRACTION PC /ROTATION NOROTATE /METHOD=CORRELATION . |
| Resources | Elapsed Time | 0:00:00.03 |
| | Maximum Memory Required | 11172 (10.910K) bytes |

**Communalities**

| | Initial | Extraction |
|---|---|---|
| lo1 | 1.000 | .713 |
| lo2 | 1.000 | .553 |
| lo3 | 1.000 | .900 |
| lo4 | 1.000 | .837 |
| lo5 | 1.000 | .724 |
| lo6 | 1.000 | .829 |
| lo7 | 1.000 | .704 |
| lo8 | 1.000 | .893 |

215

| Io9 | 1.000 | .864 |

Extraction Method: Principal Component Analysis.

**Total Variance Explained**

| Component | Initial Eigenvalues | | | Extraction Sums of Squared Loadings | | |
|---|---|---|---|---|---|---|
| | Total | % of Variance | Cumulative % | Total | % of Variance | Cumulative % |
| 1 | 7.017 | 77.967 | 77.967 | 7.017 | 77.967 | 77.967 |
| 2 | .557 | 6.185 | 84.152 | | | |
| 3 | .484 | 5.378 | 89.530 | | | |
| 4 | .374 | 4.157 | 93.687 | | | |
| 5 | .196 | 2.180 | 95.867 | | | |
| 6 | .151 | 1.674 | 97.541 | | | |
| 7 | .099 | 1.097 | 98.638 | | | |
| 8 | .074 | .823 | 99.461 | | | |
| 9 | .048 | .539 | 100.000 | | | |

Extraction Method: Principal Component Analysis.

**Component Matrix(a)**

| | Component |
|---|---|
| | 1 |
| Io1 | .844 |
| Io2 | .744 |
| Io3 | .949 |
| Io4 | .915 |
| Io5 | .851 |
| Io6 | .910 |
| Io7 | .839 |
| Io8 | .945 |
| Io9 | .929 |

Extraction Method: Principal Component Analysis.
a  1 components extracted.

# Correlations

**Notes**

| Output Created | | 16-DEC-2004 14:20:39 |
|---|---|---|
| Comments | | |
| Input | Data | E:\louis.sav |
| | Filter | <none> |
| | Weight | <none> |

|  |  | Split File |  |  |  |  | <none> |  |  |
|--|--|------------|--|--|--|--|--------|--|--|
| Missing Value Handling |  | N of Rows in Working Data File |  |  |  |  | 40 |  |  |
|  |  | Definition of Missing |  |  |  |  | User-defined missing values are treated as missing. |  |  |
|  |  | Cases Used |  |  |  |  | Statistics for each pair of variables are based on all the cases with valid data for that pair. |  |  |
| Syntax |  |  |  |  |  |  | CORRELATIONS /VARIABLES=usermean matchmean clmean presmean acmean fbmean lomean engmean /PRINT=TWOTAIL NOSIG /MISSING=PAIRWISE . |  |  |
| Resources |  | Elapsed Time |  |  |  |  | 0:00:00.05 |  |  |

|  |  | usermean | matchmean | clmean | presmean | acmean | fbmean | lomean | engmeant |
|--|--|----------|-----------|--------|----------|--------|--------|--------|----------|
| usermean | Pearson Correlation | 1 | -.386(*) | .071 | .253 | .134 | .136 | .125 | .110 |
|  | Sig. (2-tailed) | . | .018 | .690 | .148 | .442 | .443 | .481 | .534 |
|  | N | 40 | 37 | 34 | 34 | 35 | 34 | 34 | 34 |
| matchmean | Pearson Correlation | -.386(*) | 1 | .952(**) | .894(**) | .943(**) | .877(**) | .975(**) | .928(**) |
|  | Sig. (2-tailed) | .018 | . | .000 | .000 | .000 | .000 | .000 | .000 |
|  | N | 37 | 37 | 34 | 34 | 35 | 34 | 34 | 34 |
| clmean | Pearson Correlation | .071 | .952(**) | 1 | .863(**) | .935(**) | .893(**) | .953(**) | .946(**) |
|  | Sig. (2-tailed) | .690 | .000 | . | .000 | .000 | .000 | .000 | .000 |
|  | N | 34 | 34 | 34 | 34 | 34 | 34 | 34 | 34 |
| presmean | Pearson Correlation | .253 | .894(**) | .863(**) | 1 | .863(**) | .896(**) | .910(**) | .872(**) |
|  | Sig. (2-tailed) | .148 | .000 | .000 | . | .000 | .000 | .000 | .000 |
|  | N | 34 | 34 | 34 | 34 | 34 | 34 | 34 | 34 |
| acmean | Pearson Correlation | .134 | .943(**) | .935(**) | .863(**) | 1 | .864(**) | .956(**) | .928(**) |
|  | Sig. (2-tailed) | .442 | .000 | .000 | .000 | . | .000 | .000 | .000 |
|  | N | 35 | 35 | 34 | 34 | 35 | 34 | 34 | 34 |
| fbmean | Pearson Correlation | .136 | .877(**) | .893(**) | .896(**) | .864(**) | 1 | .879(**) | .886(**) |
|  | Sig. (2-tailed) | .443 | .000 | .000 | .000 | .000 | . | .000 | .000 |
|  | N | 34 | 34 | 34 | 34 | 34 | 34 | 34 | 34 |
| lomean | Pearson Correlation | .125 | .975(**) | .953(**) | .910(**) | .956(**) | .879(**) | 1 | .934(**) |
|  | Sig. (2-tailed) | .481 | .000 | .000 | .000 | .000 | .000 | . | .000 |
|  | N | 34 | 34 | 34 | 34 | 34 | 34 | 34 | 34 |
| engmean | Pearson | .110 | .928(**) | .946(**) | .872(**) | .928(**) | .886(**) | .934(**) |  |

| | | | | | | | | |
|---|---|---|---|---|---|---|---|---|
| Correlation | | | | | | | | |
| Sig. (2-tailed) | .534 | .000 | .000 | .000 | .000 | .000 | .000 | . |
| N | 34 | 34 | 34 | 34 | 34 | 34 | 34 | 34 |

**Correlations**

\* Correlation is significant at the 0.05 level (2-tailed).
\*\* Correlation is significant at the 0.01 level (2-tailed).


# Correlations

**Notes**

| | | |
|---|---|---|
| Output Created | | 16-DEC-2004 14:28:51 |
| Comments | | |
| Input | Data | E:\louis.sav |
| | Filter | <none> |
| | Weight | <none> |
| | Split File | <none> |
| | N of Rows in Working Data File | 40 |
| Missing Value Handling | Definition of Missing | User-defined missing values are treated as missing. |
| | Cases Used | Statistics for each pair of variables are based on all the cases with valid data for that pair. |
| Syntax | | CORRELATIONS /VARIABLES=connect learn /PRINT=TWOTAIL NOSIG /MISSING=PAIRWISE . |
| Resources | Elapsed Time | 0:00:00.02 |

**Correlations**

| | | connect | learn |
|---|---|---|---|
| connect | Pearson Correlation | 1 | .981(\*\*) |
| | Sig. (2-tailed) | . | .000 |
| | N | 12 | 12 |
| learn | Pearson Correlation | .981(\*\*) | 1 |
| | Sig. (2-tailed) | .000 | . |
| | N | 12 | 12 |

\*\* Correlation is significant at the 0.01 level (2-tailed).

218

# Appendix - E

# Effectiveness Correlations

## Course Evaluation

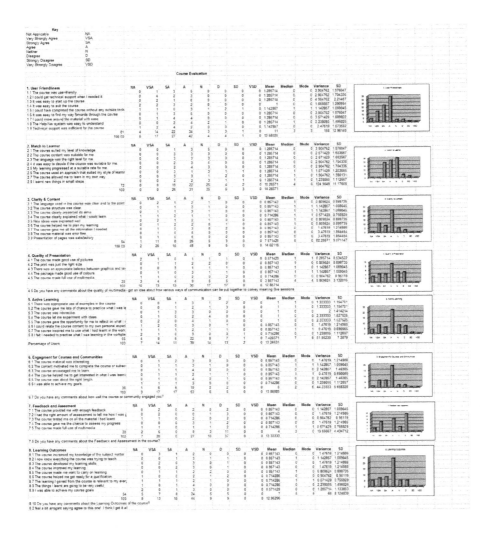

### 1. User Friendliness

| | NA | VSA | SA | A | N | D | SD | VSD | Mean | Median | Mode | Variance | SD |
|---|---|---|---|---|---|---|---|---|---|---|---|---|---|
| 1.1 The course was user-friendly | 0 | 1 | 3 | 5 | 0 | 0 | 0 | 0 | 1.285714 | | 0 | 3.904762 | 1.976047 |
| 1.2 I could get technical support when I needed it | 0 | 4 | 2 | 3 | 0 | 0 | 0 | 0 | 1.285714 | | 0 | 4.904762 | 1.704335 |
| 1.3 It was easy to start up the course | 0 | 2 | 1 | 6 | 0 | 0 | 0 | 0 | 1.285714 | | 0 | 4.904762 | 2.21467 |
| 1.4 It was easy to exit the course | 2 | 2 | 3 | 2 | 0 | 0 | 0 | 1 | | | 0 | 1.666667 | 1.290094 |
| 1.5 I could have completed the course without any outside tech | 1 | 1 | 0 | 3 | 1 | 2 | 1 | 0 | 1.142857 | | 1 | 1.142867 | 1.089045 |
| 1.6 It was easy to find my way forwards through the course | 0 | 1 | 1 | 5 | 2 | 0 | 0 | 0 | 1.285714 | | 0 | 3.904762 | 1.976047 |
| 1.7 I could move around the material with ease | 0 | 1 | 4 | 4 | 0 | 0 | 0 | 0 | 1.285714 | | 1 | 3.571429 | 1.689802 |
| 1.8 The Help/hint system was easy to understand | 0 | 0 | 2 | 4 | 2 | 1 | 0 | 0 | 1.285714 | | 0 | 2.238095 | 1.496025 |
| 1.9 Technical support was sufficient for the course | 1 | 2 | 4 | 3 | 0 | 3 | 0 | 0 | 1.142857 | | 0 | 2.47619 | 1.673592 |
| 81 | 4 | 14 | 22 | 34 | 3 | 3 | 1 | 0 | 11 | | 3 | 168 | 12.96148 |
| 100.00 | 6 | 17 | 27 | 42 | 4 | 4 | 1 | | 13.58025 | | | | |

### 2. Match to Learner

| | NA | VSA | SA | A | N | D | SD | VSD | Mean | Median | Mode | Variance | SD |
|---|---|---|---|---|---|---|---|---|---|---|---|---|---|
| 2.1 The course suited my level of knowledge | 0 | 0 | 1 | 3 | 5 | 0 | 0 | 0 | 1.285714 | | 0 | 3.904762 | 1.976047 |
| 2.2 The course content was suitable for me | 0 | 0 | 3 | 3 | 3 | 0 | 0 | 0 | 1.285714 | | 0 | 2.571429 | 1.603667 |
| 2.3 The language was the right level for me | 0 | 0 | 3 | 3 | 3 | 0 | 0 | 0 | 1.285714 | | 0 | 2.571429 | 1.603567 |
| 2.4 It was easy to decide if the course was suitable for me | 0 | 0 | 2 | 3 | 4 | 0 | 0 | 0 | 1.285714 | | 0 | 3.904762 | 1.704335 |
| 2.5 My learning progressed at a suitable rate for me | 0 | 0 | 2 | 4 | 3 | 0 | 0 | 0 | 1.285714 | | 0 | 3.904762 | 1.704335 |
| 2.6 The course used an approach that suited my style of learning | 0 | 0 | 3 | 1 | 3 | 1 | 1 | 0 | 1.285714 | | 1 | 1.571429 | 1.203665 |
| 2.7 The course allowed me to learn in my own way | 0 | 0 | 3 | 3 | 1 | 2 | 0 | 0 | 1.285714 | | 0 | 1.904762 | 1.380131 |
| 2.8 I learnt new things in small steps | 0 | 0 | 2 | 2 | 3 | 1 | 1 | 0 | 1.285714 | | 1 | 1.239095 | 1.112667 |
| 72 | 0 | 0 | 18 | 22 | 25 | 4 | 3 | 0 | 10.28571 | | 0 | 124.3048 | 11.17608 |
| 100 | 0 | 0 | 26 | 31 | 35 | 6 | 3 | | 14.28571 | | | | |

### 3. Clarity & Content

| | NA | VSA | SA | A | N | D | SD | VSD | Mean | Median | Mode | Variance | SD |
|---|---|---|---|---|---|---|---|---|---|---|---|---|---|
| 3.1 The language used in the course was clear and to the point | 0 | 2 | 1 | 3 | 1 | 0 | 0 | 0 | 0.857143 | | 1 | 0.809524 | 0.899735 |
| 3.2 The course structure was clear | 0 | 1 | 1 | 3 | 1 | 0 | 0 | 0 | 0.857143 | | 1 | 1.142867 | 1.089045 |
| 3.3 The course clearly presented its aims | 0 | 1 | 1 | 3 | 1 | 0 | 0 | 0 | 0.857143 | | 1 | 1.142867 | 1.089045 |
| 3.4 The course clearly explained what I would learn | 1 | 1 | 2 | 1 | 1 | 0 | 0 | 0 | 0.714286 | | 1 | 0.571429 | 0.755829 |
| 3.5 New ideas were explained well | 0 | 1 | 1 | 2 | 1 | 0 | 1 | 0 | 0.857143 | | 0 | 0.809524 | 0.899735 |
| 3.6 The course helped me to plan my learning | 0 | 1 | 2 | 2 | 0 | 1 | 0 | 0 | 0.857143 | | 1 | 0.809524 | 0.899735 |
| 3.7 The course gave me all the information I needed | 0 | 1 | 0 | 3 | 2 | 2 | 0 | 0 | 0.857143 | | 0 | 1.47619 | 1.214986 |
| 3.8 The course material was error free | 0 | 1 | 1 | 3 | 0 | 0 | 0 | 0 | 0.857143 | | 0 | 3.47619 | 1.864464 |
| 3.9 Presentation of pages was satisfactory | 0 | 1 | 1 | 5 | 0 | 0 | 0 | 0 | 0.857143 | | 0 | 3.47619 | 1.864464 |
| 54 | 1 | 11 | 8 | 26 | 9 | 5 | 0 | 0 | 7.571429 | | 0 | 82.28571 | 9.071147 |
| 100.00 | 0 | 20 | 18 | 48 | 9 | 6 | 0 | | 14.02116 | | | | |

### 4. Quality of Presentation

| | NA | VSA | SA | A | N | D | SD | VSD | Mean | Median | Mode | Variance | SD |
|---|---|---|---|---|---|---|---|---|---|---|---|---|---|
| 4.1 The course made good use of pictures | 2 | 1 | 1 | 3 | 0 | 1 | 0 | 0 | 0.857143 | | 1 | 0.285714 | 0.534522 |
| 4.2 The print was just the right size | 0 | 1 | 2 | 2 | 2 | 0 | 0 | 0 | 0.857143 | | 0 | 0.809524 | 0.899735 |
| 4.3 There was an appropriate balance between graphics and text | 0 | 0 | 3 | 1 | 1 | 1 | 1 | 0 | 0.857143 | | 1 | 1.142867 | 1.089045 |
| 4.4 The package made good use of colours | 0 | 1 | 1 | 1 | 1 | 1 | 1 | 0 | 0.857143 | | 1 | 1.142867 | 1.009045 |
| 4.5 The course made full use of multimedia | 1 | 1 | 0 | 2 | 0 | 2 | 0 | 0 | 0.714286 | | 0 | 0.904762 | 0.96119 |
| 20 | 3 | 4 | 4 | 9 | 6 | 5 | 0 | 0 | 2.857143 | | 4 | 3.909621 | 3.132016 |
| 100 | 15 | 20 | 20 | 45 | 30 | 25 | 0 | | 12.86714 | | | | |

4.6 Do you have any comments about the quality of multimedia - got an idea about how various ways of communication can be put together to convey meaning (live sessions

### 5. Active Learning

| | NA | VSA | SA | A | N | D | SD | VSD | Mean | Median | Mode | Variance | SD |
|---|---|---|---|---|---|---|---|---|---|---|---|---|---|
| 5.1 There was appropriate use of examples in the course | 0 | 0 | 1 | 3 | 0 | 2 | 0 | 0 | | | 1 | 1.333333 | 1.154701 |
| 5.2 The course gave me lots of chance to practice what I was learning | 0 | 0 | 1 | 2 | 1 | 3 | 0 | 0 | | | 1 | 1.333333 | 1.154701 |
| 5.3 The course was interactive | 0 | 1 | 1 | 3 | 2 | 0 | 0 | 0 | | | 2 | 1.414214 | |
| 5.4 The course let me experiment with ideas | 0 | 1 | 1 | 2 | 4 | 0 | 0 | 0 | | | 0 | 2.333333 | 1.527525 |
| 5.5 The course gave the opportunity for me to reflect on what I learnt | 0 | 2 | 0 | 4 | 1 | 0 | 0 | 0 | | | 0 | 2.333333 | 1.527525 |
| 5.6 I could relate the course content to my own personal experience | 1 | 2 | 1 | 3 | 0 | 1 | 0 | 0 | 0.857143 | | 0 | 1.47619 | 1.214986 |
| 5.7 The course inspired me to use what I had learnt in the workplace | 1 | 1 | 1 | 3 | 1 | 0 | 0 | 0 | 0.857143 | | 1 | 1.47619 | 0.690965 |
| 5.8 I felt I needed to practise what I was learning in the workplace | 2 | 1 | 0 | 3 | 0 | 0 | 1 | 0 | 0.714286 | | 0 | 1.239095 | 1.112667 |
| 55 | 4 | 8 | 6 | 22 | 9 | 7 | 0 | 0 | 7.428571 | | 7 | 8.516230 | 7.2879 |
| Percentage of Users | 100 | 10 | 13 | 10 | 39 | 14 | 13 | 2 | | 13.26531 | | | |

### 6. Engagement for Courses and Communities

| | NA | VSA | SA | A | N | D | SD | VSD | Mean | Median | Mode | Variance | SD |
|---|---|---|---|---|---|---|---|---|---|---|---|---|---|
| 6.1 The course material was interesting | 0 | 1 | 1 | 3 | 0 | 1 | 0 | 0 | 0.857143 | | 1 | 1.47619 | 1.214986 |
| 6.2 The content motivated me to complete the course of subject | 0 | 1 | 1 | 3 | 2 | 0 | 0 | 0 | 0.857143 | | 1 | 1.142867 | 1.009045 |
| 6.3 The course encouraged me to learn | 0 | 1 | 1 | 3 | 3 | 0 | 0 | 0 | 0.857143 | | 2 | 1.142867 | 1.46365 |
| 6.4 The course helped me to get interested in what I was learning | 0 | 1 | 1 | 2 | 1 | 1 | 0 | 0 | 0.857143 | | 0 | 0.47619 | 0.690965 |
| 6.5 The course was about the right length | 0 | 1 | 1 | 4 | 3 | 0 | 0 | 0 | 0.857143 | | 0 | 2.142867 | 1.46365 |
| 6.6 I was able to achieve my goals | 0 | 1 | 1 | 6 | 0 | 0 | 0 | 0 | 0.714286 | | 2 | 1.239095 | 1.112667 |
| 55 | 0 | 6 | 6 | 19 | 9 | 2 | 0 | 0 | | | 6 | 44.23333 | 6.698328 |
| 100 | 3 | 17 | 17 | 53 | 6 | 5 | 0 | | 13.60085 | | | | |

6.7 Do you have any comments about how well the course or community engaged you?

### 7. Feedback and Assessment

| | NA | VSA | SA | A | N | D | SD | VSD | Mean | Median | Mode | Variance | SD |
|---|---|---|---|---|---|---|---|---|---|---|---|---|---|
| 7.1 The course provided me with enough feedback | 2 | 1 | 2 | 2 | 0 | 2 | 0 | 0 | 0.857143 | | 0 | 1.47619 | 1.214986 |
| 7.2 I had the right amount of assessment to tell me how I was getting on | 0 | 1 | 1 | 0 | 1 | 3 | 0 | 0 | 0.857143 | | 1 | 1.47619 | 1.214986 |
| 7.3 The course tested me on all the material I had learnt | 1 | 1 | 0 | 2 | 0 | 2 | 0 | 0 | 0.714286 | | 0 | 0.904762 | 0.96119 |
| 7.4 The course gave me the chance to assess my progress | 1 | 1 | 1 | 2 | 0 | 1 | 0 | 0 | 0.714286 | | 1 | 0.571429 | 0.755829 |
| 7.5 The course made full use of multimedia | 0 | 2 | 0 | 0 | 3 | 11 | 0 | 0 | | | 4 | 15.66667 | 4.434712 |
| 30 | 2 | 6 | 0 | 8 | 3 | 11 | 0 | 0 | 13.33333 | | 0 | | |
| 100 | 7 | 20 | 0 | 27 | 10 | 37 | 0 | | | | | | |

7.6 Do you have any comments about the Feedback and Assessment in the course?

### 8. Learning Outcomes

| | NA | VSA | SA | A | N | D | SD | VSD | Mean | Median | Mode | Variance | SD |
|---|---|---|---|---|---|---|---|---|---|---|---|---|---|
| 8.1 The course increased my knowledge of the subject matter | 0 | 3 | 1 | 3 | 0 | 0 | 0 | 0 | 0.857143 | | 1 | 1.47619 | 1.214986 |
| 8.2 I now know everything the course was trying to teach | 0 | 0 | 1 | 3 | 1 | 1 | 0 | 0 | 0.857143 | | 1 | 1.142867 | 1.009045 |
| 8.3 The course developed my learning skills | 0 | 2 | 0 | 3 | 0 | 0 | 1 | 0 | 0.857143 | | 0 | 1.47619 | 1.214986 |
| 8.4 The course improved my learning | 0 | 2 | 1 | 3 | 0 | 1 | 0 | 0 | 0.857143 | | 0 | 1.47619 | 1.214986 |
| 8.5 The course made me want to carry on learning | 0 | 0 | 1 | 2 | 2 | 1 | 0 | 0 | 0.714286 | | 1 | 0.809524 | 0.899735 |
| 8.6 The course helped me get ready for a qualification | 1 | 0 | 0 | 2 | 1 | 2 | 0 | 0 | 0.714286 | | 0 | 0.904762 | 0.96119 |
| 8.7 The learning I gained from the course is relevant to my everyday | 1 | 1 | 0 | 3 | 0 | 0 | 0 | 0 | 0.714286 | | 0 | 0.571429 | 0.755829 |
| 8.8 The things I learnt are going to be very useful | 1 | 0 | 0 | 4 | 0 | 0 | 0 | 0 | 0.714286 | | 0 | 2.238095 | 1.496025 |
| 8.9 I was able to achieve my goals | 2 | 0 | 1 | 3 | 0 | 0 | 0 | 0 | 0.571429 | | 0 | 1.285714 | 1.133853 |
| 54 | 7 | 8 | 5 | 26 | 5 | 6 | 0 | 0 | | | 6 | 66 | 9.124939 |
| 100 | 13 | 15 | 10 | 44 | 9 | 11 | 0 | | 12.96296 | | | | |

8.10 Do you have any comments about the Learning Outcomes of the course?
8.2 feel a bit arrogant saying agree to this one! I think I got it all

| Key | | | Key | |
|---|---|---|---|---|
| 1. Technical - T | | | Not Applicable | NA |
| 2. Usability - U | | | Very Strongly Agree | VSA |
| 2. Operating System - O | | | Strongly Agree | SA |
| 3. Learning - L | | | Agree | A |
| 4. Motivation - M | | | Neither | N |
| | | | Disagree | D |
| | | | Strongly Disagree | SD |
| | | | Very Strongly Disagree | VSD |

**Course Evaluation**

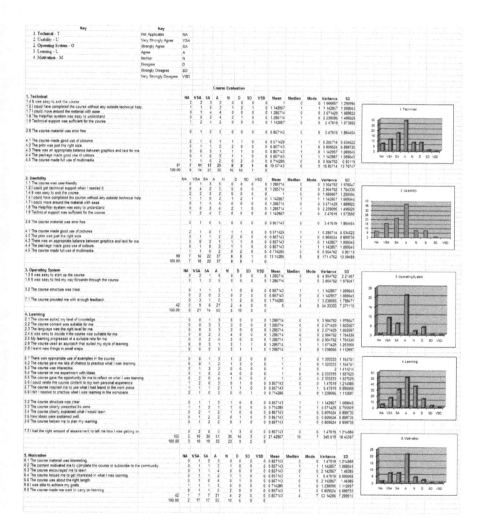

| 1. Technical | NA | VSA | SA | A | N | D | SD | VSD | Mean | Median | Mode | Variance | SD |
|---|---|---|---|---|---|---|---|---|---|---|---|---|---|
| 1.4 It was easy to exit the course | 2 | 2 | 3 | 2 | 0 | 0 | 0 | 0 | 1 | | 0 | 1.666667 | 1.290994 |
| 1.5 I could have completed the course without any outside technical help | 1 | 1 | 0 | 3 | 1 | 2 | 1 | 0 | 1.142857 | | 1 | 1.142857 | 1.069045 |
| 1.7 I could move around the material with ease | 0 | 1 | 4 | 4 | 0 | 0 | 0 | 0 | 1.285714 | | 0 | 3.571429 | 1.889822 |
| 1.8 The Help/Nav system was easy to understand | 0 | 0 | 4 | 2 | 1 | 0 | 0 | 0 | 1.285714 | | 0 | 2.238095 | 1.496026 |
| 1.9 Technical support was sufficient for the course | 1 | 2 | 4 | 2 | 0 | 0 | 0 | 0 | 1.142857 | | 0 | 2.47619 | 1.573592 |
| 3.8 The course material was error free | 0 | 1 | 0 | 5 | 0 | 0 | 0 | 0 | 0.857143 | | 0 | 3.47619 | 1.864454 |
| 4.1 The course made good use of pictures | 2 | 1 | 0 | 1 | 1 | 1 | 0 | 0 | 0.571429 | | 1 | 1.285714 | 0.634522 |
| 4.2 The print was just the right size | 0 | 1 | 1 | 2 | 2 | 0 | 0 | 0 | 0.857143 | | 1 | 0.809524 | 0.899735 |
| 4.3 There was an appropriate balance between graphics and text for me | 0 | 0 | 3 | 1 | 1 | 1 | 0 | 0 | 0.857143 | | 1 | 1.142857 | 1.069045 |
| 4.4 The package made good use of colours | 0 | 1 | 0 | 3 | 1 | 1 | 0 | 0 | 0.857143 | | 1 | 1.142857 | 1.069045 |
| 4.5 The course made full use of multimedia | 1 | 1 | 0 | 2 | 0 | 2 | 0 | 0 | 0.714286 | | 0 | 0.904762 | 0.95119 |
| | 81 | 7 | 11 | 17 | 29 | 8 | 8 | 1 | 0 | 10.57143 | | 6 | 3 | 18.95714 | 13.70747 |
| | 100.00 | 9 | 14 | 21 | 36 | 10 | 10 | 1 | 0 | | | | |

| 2. Usability | NA | VSA | SA | A | N | D | SD | VSD | Mean | Median | Mode | Variance | SD |
|---|---|---|---|---|---|---|---|---|---|---|---|---|---|
| 1.1 The course was user-friendly | 0 | 1 | 3 | 5 | 0 | 0 | 0 | 0 | 1.285714 | | 0 | 3.904762 | 1.976047 |
| 1.2 I could get technical support when I needed it | 0 | 4 | 2 | 3 | 0 | 0 | 0 | 0 | 1.285714 | | 0 | 2.904762 | 1.704336 |
| 1.4 It was easy to exit the course | 2 | 2 | 3 | 2 | 0 | 0 | 0 | 0 | 1 | | 0 | 1.666667 | 1.290994 |
| 1.5 I could have completed the course without any outside technical help | 1 | 1 | 0 | 3 | 1 | 2 | 1 | 0 | 1.142857 | | 1 | 1.142857 | 1.069045 |
| 1.7 I could move around the material with ease | 0 | 1 | 4 | 4 | 0 | 0 | 0 | 0 | 1.285714 | | 0 | 3.571429 | 1.889822 |
| 1.8 The Help/Nav system was easy to understand | 0 | 0 | 4 | 2 | 1 | 0 | 0 | 0 | 1.285714 | | 0 | 2.238095 | 1.496026 |
| 1.9 Technical support was sufficient for the course | 1 | 2 | 4 | 2 | 0 | 0 | 0 | 0 | 1.142857 | | 0 | 2.47619 | 1.573592 |
| 3.8 The course material was error free | 0 | 1 | 0 | 5 | 0 | 0 | 0 | 0 | 0.857143 | | 0 | 3.47619 | 1.864454 |
| 4.1 The course made good use of pictures | 2 | 1 | 0 | 1 | 1 | 1 | 0 | 0 | 0.571429 | | 1 | 1.285714 | 0.634522 |
| 4.2 The print was just the right size | 0 | 1 | 1 | 2 | 2 | 0 | 0 | 0 | 0.857143 | | 1 | 0.809524 | 0.899735 |
| 4.3 There was an appropriate balance between graphics and text for me | 0 | 0 | 3 | 1 | 1 | 1 | 0 | 0 | 0.857143 | | 1 | 1.142857 | 1.069045 |
| 4.4 The package made good use of colours | 0 | 1 | 0 | 3 | 1 | 1 | 0 | 0 | 0.857143 | | 1 | 1.142857 | 1.069045 |
| 4.5 The course made full use of multimedia | 1 | 1 | 0 | 2 | 0 | 2 | 0 | 0 | 0.714286 | | 0 | 0.904762 | 0.95119 |
| | 99 | 7 | 16 | 22 | 37 | 8 | 8 | 1 | 1 | 13.14286 | | 8 | 171.4762 | 13.09489 |
| | 100.00 | 7 | 16 | 22 | 37 | 8 | 8 | 1 | 1 | | | | |

| 3. Operating System | NA | VSA | SA | A | N | D | SD | VSD | Mean | Median | Mode | Variance | SD |
|---|---|---|---|---|---|---|---|---|---|---|---|---|---|
| 1.3 It was easy to start up the course | 0 | 2 | 1 | 6 | 0 | 0 | 0 | 0 | 1.285714 | | 0 | 4.904762 | 2.21467 |
| 1.6 It was easy to find my way forwards through the course | 0 | 1 | 3 | 5 | 0 | 0 | 0 | 0 | 1.285714 | | 0 | 3.904762 | 1.976047 |
| 3.2 The course structure was clear | 0 | 1 | 1 | 3 | 1 | 0 | 0 | 0 | 0.857143 | | 0 | 1.142857 | 1.069045 |
| 7.1 The course provided me with enough feedback | 0 | 2 | 0 | 2 | 0 | 2 | 0 | 0 | 0.857143 | | 0 | 1.142857 | 1.069045 |
| | | 0 | 3 | 1 | 5 | 1 | 2 | 0 | 0 | 0.714286 | | 0 | 1.238095 | 1.75947 |
| | 42 | 0 | 9 | 6 | 21 | 2 | 4 | 0 | 0 | 6 | | 4 | 54.33333 | 7.371115 |
| | 100.00 | 9 | 21 | 14 | 50 | 5 | 10 | 0 | 0 | | | | |

| 4. Learning | NA | VSA | SA | A | N | D | SD | VSD | Mean | Median | Mode | Variance | SD |
|---|---|---|---|---|---|---|---|---|---|---|---|---|---|
| 2.1 The course suited my level of knowledge | 0 | 0 | 1 | 3 | 6 | 0 | 0 | 0 | 1.285714 | | 0 | 3.904762 | 1.976047 |
| 2.2 The course content was suitable for me | 0 | 0 | 3 | 3 | 3 | 0 | 0 | 0 | 1.285714 | | 0 | 2.571429 | 1.603567 |
| 2.3 The language was the right level for me | 0 | 0 | 3 | 3 | 3 | 0 | 0 | 0 | 1.285714 | | 0 | 2.571429 | 1.603567 |
| 2.4 It was easy to decide if the course was suitable for me | 0 | 0 | 2 | 3 | 4 | 0 | 0 | 0 | 1.285714 | | 0 | 2.904762 | 1.704336 |
| 2.6 My learning progressed at a suitable rate for me | 0 | 0 | 2 | 4 | 3 | 0 | 0 | 0 | 1.285714 | | 0 | 2.904762 | 1.704336 |
| 2.6 The course used an approach that suited my style of learning | 0 | 0 | 3 | 1 | 3 | 1 | 1 | 0 | 1.285714 | | 1 | 1.571429 | 1.253566 |
| 2.8 I learnt new things in small steps | 0 | 0 | 2 | 1 | 2 | 0 | 0 | 1 | 1.285714 | | 1 | 1.238095 | 1.112697 |
| 5.1 There was appropriate use of examples in the course | 0 | 0 | 1 | 3 | 1 | 2 | 0 | 0 | 1 | | 1 | 1.333333 | 1.154701 |
| 5.2 The course gave me lots of chance to practice what I was learning | 0 | 0 | 1 | 2 | 1 | 3 | 0 | 0 | 1 | | 1 | 1.333333 | 1.164701 |
| 5.3 The course was interactive | 2 | 1 | 3 | 3 | 0 | 0 | 0 | 0 | 1 | | 1 | 1.414214 |
| 5.4 The course let me experiment with ideas | 0 | 1 | 0 | 2 | 4 | 0 | 0 | 0 | 1 | | 0 | 2.333333 | 1.527525 |
| 5.5 The course gave the opportunity for me to reflect on what I was learning | 0 | 2 | 0 | 4 | 1 | 0 | 0 | 0 | 1 | | 0 | 2.333333 | 1.527525 |
| 5.6 I could relate the course content to my own personal experience | 1 | 2 | 0 | 3 | 0 | 1 | 0 | 0 | 0.857143 | | 0 | 1.47619 | 1.214986 |
| 5.7 The course inspired me to use what I had learnt in the work place | 1 | 1 | 1 | 2 | 1 | 1 | 0 | 0 | 0.857143 | | 1 | 0.47619 | 0.690065 |
| 5.8 I felt I needed to practise what I was learning in the workplace | 2 | 1 | 0 | 3 | 0 | 0 | 1 | 0 | 0.714286 | | 0 | 1.238095 | 1.112697 |
| 3.2 The course structure was clear | 0 | 1 | 1 | 3 | 1 | 0 | 0 | 0 | 0.857143 | | 1 | 1.142857 | 1.069045 |
| 3.3 The course clearly presented its aims | 1 | 1 | 2 | 1 | 1 | 0 | 0 | 0 | 0.714286 | | 1 | 0.571429 | 0.755929 |
| 3.4 The course clearly explained what I would learn | 0 | 2 | 1 | 2 | 1 | 0 | 0 | 0 | 0.857143 | | 1 | 0.809524 | 0.899735 |
| 3.5 New ideas were explained well | 0 | 1 | 2 | 2 | 0 | 1 | 0 | 0 | 0.857143 | | 0 | 0.809524 | 0.899735 |
| 3.6 The course helped me to plan my learning | 0 | 1 | 2 | 2 | 0 | 1 | 0 | 0 | 0.857143 | | 0 | 0.809524 | 0.899735 |
| 7.2 I had the right amount of assessment to tell me how I was getting on | 0 | 2 | 0 | 1 | 3 | 0 | 0 | 0 | 0.857143 | | 0 | 1.47619 | 1.214986 |
| | 155 | 5 | 16 | 30 | 51 | 36 | 14 | 3 | 1 | 21.42857 | | 16 | 7 | 340.619 | 18.45697 |
| | 100.00 | 3 | 10 | 19 | 33 | 23 | 9 | 2 | 0 | | | | |

| 5. Motivation | NA | VSA | SA | A | N | D | SD | VSD | Mean | Median | Mode | Variance | SD |
|---|---|---|---|---|---|---|---|---|---|---|---|---|---|
| 6.1 The course material was interesting | 0 | 1 | 2 | 3 | 0 | 0 | 0 | 0 | 0.857143 | | 0 | 1.47619 | 1.214986 |
| 6.2 The content motivated me to complete the course or subscribe to the community | 0 | 0 | 1 | 3 | 1 | 0 | 0 | 0 | 0.857143 | | 0 | 1.142857 | 1.069045 |
| 6.3 The course encouraged me to learn | 0 | 1 | 1 | 4 | 0 | 0 | 0 | 0 | 0.857143 | | 0 | 2.142857 | 1.46385 |
| 6.4 The course helped me to get interested in what I was learning | 0 | 0 | 3 | 1 | 1 | 0 | 0 | 0 | 0.857143 | | 1 | 0.47619 | 0.690065 |
| 6.5 The course was about the right length | 0 | 0 | 4 | 0 | 1 | 0 | 0 | 0 | 0.857143 | | 0 | 2.142857 | 1.46385 |
| 6.6 I was able to achieve my goals | 1 | 1 | 1 | 2 | 0 | 0 | 0 | 0 | 0.714286 | | 0 | 1.230095 | 1.112697 |
| 6.8 The course made me want to carry on learning | 1 | 1 | 3 | 2 | 0 | 0 | 0 | 0 | 0.857143 | | 1 | 0.809524 | 0.899735 |
| | 42 | 1 | 7 | 21 | 4 | 0 | 0 | 0 | 5.857143 | | 4 | 7 | 53.14286 | 7.209915 |
| | 100.00 | 2 | 17 | 17 | 50 | 10 | 6 | 0 | 0 | | | | |

## Course Evaluation

### 1. Technical

| | NA | VSA | SA | A | N | D | SD | VSD | Mean | Median | Mode | Variance | SD |
|---|---|---|---|---|---|---|---|---|---|---|---|---|---|

### 2. Usability

| | NA | VSA | SA | A | N | D | SD | VSD | Mean | Median | Mode | Variance | SD |
|---|---|---|---|---|---|---|---|---|---|---|---|---|---|

### 3. Operating System

| | NA | VSA | SA | A | N | D | SD | VSD | Mean | Median | Mode | Variance | SD |
|---|---|---|---|---|---|---|---|---|---|---|---|---|---|

### 4. Learning

| | NA | VSA | SA | A | N | D | SD | VSD | Mean | Median | Mode | Variance | SD |
|---|---|---|---|---|---|---|---|---|---|---|---|---|---|

### 5. Motivation

| | NA | VSA | SA | A | N | D | SD | VSD | Mean | Median | Mode | Variance | SD |
|---|---|---|---|---|---|---|---|---|---|---|---|---|---|

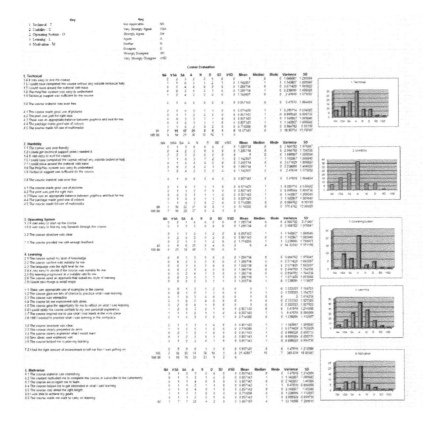

# Appendix - F

# Adaptation of Blooms Taxonomy Cognitive, Affective and Psycho-motive Factors

## Adaptation of Blooms Taxonomy Cognitive, Affective and Psychomotive Factors

| *Cognitive* | |
|---|---|
| The cognitive domain involves knowledge and the development of intellectual skills. This includes the recall or recognition of specific facts, procedural patterns, and concepts that serve in the development of intellectual abilities and skills. There are six major categories, which are listed in order below, starting from the simplest behaviour to the most complex. The categories can be thought of as degrees of difficulties. That is, the first one must be mastered before the next one can take place. | |
| Knowledge: Recall of data | Examples: Recite a policy. Quote prices from memory to a customer. Knows the safety rules. Key Words: defines, describes, identifies, knows, labels, lists, matches, names, outlines, recalls, recognizes, reproduces, selects, states. |
| Comprehension: Understand the meaning, translation, interpolation, and interpretation of instructions and problems. State a problem in one's own words. | Examples: Rewrites the principles of test writing. Explain in one's own words the steps for performing a complex task. Translates an equation into a computer spreadsheet. Key words: comprehends, converts, defends, distinguishes, estimates, explains, extends, generalizes, gives examples, infers, interprets, paraphrases, predicts, rewrites, summarizes, translates. |
| Application: Use a concept in a new situation or unprompted use of an abstraction. Applies what was learned in the classroom into novel situations in the workplace. | Examples: Use a manual to calculate an employee's vacation time. Apply laws of statistics to evaluate the reliability of a written test. Key Words: applies, changes, computes, constructs, demonstrates, discovers, manipulates, modifies, operates, predicts, prepares, produces, relates, shows, solves, uses. |
| Analysis: Separates material or concepts into component parts so that its organizational structure may be understood. Distinguishes between facts and inferences. | Examples: Troubleshoot a piece of equipment by using logical deduction. Recognize logical fallacies in reasoning. Gathers information from a department and selects the required tasks |

225

| | |
|---|---|
| | for training.<br>Keywords: analyzes, breaks down, compares, contrasts, diagrams, deconstructs, differentiates, discriminates, distinguishes, identifies, illustrates, infers, outlines, relates, selects, separates. |
| Synthesis: Builds a structure or pattern from diverse elements. Put parts together to form a whole, with emphasis on creating a new meaning or structure. | Examples: Write a company operations or process manual. Design a machine to perform a specific task. Integrates training from several sources to solve a problem. Revises and process to improve the outcome.<br>Keywords: categorizes, combines, compiles, composes, creates, devises, designs, explains, generates, modifies, organizes, plans, rearranges, reconstructs, relates, reorganizes, revises, rewrites, summarizes, tells, writes. |
| Evaluation: Make judgments about the value of ideas or materials. | Examples: Select the most effective solution. Hire the most qualified candidate. Explain and justify a new budget.<br>Keywords: appraises, compares, concludes, contrasts, criticizes, critiques, defends, describes, discriminates, evaluates, explains, interprets, justifies, relates, summarizes, supports. |

## Affective

This domain includes the manner in which we deal with things emotionally, such as feelings, values, appreciation, enthusiasms, motivations, and attitudes. The five major categories listed in order are:

| | |
|---|---|
| Receiving phenomena: Awareness, willingness to hear, selected attention. | Examples: Listen to others with respect. Listen for and remember the name of newly introduced people.<br>Keywords: asks, chooses, describes, follows, gives, holds, identifies, locates, names, points to, selects, sits, erects, replies, uses. |
| Responding to phenomena: Active participation on the part of the learners. Attends and reacts to a particular phenomenon. Learning outcomes may | Examples: Participates in class discussions. Gives a presentation. Questions new ideals, concepts, models, etc. in order to fully understand them. |

| | |
|---|---|
| emphasize compliance in responding, willingness to respond, or satisfaction in responding (motivation). | Know the safety rules and practices them. Keywords: answers, assists, aids, complies, conforms, discusses, greets, helps, labels, performs, practices, presents, reads, recites, reports, selects, tells, writes. |
| Valuing: The worth or value a person attaches to a particular object, phenomenon, or behaviour. This ranges from simple acceptance to the more complex state of commitment. Valuing is based on the internalization of a set of specified values, while clues to these values are expressed in the learner's overt behaviour and are often identifiable. | Examples: Demonstrates belief in the democratic process. Is sensitive towards individual and cultural differences (value diversity). Shows the ability to solve problems. Proposes a plan to social improvement and follows through with commitment. Informs management on matters that one feels strongly about. Keywords: completes, demonstrates, differentiates, explains, follows, forms, initiates, invites, joins, justifies, proposes, reads, reports, selects, shares, studies, works. |
| Organization: Organizes values into priorities by contrasting different values, resolving conflicts between them, and creating a unique value system. The emphasis is on comparing, relating, and synthesizing values. | Examples: Recognizes the need for balance between freedom and responsible behaviour. Accepts responsibility for one's behaviour. Explains the role of systematic planning in solving problems. Accepts professional ethical standards. Creates a life plan in harmony with abilities, interests, and beliefs. Prioritizes time effectively to meet the needs of the organization, family, and self. Keywords: adheres, alters, arranges, combines, compares, completes, defends, explains, formulates, generalizes, identifies, integrates, modifies, orders, organizes, prepares, relates, synthesizes. |

## Psychomotor

The psychomotor domain includes physical movement, coordination, and use of the motor-skill areas. Development of these skills requires practice and is measured in terms of speed, precision, distance, procedures, or techniques in execution. The seven major categories listed in order are:

| | |
|---|---|
| Perception: The ability to use sensory cues to guide motor activity. This ranges | Examples: Detects non-verbal communication cues. Estimate where a ball |

| | |
|---|---|
| from sensory stimulation, through cue selection, to translation. | will land after it is thrown and then moving to the correct location to catch the ball. Adjusts heat of stove to correct temperature by smell and taste of food. Adjusts the height of the forks on a forklift by comparing where the forks are in relation to the pallet.<br>Keywords: chooses, describes, detects, differentiates, distinguishes, identifies, isolates, relates, selects. |
| Set: Readiness to act. It includes mental, physical, and emotional sets. These three sets are dispositions that predetermine a person's response to different situations (sometimes called mindsets). | Examples: Knows and acts upon a sequence of steps in a manufacturing process. Recognize one's abilities and limitations. Shows desire to learn a new process (motivation). NOTE: This subdivision of Psychomotor is closely related with the "Responding to phenomena" subdivision of the Affective domain.<br>Keywords: begins, displays, explains, moves, proceeds, reacts, shows, states, volunteers. |
| Guided response: The early stages in learning a complex skill that includes imitation and trial and error. Adequacy of performance is achieved by practicing. | |
| | Examples: Performs a mathematical equation as demonstrated. Follows instructions to build a model. Responds hand-signals of instructor while learning to operate a forklift.<br>Keywords: copies, traces, follows, react, reproduce, responds |
| Mechanism: This is the intermediate stage in learning a complex skill. Learned responses have become habitual and the movements can be performed with some confidence and proficiency. | Examples: Use a personal computer. Repair a leaking faucet. Drive a car.<br>Keywords: assembles, calibrates, constructs, dismantles, displays, fastens, fixes, grinds, heats, manipulates, measures, mends, mixes, organizes, sketches. |
| Complex Overt Response: The skilful performance of motor acts that involve complex movement patterns. Proficiency is indicated by a quick, accurate, and highly coordinated performance, requiring a minimum of energy. This category includes performing without hesitation, and automatic performance. For example, players are often utter sounds of satisfaction or | Examples: Manoeuvres a car into a tight parallel parking spot. Operates a computer quickly and accurately. Displays competence while playing the piano.<br>Keywords: assembles, builds, calibrates, constructs, dismantles, displays, fastens, fixes, grinds, heats, manipulates, measures, mends, mixes, organizes, sketches. NOTE: The key words are the same as Mechanism, but will have adverbs or adjectives that |

| | |
|---|---|
| expletives as soon as they hit a tennis ball or throw a football, because they can tell by the feel of the act what the result will produce | indicate that the performance is quicker, better, more accurate, etc. |
| Adaptation: Skills are well developed and the individual can modify movement patterns to fit special requirements. | Examples: Responds effectively to unexpected experiences. Modifies instruction to meet the needs of the learners. Perform a task with a machine that it was not originally intended to do (machine is not damaged and there is no danger in performing the new task).<br>Keywords: adapts, alters, changes, rearranges, reorganizes, revises, varies. |
| Origination: Creating new movement patterns to fit a particular situation or specific problem. Learning outcomes emphasize creativity based upon highly developed skills. | Examples: Constructs a new theory. Develops a new and comprehensive training programming. Creates a new gymnastic routine.<br>Keywords: arranges, builds, combines, composes, constructs, creates, designs, initiate, makes, originates. |

## Reference

Bengamin S. Bloom, Bertram B. Mesia, and David R. Krathwohl (1964). Taxonomy of Educational Objectives (two vols: The Affective Domain & The Cognitive Domain). New York. David McKay.